RIVERSIDE LITERATURE SERIES

GENERAL EDITORS:

Kenneth S. Lynn
Arno Jewett

Literature from the Old Testament

Selections from the
King James Version

With drawings by
Rembrandt van Rijn, 1606–1669

HOUGHTON MIFFLIN COMPANY · BOSTON

New York · Atlanta · Geneva, Ill. · Dallas · Palo Alto

Introduction by
Mary Ellen Chase
Formerly of Smith College
Northampton, Massachusetts

Suggestions for Reading and Discussion by
Harvey Granite
Rochester Public Schools
Rochester, New York
and
Charles Griffith
Monroe High School
Rochester, New York

Library of Congress Catalog Card Number: 70-128708
Hardcover ISBN: 0-395-03432-9
Softcover ISBN: 0-395-03515-5

Contents

The Riches of the
Old Testament

*The Old Testament is many things. It is a history; and thanks
to archaeologists as well as historians, we are constantly
discovering how accurate a history it is. It is also fiction and
biography. It is poetry in many forms.*

*As to people, where else can we find such memorable characters
as in the Old Testament narratives? Cain, the exiled murderer,
who complains, "My punishment is greater than I can bear";
Sarah, who laughs when God promises her a son in her old age;
the wily and smooth-faced Jacob, who tricks his brother Esau
out of birthright and blessing; Joseph, who at seventeen is such
a conceited talebearer his brothers plot to kill him; that
remarkable lawgiver Moses, who leads his people to a promised
land he himself cannot enter; the blind and shaven Samson, who
is made sport of by the Philistines; that "choice young man" Saul,
who hides in the baggage when Samuel prepares to anoint him
king; the young and handsome David, who is "a cunning player
on an harp" and a master hand with a slingshot; the old and
saddened David, who weeps, "Would God I had died for thee, O
Absalom, my son, my son!"; Boaz, who watches Ruth gleaning
in the fields and asks, "Whose damsel is this?"; Jonah, the
preacher of doom who sulks when the people repent and are
saved; Job, who cries out in his misery, "Have pity upon me,
have pity upon me, O ye my friends" — all these have lived for
centuries because of the genius of the Old Testament writers.*

What is it that makes the stories and people of the Old Testament so memorable? Among the many reasons two stand out: the storytelling skill of the Hebrew writers and their use of a concrete, simple language whose poetical quality is conveyed even in translation.

In their storytelling, the Old Testament narrators are notable for brevity and sparing use of descriptive details. Often they do not tell us the time or place of important events. The physical appearance of characters is rarely mentioned. David is an exception since he is accorded two adjectives: he is *ruddy,* that is, red-haired, and of a *beautiful* countenance. What did Abraham look like? Or Isaac? Or Jacob? We do not know. The only house described in any detail is the temple built by Solomon in Jerusalem. Yet by omitting all but the most important details, the narrators focus your attention on the story line. You learn about people from what they do and say, and you fill in imaginatively what the narrator omits.

Take, for instance, the scene of Abraham sacrificing Isaac at God's command. The story is short, only a page or so. You are not told what Abraham is thinking and feeling, but when you read "And Abraham stretched forth his hand, and took the knife to slay his son," you yourself fill in the details — the anguish in the father's heart and the slow arc made by his reluctant hand. By its very simplicity and understatement, the story is one of the most moving and forceful in literature.

Another example of the power of simplicity is David's lament for Jonathan, which concludes:

> How are the mighty fallen in the midst of battle!
> O Jonathan, thou wast slain in thine high places.

> I am distressed for thee, my brother Jonathan, very pleasant hast thou been unto me: thy love to me was wonderful, passing the love of women.

> How are the mighty fallen, and the weapons of war perished!

Understated and simple, this is one of the famous elegies in our literature.

The language of the Old Testament writers, like their story-telling technique, is simple and direct. It is full of concrete nouns: bread, cakes, honey, milk, water, wine, oil, oxen, goats, mules, sheep, lambs. The Old Testament writers tell of everyday things, but as the scholar Eric Auerbach points out, they invest the every-day and the low with sublimity. The simple and the obvious are endowed with inner spiritual significance. The literal becomes the figurative as well; the concrete loses its sharp outlines in the abstract. Nothing is seen alone, but is forever attended by its meaning, like a surrounding light or a reflected shadow. This power of transcending the ordinary and endowing it with imagina-tive significance is perhaps most clearly illustrated by the symbolic use of hands and feet in the Old Testament.

Hands are referred to countless times in the Bible. God delivers into Noah's *hand* all the beasts of the field and the fowls of the air. Jacob in his reproaches to Laban speaks not only of his labor in the drought by day and the frost by night, but of the *labor of his hands*. Pharaoh leaves all his responsibilities *in Joseph's hand*. One is delivered from the *hands* of one's enemies, just as the de-feated are given over into the *hands* of their conquerors. Accord-ing to Proverbs, one of the characteristics of a virtuous woman is that she "worketh willingly with her hands." Symbolically, hands stand for many things — creativity, industry, power, re-sponsibility.

Feet are even more symbolic than hands in the Old Testament. They are practically always used in a connotative, imaginative sense. In constant remembrance of the rough and perilous roads over which bare or sandaled feet must walk, the poets and prophets see feet as slipping or stumbling, or falling into snares or nets. Such stumbling and backsliding is often the symbol for a spiritual fall from grace. Contrarily, sureness of footing often refers to uprightness and stability in a moral as well as a physical sense, as when a Psalmist says of the Lord, "He brought me up also out of a horrible pit, out of the miry clay, and set my feet upon a rock, and established my goings."

The concrete yet symbolic language of the Hebrew writers made it particularly suitable for translation. And by a lucky coincidence the translators of the first printed English Bibles were men of the sixteenth-century Renaissance in England, for as Roland Frye points out, "Of all the periods in our literary history, only the English Renaissance contained within itself so full an appreciation of literary style and expression as to allow its translators and editors to do full justice to the tone as well as the meaning of the Bible." In 1611 several English translations were combined into an Authorized Version, the King James Bible.

For more than three hundred years the King James Bible has been read and loved by millions of people. In many households it was the only book possessed. Its words and its rhythms became woven into the very fabric of English literature. Its influence resounds in the works of the greatest writers in English: Milton, Dickens, Hardy, Emerson, Hawthorne, Melville, to name only a few. If we know the Bible in the translation they knew, we can more fully understand and appreciate their work.

Nor do we realize how in the course of a single day we use many expressions from the King James Bible to record or to describe our doings, our moods and feelings, our hopes and fears, our narrow escapes, the demands made upon us on "our right hand and our left." Such expressions have become so much a part of our common speech that we have forgotten their ancient origin. Thus — we are hewers of wood and drawers of water; we earn our bread by the sweat of our faces and by the work of our hands; we rest from our labors; and we tolerate or welcome strangers within our gates. We sit in sackcloth and ashes; we eat sour grapes; we discover that like the leopard we cannot change our spots; we long to be giants in the earth but are satisfied if we can quit ourselves like men. We escape by the skin of our teeth, and we take our lives in our hands. Whether we know it or not, in all these phrases we are using the language of the King James Bible.

The making of the King James Bible is itself a fascinating story. The story begins with William Tyndale, who is sometimes called the Father of the English Bible. A teacher and a preacher who had studied at Oxford and Cambridge, Tyndale was outspokenly critical of the ignorance of the English clergy. To reveal how far the church had deviated from the early teaching of Christianity, Tyndale decided to translate the New Testament into English directly from the original Greek. (Any previous translations, which existed only in unprinted manuscript form, had been made from the Latin version, itself a translation.) In 1523 Tyndale asked the Bishop of London for permission to make the new translation. He encountered powerful resistance to his proposal, finding not only "that there were no rowme in my lorde of londons palace to translate the new Testament but also that there was no place to do it in all englonde."

Undaunted, Tyndale went to Germany, and in 1526 the first printing of his New Testament was completed. Copies were smuggled into England despite the Church and royal authorities who prohibited their use and ordered them burned. Tyndale then set to work translating the first five books of the Old Testament, which were published in 1530. Hunted down by enemies of the Reformation, Tyndale was finally convicted of heresy and sentenced to death. In 1536 he was burned at the stake in Belgium, crying out, "Lord, open the King of England's eyes."

It was Tyndale's translation, though incomplete, that determined the style of other translators, and the King James Bible is based more on his work than on any other. Significantly, Tyndale was the first to translate the Bible into English directly from Hebrew and Greek. Perhaps this accounts for the simplicity and vigor of his style, a style which shaped "the noblest monument of English prose," as the King James Bible has been called.

The persecution and martyrdom of Tyndale coincided with a rush of other printed English Bibles. The first *complete* translation, based largely on Tyndale's work, was prepared by Miles Coverdale and printed in 1535. About this time the Reformation was well under way in England, and the English clergy were eager for a translation authorized to be read in churches. In 1539 appeared the Great Bible — so called because of its size — edited largely by Miles Coverdale. In this version Coverdale again relied heavily on Tyndale's translation, as well as Hebrew, Greek, Latin, and German versions.

During the reign of the Catholic Queen Mary there were no Bibles printed in England. To escape Mary's persecution, many Protestant scholars fled to the Continent. One group, later to be known as Puritans, settled in Geneva. There, in 1560, they published their own translation of the Bible, based on Tyndale and Coverdale, as well as the latest biblical scholarship.

This Geneva Bible is important in the history of English Bibles. Moderate in size and price, it was the Bible used in most English homes until it was eventually superseded by the King James Version. It was the first to be printed in roman type and the first to divide the text into numbered verses. Most important, it provided many of the most beautiful passages in the King James Bible. Other passages were not so felicitous, as Genesis 3:7: "They sewed fig leaves together and made themselves breeches." From this verse came the commonly used nickname of the Geneva Bible — the "Breeches" Bible.

With the accession of the Protestant Queen Elizabeth, the Great Bible was again officially sanctioned to be read in the churches. However, the Geneva Bible remained the most popular among laymen. Its popularity disturbed the bishops — it overshadowed the Great Bible, and it had marginal notes that were too nonconformist for the Church of England. To compete with the Geneva Bible, the church authorities revised the Great Bible and published in 1568 the version known as the Bishop's Bible. Large and pretentious and illustrated by woodcuts, it nevertheless did not dim the popularity of the Geneva Bible.

In 1604 a scholar by the name of John Reynolds proposed a new translation to King James, who had succeeded to the English throne in 1603. The king was enthusiastic about the proposal and appointed fifty-four "learned men . . . having especial skill in the Hebrew and Greek tongues" to make the new translation. The scholars were divided into six companies of nine men each, and each company was assigned a portion of the Bible.

Of the task before them, the translators "never thought from the beginning that we should need to make a new translation, nor yet to make of a bad one a good one; but to make a good one better, or out of many good ones one principal good one. . . ." They worked with biblical texts in the original languages and with the existing English translations, most of which traced back to Tyndale and Coverdale. After comparing texts, the editors chose the best reading, or if necessary, made up a new one.

It is interesting to compare the renderings of the earlier Bibles with those of the King James Bible, as in the opening words of Psalm 23:

COVERDALE:
The Lord is my shepherd, I can want nothing. He feedeth me in a green pasture,
GREAT BIBLE:
The Lord is my shepherd, therefore can I lack nothing. He shall feed me in a green pasture,
GENEVA:
The Lord is my shepherd, I shall not want. He maketh me to rest in green pasture,
BISHOPS:
God is my sheepherd, therefore I can lack nothing: He will cause me to repose myself in pasture full of grass,
KING JAMES:
The Lord is my shepherd, I shall not want. He maketh me to lie down in green pastures:

Here the scholars have essentially used the Geneva wording, with the improvement of substituting "lie down" for "rest" and of using the plural "green pastures." The changes are an example of what John Livingstone Lowes describes as the "winnowing of words" by the King James translators until they found the perfect one.

Thus the fifty-four learned men went through the entire Bible, working passage by passage to achieve the most correct translation and the most felicitous phrasing. The result was a masterpiece of literary taste and sound scholarship. The actual revision took two years and nine months, and the preparation for press another nine months. The edition appeared in 1611, and to this day no one has explained the mystery of how a committee could have produced such a unified and inspired work.

"It is the great good fortune of English-speaking people to have an English version of the Bible which stands with the original in literary power and excellence." So remarked the great English poet Coleridge. It is indeed good fortune that we can read the works of the Hebrew writers in a style so close to their own. We can better appreciate the riches that the Old Testament has to offer us.

The Old Testament is the history of a race, the revelation of its mind, the record of its eternal, restless search after "the things of God." If it were only that, in the hands and minds of gifted men, it would rightly deserve immortality. But it is more. For these ancient men by their wisdom, desire, and compassion, by their understanding of the power of language, and by their imagination which carried them from their bare Judean hills to the uttermost parts of the earth, have transformed the story of a particular people into the story of all mankind. It is surely not by chance that the term *every man* occurs numberless times in both prose and poetry in the Old Testament. For the Old Testament is the record of the life of every man, in every age and place, throughout all the perils and the compensations of his threescore years and ten.

MARY ELLEN CHASE

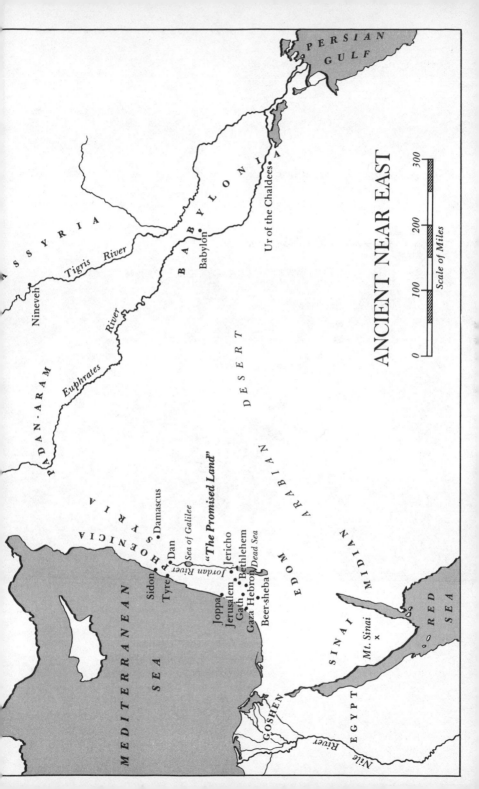

Cain Killing Abel
The Royal Museum of Fine Arts, Copenhagen

In
the
Beginning

When the astronauts who first circled the moon saw the light of the sun rising above the moon's horizon, they shared their feeling of awe with the rest of mankind by reading the opening verses of Genesis. This selection was appropriate. Whether we accept the biblical story of Creation as literal truth or as an awesome allegory of the origins of all things, it expresses man's wonder at the glories and mysteries of the universe.

In the opening chapters of Genesis are some of the most fascinating and famous stories of the Bible — the creation and fall of man, the murder of Abel by his brother Cain, the great flood, and the building of the Tower of Babel. All these stories are an attempt to answer some of the questions that puzzled and excited men thousands of years ago — and still do: what are the origins of the universe? where did life come from? how did evil enter the world?

Genesis

The Creation

One In the beginning God created the heaven and the earth. And the earth was without form, and void, and darkness was upon the face of the deep. And the spirit of God moved upon the face of the waters. And God said, "Let there be light": and there was light. And God saw the light, that it was good: and God divided the light from the darkness. And God called the light Day, and the darkness he called Night: and the evening and morning were the first day.

And God said, "Let there be a firmament in the midst of the waters; and let it divide the waters from the waters." And God made the firmament, and divided the waters which were under the firmament from the waters which were above the firmament: and it was so. And God called the firmament Heaven: and the evening and the morning were the second day.

> THE LORD BY WISDOM HATH FOUNDED THE EARTH; BY
> UNDERSTANDING HATH HE ESTABLISHED THE HEAVENS.
>
> PROVERBS 3:1

And God said, "Let the waters under the heaven be gathered together unto one place, and let the dry land appear": and it was so. And God called the dry land Earth, and the gathering together of the waters called he Seas: and God saw that it was good. And God said, "Let the earth bring forth grass, the herb yielding seed,

2

and the fruit tree yielding fruit after his kind, whose seed is in itself, upon the earth": and it was so. And the earth brought forth grass, and herb yielding seed after his kind, and the tree yielding fruit, whose seed was in itself, after his kind: and God saw that it was good. And the evening and the morning were the third day.

And God said, "Let there be lights in the firmament of the heaven, to divide the day from the night: and let them be for signs and for seasons, and for days and years. And let them be for lights in the firmament of the heaven, to give light upon the earth": and it was so. And God made two great lights; the greater light to rule the day, and the lesser light to rule the night: he made the stars also. And God set them in the firmament of the heaven to give light upon the earth, and to rule over the day and over the night, and to divide the light from the darkness: and God saw that it was good. And the evening and the morning were the fourth day.

And God said, "Let the waters bring forth abundantly the moving creature that hath life, and fowl that may fly above the earth in the open firmament of heaven." And God created great whales, and every living creature that moveth, which the waters brought forth abundantly after their kind, and every winged fowl after his kind: and God saw that it was good. And God blessed them, saying, "Be fruitful, and multiply, and fill the waters in the sea, and let fowl multiply in the earth." And the evening and the morning were the fifth day.

And God said, "Let the earth bring forth the living creature after his kind, cattle,[1] and creeping thing, and beast of the earth after his kind": and it was so. And God made the beast of the earth after his kind, and cattle after their kind, and every thing that creepeth upon the earth after his kind: and God saw that it was good.

And God said, "Let us make man in our image, after our likeness: and let them have dominion over the fish of the sea, and over the fowl of the air, and over the cattle, and over all the earth, and over every creeping thing that creepeth upon the earth." So God

---

[1] *cattle:* a collective noun for several kinds of animals — oxen, camels, sheep, goats.

created man in his own image, in the image of God created he him; male and female created he them. And God blessed them, and God said unto them, "Be fruitful, and multiply, and replenish the earth, and subdue it, and have dominion over the fish of the sea, and over the fowl of the air, and over every living thing that moveth upon the earth."

And God said, "Behold, I have given you every herb bearing seed, which is upon the face of all the earth, and every tree, in the which is the fruit of a tree yielding seed; to you it shall be for meat. And to every beast of the earth, and to every fowl of the air, and to every thing that creepeth upon the earth, wherein there is life, I have given every green herb for meat": and it was so. And God saw every thing that he had made: and behold, it was very good. And the evening and the morning were the sixth day.

Two Thus the heavens and the earth were finished, and all the host of them. And on the seventh day God ended his work which he had made; and he rested on the seventh day from all his work which he had made. And God blessed the seventh day, and sanctified it: because that in it he had rested from all his work which God created and made.

These are the generations of the heavens and of the earth when they were created, in the day that the Lord God made the earth and the heavens, and every plant of the field before it was in the earth and every herb of the field before it grew: for the Lord God had not caused it to rain upon the earth, and there was not a man to till the ground. But there went up a mist from the earth, and watered the whole face of the ground. And the Lord God formed man of the dust of the ground, and breathed into his nostrils the breath of life; and man became a living soul.

The Garden of Eden

And the Lord God planted a garden eastward in Eden; and there he put the man whom he had formed. And out of the ground made the Lord God to grow every tree that is pleasant to the sight and good for food; the tree of life also in the midst of the garden, and the tree of knowledge of good and evil.

And a river went out of Eden to water the garden; and from thence it was parted, and became into four heads. The name of the first is Pison: that is it which compasseth the whole land of Havilah, where there is gold; and the gold of that land is good: there is bdellium[2] and the onyx stone. And the name of the second river is Gihon: the same is it that compasseth the whole land of Ethiopia. And the name of the third river is Hiddekel: that is it which goeth toward the east of Assyria. And the fourth river is Euphrates.

And the Lord God took the man, and put him into the garden of Eden, to dress it and to keep it. And the Lord God commanded the man, saying, "Of every tree of the garden thou mayest freely eat. But of the tree of the knowledge of good and evil, thou shalt not eat of it: for in the day that thou eatest thereof thou shalt surely die."

And the Lord God said, "It is not good that the man should be alone; I will make him an help meet for him." And out of the ground the Lord God formed every beast of the field, and every fowl of the air, and brought them unto Adam, to see what he would call them: and whatsoever Adam called every living creature, that was the name thereof. And Adam gave names to all cattle, and to the fowl of the air, and to every beast of the field: but for Adam there was not found an help meet for him.

And the Lord God caused a deep sleep to fall upon Adam, and he slept: and he took one of his ribs, and closed up the flesh instead thereof. And the rib which the Lord God had taken from man, made he a woman, and brought her unto the man. And Adam said, "This is now bone of my bones, and flesh of my flesh: she shall be called Woman, because she was taken out of Man." Therefore shall a man leave his father and his mother, and shall cleave unto his wife: and they shall be one flesh. And they were both naked, the man and his wife, and were not ashamed.

Three Now the serpent was more subtle than any beast of the field which the Lord God had made, and he said unto the woman, "Yea, hath God said, 'Ye shall not eat of every tree of the garden'?" And the woman said unto the serpent, "We may eat of the fruit of

2 *bdellium:* a fragrant yellow gum resin much valued as a spice in antiquity.

the trees of the garden, but of the fruit of the tree which is in the midst of the garden, God hath said, 'Ye shall not eat of it, neither shall ye touch it, lest ye die.' " And the serpent said unto the woman, "Ye shall not surely die. For God doth know that in the day ye eat thereof, then your eyes shall be opened: and ye shall be as gods, knowing good and evil."

And when the woman saw that the tree was good for food, and that it was pleasant to the eyes, and a tree to be desired to make one wise, she took of the fruit thereof, and did eat, and gave also unto her husband with her; and he did eat. And the eyes of them both were opened, and they knew that they were naked, and they sewed fig leaves together, and made themselves aprons. And they heard the voice of the Lord God walking in the garden in the cool of the day: and Adam and his wife hid themselves from the presence of the Lord God amongst the trees of the garden.

And the Lord God called unto Adam, and said unto him, "Where art thou?" And he said, "I heard thy voice in the garden, and I was afraid, because I was naked; and I hid myself." And he said, "Who told thee that thou wast naked? Hast thou eaten of the tree whereof I commanded thee that thou shouldst not eat?" And the man said, "The woman whom thou gavest to be with me, she gave me of the tree, and I did eat." And the Lord God said unto the woman, "What is this that thou hast done?" And the woman said, "The serpent beguiled me, and I did eat."

And the Lord God said unto the serpent, "Because thou hast done this, thou art cursed above all cattle, and above every beast of the field; upon thy belly shalt thou go, and dust shalt thou eat all the days of thy life. And I will put enmity between thee and the woman, and between thy seed and her seed; it shall bruise thy head, and thou shalt bruise his heel." Unto the woman he said, "I will greatly multiply thy sorrow and thy conception; in sorrow thou shalt bring forth children; and thy desire shall be to thy husband, and he shall rule over thee."

And unto Adam he said, "Because thou hast hearkened unto the voice of thy wife, and hast eaten of the tree, of which I commanded thee, saying, 'Thou shalt not eat of it': cursed is the ground for thy sake; in sorrow shalt thou eat of it all the days of thy life.

Thorns also and thistles shall it bring forth to thee; and thou shalt eat the herb of the field. In the sweat of thy face shalt thou eat bread, till thou return unto the ground; for out of it wast thou taken, for dust thou art, and unto dust shalt thou return." And Adam called his wife's name Eve, because she was the mother of all living. Unto Adam also, and to his wife did the Lord God make coats of skins, and clothed them.

And the Lord God said, "Behold, the man is become as one of us, to know good and evil: and now, lest he put forth his hand, and take also of the tree of life, and eat, and live for ever": therefore the Lord God sent him forth from the garden of Eden, to till the ground from whence he was taken. So he drove out the man; and he placed at the east of the garden of Eden cherubim, and a flaming sword which turned every way, to keep the way of the tree of life.

Cain and Abel

Four And Adam knew Eve his wife; and she conceived, and bare Cain, and said, "I have gotten a man from the Lord." And she again bare his brother Abel. And Abel was a keeper of sheep, but Cain was a tiller of the ground. And in process of time it came to pass, that Cain brought of the fruit of the ground an offering unto the Lord. And Abel, he also brought of the firstlings of his flock and of the fat thereof. And the Lord had respect unto Abel and to his offering: but unto Cain and to his offering he had not respect. And Cain was very wroth, and his countenance fell. And the Lord said until Cain, "Why art thou wroth? And why is thy countenance fallen? If thou do well, shalt thou not be accepted? and if thou doest not well, sin lieth at the door. And unto thee shall be his desire, and thou shalt rule over him." And Cain talked with Abel his brother: and it came to pass when they were in the field, that Cain rose up against Abel his brother, and slew him.

And the Lord said unto Cain, "Where is Abel thy brother?" And he said, "I know not: am I my brother's keeper?" And he said, "What hast thou done? the voice of thy brother's blood crieth unto me from the ground. And now art thou cursed from the earth, which hath opened her mouth to receive thy brother's blood from thy hand. When thou tillest the ground, it shall not henceforth yield unto thee her strength; a fugitive and a vagabond shalt thou be in the earth." And Cain said unto the Lord, "My punishment is greater than I can bear. Behold, thou hast driven me out this day from the face of the earth; and from thy face shall I be hid; and I shall be a fugitive and a vagabond in the earth; and it shall come to pass, that every one that findeth me shall slay me." And the Lord said unto him, "Therefore whosoever slayeth Cain, vengeance shall be taken on him sevenfold." And the Lord set a mark upon Cain, lest any finding him should kill him.

And Cain went out from the presence of the Lord, and dwelt in the land of Nod, on the east of Eden. . . .

Noah and the Ark

Six And it came to pass, when men began to multiply on the face of the earth, and daughters were born unto them, that the sons of God saw the daughters of men, that they were fair; and they took them wives of all which they chose. And the Lord said, "My spirit shall not always strive with man, for that he also is flesh: yet his days shall be an hundred and twenty years." There were giants in the earth in those days; and also after that, when the sons of God came in unto the daughters of men, and they bare children to them, the same became mighty men, which were of old, men of renown.

And God saw that the wickedness of men was great in the earth, and that every imagination of the thoughts of his heart was only evil continually. And it repented the Lord that he had made man on the earth, and it grieved him at his heart. And the Lord said, "I will destroy man whom I have created from the face of the earth; both man, and beast, and the creeping thing, and the fowls of the air; for it repenteth me that I have made them." But Noah found grace in the eyes of the Lord.

These are the generations of Noah: Noah was a just man and perfect in his generations, and Noah walked with God. And Noah begat three sons, Shem, Ham, and Japheth. The earth also was corrupt before God, and the earth was filled with violence. And God looked upon the earth, and, behold, it was corrupt; for all flesh had corrupted his way upon the earth. And God said unto Noah, "The end of all flesh is come before me; for the earth is filled with violence through them; and, behold, I will destroy them with the earth."

"Make thee an ark of gopher wood;³ rooms shalt thou make in the ark, and shalt pitch it within and without with pitch. And this is the fashion which thou shalt make it of: The length of the ark shall be three hundred cubits,⁴ the breadth of it fifty cubits, and the height of it thirty cubits. A window shalt thou make to the ark, and in a cubit shalt thou finish it above; and the door of the ark shalt thou set in the side thereof; with lower, second, and third stories shalt thou make it. And, behold, I, even I do bring a flood of waters upon the earth, to destroy all flesh wherein is the breath of life from under heaven; and every thing that is in the earth shall die. But with thee will I establish my covenant; and thou shalt come into the ark, thou, and thy sons, and thy wife, and thy sons' wives with thee. And of every living thing of all flesh, two of every sort shalt thou bring into the ark, to keep them alive with thee; they shall be male and female. Of fowls after their kind, and of cattle after their kind, of every creeping thing of the earth after his kind, two of every sort shall come unto thee, to keep them alive. And take thou unto thee of all food that is eaten, and thou shalt gather it to thee; and it shall be for food for thee, and for them." Thus did Noah; according to all that God commanded him, so did he.

Seven And the Lord said unto Noah, "Come thou and all thy house into the ark; for thee have I seen righteous before me in this generation. Of every clean beast thou shalt take to thee by sevens,⁵ the male and the female: and of beasts that are not clean by two, the male and the female. Of fowls also of the air, by sevens, the male and female; to keep seed alive upon the face of all the earth. For yet seven days, and I will cause it to rain

³ *gopher wood:* cypress.
⁴ *cubits:* a cubit is a measurement of length, approximately 18 inches.
⁵ *sevens:* perhaps seven pairs.

upon the earth forty days and forty nights; and every living substance that I have made will I destroy from off the face of the earth." And Noah did according unto all that the Lord commanded him. And Noah was six hundred years old when the flood of waters was upon the earth.

And Noah went in, and his sons, and his wife, and his sons' wives with him, into the ark, because of the waters of the flood. Of clean beasts, and of beasts that are not clean, and of fowls, and of every thing that creepeth upon the earth, there went in two and two unto Noah into the ark, the male and the female, as God had commanded Noah. And it came to pass after seven days, that the waters of the flood were upon the earth.

In the six hundredth year of Noah's life, in the second month, the seventeenth day of the month, the same day were all the fountains of the great deep broken up, and the windows of heaven were opened. And the rain was upon the earth forty days and forty nights. In the selfsame day entered Noah, and Shem, and Ham, and Japheth, the sons of Noah, and Noah's wife, and the three wives of his sons with them, into the ark; they, and every beast after his kind, and all the cattle after their kind, and every creeping thing that creepeth upon the earth after his kind, and every fowl after his kind, every bird of every sort. And they went in unto Noah into the ark, two and two of all flesh, wherein is the breath of life. And they that went in, went in male and female of all flesh, as God had commanded him: and the Lord shut him in.

And the flood was forty days upon the earth; and the waters increased, and bare up the ark, and it was lifted up above the earth. And the waters prevailed, and were increased greatly upon the earth; and the ark went upon the face of the waters. And the waters prevailed exceedingly upon the earth; and all the high hills that were under the whole heaven were covered. Fifteen cubits upward did the waters prevail; and the mountains were covered.

And all flesh died that moved upon the earth, both of fowl, and of cattle, and of beast, and of every creeping thing that creepeth upon the earth, and every man. All in whose nostrils was the breath of life, of all that was in the dry land, died. And every living substance was destroyed which was upon the face of the ground, both man and cattle, and the creeping things, and the fowl of the heaven; and they were destroyed from the earth: and Noah only remained alive, and they that were with him in the ark. And the waters prevailed upon the earth an hundred and fifty days.

Eight And God remembered Noah, and every living thing, and all the cattle that was with him in the ark: and God made a wind to pass over the earth, and the waters assuaged. The fountains also of the deep and the windows of heaven were stopped, and the rain from heaven was restrained. And the waters returned from off the earth continually: and after the end of the hundred and fifty days the waters were abated. And the ark rested in the seventh month, on the seventeenth day of the month, upon the mountains of Ararat. And the waters decreased continually until the tenth month: in the tenth month, on the first day of the month, were the tops of the mountains seen.

And it came to pass at the end of forty days, that Noah opened the window of the ark which he had made: and he sent forth a raven, which went forth to and fro, until the waters were dried up from off the earth. Also he sent forth a dove from him, to see if the waters were abated from off the face of the ground; but the dove found no rest for the sole of her foot, and she returned unto him into the ark: for the waters were on the face of the whole earth. Then he put forth his hand, and took her, and pulled her in unto him, into the ark. And he stayed yet other seven days; and again he sent forth the dove out of the ark. And the dove came in to him in the evening; and lo, in her mouth was an olive leaf plucked off: so Noah knew that the waters were abated from off the earth. And he stayed yet other seven days, and sent forth the dove, which returned not again unto him any more.

And it came to pass in the six hundredth and one year, in the first month, the first day of the month, the waters were dried up from off the earth: and Noah removed the covering of the ark, and looked, and behold, the face of the ground was dry. And in the second month, on the seven and twentieth day of the month, was the earth dried.

And God spake unto Noah, saying, "Go forth of the ark, thou, and thy wife, and thy sons and thy sons' wives with thee. Bring forth with thee every living thing that is with thee, of all flesh, both of fowl, and of cattle, and of every creeping thing that creepeth upon the earth; that they may breed abundantly in the earth, and be fruitful, and multiply upon the earth." And Noah went forth, and his sons, and his wife, and his sons' wives with him: every beast, every creeping thing, and every fowl, and whatsoever creepeth upon the earth, after their kinds, went forth out of the ark.

And Noah builded an altar unto the Lord, and took of every clean beast, and of every clean fowl, and offered burnt offerings on the altar. And the Lord smelled a sweet savour; and the Lord said in his heart, "I will not again curse the ground any more for man's sake, for the imagination of man's heart is evil from his youth; neither will I again smite any more every thing living, as I have done. While the earth remaineth, seedtime and harvest, and cold and heat, and summer and winter, and day and night shall not cease."

Nine   And God blessed Noah and his sons, and said unto them, "Be fruitful and multiply, and replenish the earth. And the fear of you and the dread of you shall be upon every beast of the earth, and upon every fowl of the air, upon all that moveth upon the earth, and upon all the fishes of the sea; into your hand are they delivered. Every moving thing that liveth shall be meat for you; even as the green herb have I given you all things. But flesh with the life thereof, which is the blood thereof, shall you not eat. And surely your blood of your lives will I require; at the hand of every beast will I require it, and at the hand of man; at the hand of every man's brother will I require the life of man. Whoso sheddeth man's blood, by man shall his blood be shed: for in the image of God made he man. And you, be ye fruitful and multiply; bring forth abundantly in the earth, and multiply therein."

And God spake unto Noah, and to his sons with him, saying, "And I, behold, I establish my covenant with you and with your seed after you; and with every living creature that is with you, of the fowl, of cattle, and of every beast of the earth with you; from all that go out of the ark, to every beast of the earth. And I will establish my covenant with you; neither shall all flesh be cut off any more by the waters of a flood; neither shall there any more be a flood to destroy the earth."

And God said, "This is the token of the covenant which I make between me and you and every living creature that is with you, for perpetual generations. I do set my bow in the cloud, and it shall be for a token of a covenant between me and the earth. And it shall come to pass, when I bring a cloud over the earth, that the bow shall be seen in the cloud: And I will remember my covenant, which is between me and you, and every living creature of all flesh; and the waters shall no more become a flood to destroy all flesh. And the bow shall be in the cloud; and I will look upon it, that I may remember the everlasting covenant between God and every living creature of all flesh that is upon the earth." And God said unto Noah, "This is the token of the covenant which I have established between me and all flesh that is upon the earth."

And the sons of Noah that went forth of the ark were Shem, and Ham, and Japheth: and Ham is the father of Canaan. These are the three sons of Noah: and of them was the whole earth overspread. . . .

The Tower of Babel

Eleven And the whole earth was of one language, and of one speech. And it came to pass, as they journeyed from the east, that they found a plain in the land of Shinar,[6] and they dwelt there. And they said one to another, "Go to, let us make brick, and burn them thoroughly." And they had brick for stone, and slime had they for mortar. And they said, "Go to, let us build us a city and a tower, whose top may reach unto heaven; and let us make us a name, lest we be scattered abroad upon the face of the whole earth." And the Lord came down to see the city and the tower, which the children of men builded. And the Lord said,

6 *Shinar:* Babylonia.

"Behold, the people is one, and they have all one language: and this they began to do: and now nothing will be restrained from them, which they have imagined to do. Go to, let us go down, and there confound their language, that they may not understand one another's speech." So the Lord scattered them abroad from thence upon the face of all the earth: and they left off to build the city. Therefore is the name of it called Babel, because the Lord did there confound the language of all the earth: and from thence did the Lord scatter them abroad upon the face of all the earth. . . .

Abraham Conversing with the Angel
C. Robert Rudolf, London

Abraham and Isaac

The earliest Hebrews were nomads who moved from place to place with their flocks and lived in tents. At the head of each tribe was a patriarch, or tribal leader. The first of the great patriarchs whose lives are recorded in the Old Testament was Abraham, who probably lived around 1850 B.C. When he was an old man, the Lord commanded Abraham to move from Ur, in Babylonia, to Canaan, 700 miles westward on the shores of the Mediterranean. Abraham obeyed the command, for he was the man of absolute faith. When God directed him to sacrifice the son of his old age, Abraham was again obedient to the Lord's will. Abraham was also a man of compassion, who pleaded with God not to destroy Sodom and Gomorrah. More than any other biblical figure, Abraham dealt directly with God in the fulfillment of God's plan for mankind.

Genesis

God's Covenant with Abraham

Seventeen And when Abram was ninety years old and nine, the Lord appeared to Abram, and said unto him, "I am the almighty God, walk before me, and be thou perfect. And I will make my covenant between me and thee, and will multiply thee exceedingly." And Abram fell on his face, and God talked with him, saying, "As for me, behold, my covenant is with thee, and thou shalt be a father of many nations. Neither shall thy name any more be called Abram, but thy name shall be Abraham: for a father of many nations have I made thee. And I will make thee exceeding fruitful, and I will make nations of thee, and kings shall come out of thee. And I will establish my covenant between me and thee, and thy seed after thee, in their generations for an everlasting covenant, to be a God unto thee, and to thy seed after thee. And I will give unto thee, and to thy seed after thee, the land wherein thou art a stranger, all the land of Canaan, for an everlasting possession, and I will be their God."

And God said unto Abraham, "Thou shalt keep my covenant therefore, thou, and thy seed after thee, in their generations. This is my covenant, which ye shall keep between me and you, and thy seed after thee: every man child among you shall be circumcised. And ye shall circumcise the flesh of your foreskin; and it shall be a token of the covenant betwixt me and you. And he that is eight days old shall be circumcised among you, every man child in your generations, he that is born in the house, or bought with money of any stranger, which is not of thy seed. He that is born in thy house, and he that is bought with thy money, must needs be circumcised: and my covenant shall be in your flesh for an everlasting covenant. And the uncircumcised man child whose flesh of his foreskin is not circumcised, that soul shall be cut off from his people: he hath broken my covenant." . . .

A Son Is Promised

Eighteen And the Lord appeared unto him in the plains of Mamre: and he sat in the tent door, in the heat of the day. And he lifted up his eyes and looked, and lo, three men stood by him: and when he saw them, he ran to meet them from the tent door, and bowed himself toward the ground, and said, "My Lord, if now I have found favour in thy sight, pass not away, I pray thee, from thy servant: let a little water, I pray you, be fetched, and wash your feet, and rest yourselves under the tree: and I will fetch a morsel of bread; and comfort ye your hearts, after that ye shall pass on: for therefore are you come to your servant." And they said, "So do, as thou hast said." And Abraham hastened into the tent, unto Sarah, and said, "Make ready quickly three measures of fine meal, knead it, and make cakes upon the hearth." And Abraham ran unto the herd, and fetched a calf, tender and good, and gave it unto a young man: and he hasted to dress it. And he took butter, and milk, and the calf which he had dressed, and set it before them, and he stood by them under the tree: and they did eat.

And they said unto him, "Where is Sarah thy wife?" And he said, "Behold, in the tent." And he said, "I will certainly return unto thee according to the time of your life; and lo, Sarah thy wife shall have a son." And Sarah heard it in the tent door, which was behind him. Now Abraham and Sarah were old, and well stricken in age: and it ceased to be with Sarah after the manner of women. Therefore Sarah laughed within herself, saying, "After I am waxed old shall I have pleasure, my lord being old also?" And the Lord said unto Abraham, "Wherefore did Sarah laugh, saying, 'Shall I of a surety bear a child, which am old?' Is any thing too hard for the Lord? At the time appointed will I return unto thee, according to the time of life, and Sarah shall have a son." Then Sarah denied, saying, "I laughed not": for she was afraid. And he said, "Nay, but thou didst laugh."

Sodom and Gomorrah

And the men rose up from thence, and looked toward Sodom: and Abraham went with them, to bring them on the way. And the Lord said, "Shall I hide from Abraham that thing which I do; seeing that Abraham shall surely become a great and mighty nation, and all the nations of the earth shall be blessed in him? For I know him, that he will command his children, and his household after him, and they shall keep the way of the Lord, to do justice and judgment, that the Lord may bring upon Abraham that which he hath spoken of him." And the Lord said, "Because the cry of Sodom and Gomorrah is great, and because their sin is very grievous: I will go down now, and see whether they have done altogether according to the cry of it, which is come unto me: and if not, I will know." And the men turned their faces from thence, and went toward Sodom: but Abraham stood yet before the Lord.

And Abraham drew near, and said, "Wilt thou also destroy the righteous with the wicked? Peradventure there be fifty righteous within the city; wilt thou also destroy, and not spare the place for the fifty righteous that are therein? That be far from thee, to do after this manner, to slay the righteous with the wicked; and that the righteous should be as the wicked, that be far from thee: shall not the judge of all the earth do right?" And the Lord said, "If I find in Sodom fifty righteous within the city, then I will spare all the place for their sakes." And Abraham answered, and said, "Behold now, I have taken upon me to speak unto the Lord, which am but dust and ashes. Peradventure there shall lack five of the fifty righteous: wilt thou destroy all the city for lack of five?" And he said, "If I find there forty and five, I will not destroy it." And he spake unto him yet again, and said, "Peradventure there shall be forty found there." And he said, "I will not do it for forty's sake." And he said unto him, "Oh let not the Lord be angry, and I will speak: peradventure there shall thirty be found there." And he said, "I will not do it, if I find thirty there." And he said, "Behold now, I have taken upon me to speak unto the Lord: peradventure there shall be twenty found there." And he said, "I will not destroy it for twenty's sake." And he said, "Oh let not the Lord be angry, and I will speak yet but this once: peradventure ten shall be found there." And he said, "I will not destroy it for ten's sake." And the Lord went his way, as soon as he had left communing with Abraham: and Abraham returned unto his place.

Nineteen And there came two angels to Sodom at even, and Lot sat in the gate of Sodom: and Lot seeing them rose up to meet them, and he bowed himself with his face toward the ground. And he said, "Behold now my lords, turn in, I pray you, into your servant's house, and tarry all night, and wash your feet, and ye shall rise up early and go on your ways." And they said, "Nay: but we will abide in the street all night." And he pressed upon them greatly, and they turned in unto him, and entered into his house: and he made them a feast, and did bake unleavened bread, and they did eat.

But before they lay down, the men of the city, even the men of Sodom, compassed the house round, both old and young, all the people from every quarter. And they called unto Lot, and said unto him, "Where are the men which came in to thee this night? bring them out unto us, that we may know them." And Lot went out at the door unto them, and shut the door after him, and said, "I pray you, brethren, do not so wickedly. Behold now, I have two daughters, which have not known man; let me, I pray you, bring them out unto you, and do ye to them as is good in your eyes: only unto these men do nothing: for therefore came they under the shadow of my roof." And they said, "Stand back." And they said again, "This one fellow came in to sojourn, and he will needs be a judge: now will we deal worse with thee than with them." And they pressed sore upon the man, even Lot, and came near to break the door. But the men put forth their hand, and pulled Lot into the house to them, and shut to the door.

And they smote the men that were at the door of the house with blindness, both small and great: so that they wearied themselves to find the door.

And the men said unto Lot, "Hast thou here any besides? Son-in-law, and thy sons, and thy daughters, and whatsoever thou hast in the city, bring them out of this place. For we will destroy this place, because the cry of them is waxen great before the face of the Lord: and the Lord hath sent us to destroy it." And Lot went out, and spake unto his sons-in-law, which married his daughters, and said, "Up, get ye out of this place: for the Lord will destroy this city": but he seemed as one that mocked unto his sons-in-law.

And when the morning arose, then the angels hastened Lot, saying, "Arise, take thy wife, and thy two daughters, which are here, lest thou be consumed in the iniquity of the city." And while he lingered, the men laid hold upon his hand, and upon the hand of his wife, and upon the hand of his two daughters, the Lord being merciful unto him: and they brought him forth, and set him without the city.

And it came to pass, when they had brought them forth abroad, that he said, "Escape for thy life, look not behind thee, neither stay thou in all the plain: escape to the mountains, lest thou be consumed." And Lot said unto them, "Oh, not so, my Lord. Behold now, thy servant hath found grace in thy sight, and thou hast magnified thy mercy, which thou hast showed unto me in saving my life, and I cannot escape to the mountains, lest some evil take me, and I die. Behold now, this city is near to flee unto, and it is a little one. Oh, let me escape thither (is it not a little one?), and my soul shall live." And he said unto him, "See, I have accepted thee concerning this thing also, that I will not overthrow this city, for the which thou hast spoken. Haste thee, escape thither: for I cannot do any thing till thou be come thither": therefore the name of the city was called Zoar.

The sun was risen upon the earth when Lot entered into Zoar. Then the Lord rained upon Sodom and upon Gomorrah brimstone and fire from the Lord out of heaven. And he overthrew those cities, and all the plain, and all the inhabitants of the cities, and that which grew upon the ground. But his wife looked back from behind him, and she became a pillar of salt.

And Abraham got up early in the morning to the place where he stood before the Lord. And he looked toward Sodom and Gomorrah, and toward all the land of the plain, and beheld, and lo, the smoke of the country went up as the smoke of a furnace. And it came to pass, when God destroyed the cities of the plain, that God remembered Abraham, and sent Lot out of the midst of the overthrow, when he overthrew the cities in the which Lot dwelt. . . .

Birth and Youth of Isaac

Twenty-one And the Lord visited Sarah as he had said, and the Lord did unto Sarah as he had spoken. For Sarah conceived, and bare Abraham a son in his old age, at the set time of which God had spoken to him. And Abraham called the name of his son that was born unto him, whom Sarah bare to him, Isaac. And Abraham circumcised his son Isaac, being eight days old, as God had commanded him.

And Abraham was an hundred years old when his son Isaac was born unto him. And Sarah said, "God hath made me to laugh, so that all that hear will laugh with me." And she said, "Who would have said unto Abraham that Sarah should have given children suck? for I have borne him a son in his old age." And the child grew, and was weaned: and Abraham made a great feast the same day that Isaac was weaned.

> HOPE DEFERRED MAKETH THE HEART SICK: BUT WHEN
> THE DESIRE COMETH, IT IS A TREE OF LIFE.
> PROVERBS 13:12

And Sarah saw the son of Hagar the Egyptian, which she had borne unto Abraham, mocking. Wherefore she said unto Abraham, "Cast out this bondwoman and her son: for the son of this bondwoman shall not be heir with my son, even with Isaac." And the thing was very grievous in Abraham's sight, because of his son.

And God said unto Abraham, "Let it not be grievous in thy sight because of the lad, and because of thy bondwoman. In all that Sarah hath said unto thee, hearken unto her voice; for in

Isaac shall thy seed be called. And also of the son of the bond-woman will I make a nation, because he is thy seed." And Abraham rose up early in the morning, and took bread, and a bottle of water, and gave it unto Hagar, putting it on her shoulder, and the child, and sent her away: and she departed, and wandered in the wilderness of Beer-sheba. And the water was spent in the bottle, and she cast the child under one of the shrubs. And she went, and sat her down over against[1] him, a good way off, as it were a bowshot: for she said, "Let me not see the death of the child." And she sat over against him, and lifted up her voice, and wept. And God heard the voice of the lad; and the angel of God called to Hagar out of heaven, and said unto her, "What aileth thee, Hagar? fear not; for God hath heard the voice of the lad, where he is. Arise, lift up the lad, and hold him in thine hand; for I will make him a great nation." And God opened her eyes, and she saw a well of water, and she went, and filled the bottle with water, and gave the lad drink. And God was with the lad, and he grew, and dwelt in the wilderness, and became an archer. And he dwelt in the wilderness of Paran: and his mother took him a wife out of the land of Egypt. . . .

Twenty-two   And it came to pass after these things, that God did tempt[2] Abraham, and said unto him, "Abraham": and he said, "Behold, here I am." And he said, "Take now thy son, thine only son Isaac, whom thou lovest, and get thee into the land of Moriah; and offer him there for a burnt offering upon one of the mountains which I will tell thee of."

And Abraham rose up early in the morning, and saddled his ass, and took two of his young men with him, and Isaac his son, and clave the wood for the burnt offering, and rose up, and went unto the place of which God had told him. Then on the third day Abraham lifted up his eyes, and saw the place afar off. And Abraham said unto his young men, "Abide ye here with the ass; and I and the lad will go yonder and worship, and come again to you."

And Abraham took the wood of the burnt offering, and laid it

---

1 *against:* opposite.
2 *tempt:* test.

upon Isaac his son; and he took the fire in his hand, and a knife; and they went both of them together. And Isaac spake unto Abraham his father, and said, "My father": and he said, "Here am I, my son." And he said, "Behold the fire and the wood: but where is the lamb for a burnt offering?" And Abraham said, "My son, God will provide himself a lamb for a burnt offering": so they went both of them together. And they came to the place which God had told him of, and Abraham built an altar there, and laid the wood in order, and bound Isaac his son, and laid him on the altar upon the wood. And Abraham stretched forth his hand, and took the knife to slay his son.

And the angel of the Lord called unto him out of heaven, and said, "Abraham, Abraham." And he said, "Here am I." And he said, "Lay not thine hand upon the lad, neither do thou any thing unto him: for now I know that thou fearest God, seeing thou hast not withheld thy son, thine only son from me." And Abraham lifted up his eyes, and looked, and behold, behind him a ram caught in a thicket by his horns: and Abraham went and took the ram, and offered him up for a burnt offering in the stead of his son. And Abraham called the name of that place Jehovah-jireh, as it is said to this day, "In the mount of the Lord it shall be seen."

And the angel of the Lord called unto Abraham out of heaven the second time, and said, "By myself have I sworn, saith the Lord, for because thou hast done this thing, and hast not withheld thy son, thine only son, that in blessing I will bless thee, and in multiplying I will multiply thy seed as the stars of the heaven, and as the sand which is upon the sea shore; and thy seed shall possess the gate of his enemies. And in thy seed shall all the nations of the earth be blessed, because thou hast obeyed my voice." So Abraham returned unto his young men, and they rose up, and went together to Beer-sheba, and Abraham dwelt at Beer-sheba. . . .

The Search for a Bride: Rebekah

Twenty-four And Abraham was old and well stricken in age: and the Lord had blessed Abraham in all things. And Abraham said unto his eldest servant of his house, that ruled over all that he had, "Put, I pray thee, thy hand under my thigh:[3] and I will make thee swear by the Lord, the God of heaven, and the God of the earth, that thou shalt not take a wife unto my son of the daughters of the Canaanites, among whom I dwell. But thou shalt go unto my country, and to my kindred, and take a wife unto my son Isaac."

And the servant said unto him, "Peradventure the woman will not be willing to follow me unto this land: must I needs bring thy son again unto the land from whence thou camest?"

And Abraham said unto him, "Beware thou, that thou bring not my son thither again. The Lord God of heaven which took me from my father's house, and from the land of my kindred, and which spake unto me, and that sware unto me, saying, "Unto thy seed will I give this land'; he shall send his angel before thee, and thou shalt take a wife unto my son from thence. And if the woman will not be willing to follow thee, then thou shalt be clear from this my oath: only bring not my son thither again." And the servant put his hand under the thigh of Abraham his master, and sware to him concerning that matter.

And the servant took ten camels of the camels of his master, and departed; for all the goods of his master were in his hand: and he arose, and went to Mesopotamia, unto the city of Nahor. And he made his camels to kneel down without the city, by a well of water, at the time of the evening, even the time that women go out to draw water. And he said, "O Lord, God of my master Abraham, I pray thee send me good speed this day, and show kindness unto my master Abraham. Behold, I stand here by the well of water, and the daughters of the men of the city come out to draw water. And let it come to pass, that the damsel to whom I shall say, 'Let down thy pitcher, I pray thee, that I may drink,' and she shall say, 'Drink, and I will give thy camels drink also'; let the same be she that thou hast appointed for thy servant Isaac; and thereby shall I know that thou hast showed kindness unto my master."

And it came to pass, before he had done speaking, that behold, Rebekah came out, who was born to Bethuel, son of Milcah, the wife of Nahor, Abraham's brother, with her pitcher upon her

---

[3] *"Put . . . my thigh":* an ancient custom for solemnizing an oath.

shoulder. And the damsel was very fair to look upon, a virgin, neither had any man known her; and she went down to the well, and filled her pitcher, and came up. And the servant ran to meet her, and said, "Let me, I pray thee, drink a little water of thy pitcher." And she said, "Drink, my lord": and she hasted, and let down her pitcher upon her hand, and gave him drink. And when she had done giving him drink, she said, "I will draw water for thy camels also, until they have done drinking." And she hasted, and emptied her pitcher into the trough, and ran again unto the well to draw water, and drew for all his camels. And the man wondering at her held his peace, to wit whether the Lord had made his journey prosperous or not.

And it came to pass as the camels had done drinking, that the man took a golden earring of half a shekel weight, and two bracelets for her hands of ten shekels' weight of gold, and said, "Whose daughter art thou? tell me, I pray thee: is there room in thy father's house for us to lodge in?" And she said unto him, "I am the daughter of Bethuel the son of Milcah, which she bare unto Nahor." She said moreover unto him, "We have both straw and provender enough, and room to lodge in." And the man bowed down his head, and worshipped the Lord. And he said, "Blessed be the Lord God of my master Abraham, who hath not left destitute my master of his mercy and his truth: I being in the way, the Lord led me to the house of my master's brethren." And the damsel ran, and told them of her mother's house these things.

And Rebekah had a brother, and his name was Laban: and Laban ran out unto the man, unto the well. And it came to pass when he saw the earring, and bracelets upon his sister's hands, and when he heard the words of Rebekah his sister, saying, "Thus spake the man unto me," that he came unto the man; and behold, he stood by the camels at the well. And he said, "Come in, thou blessed of the Lord; wherefore standest thou without? for I have prepared the house, and room for the camels."

And the man came into the house: and he ungirded his camels, and gave straw and provender for the camels, and water to wash his feet, and the men's feet that were with him. And there was set meat before him to eat: but he said, "I will not eat until I have told mine errand." And he said, "Speak on." And he said, "I am Abraham's servant. And the Lord hath blessed my master greatly, and he is become great: and he hath given him flocks, and herds, and silver, and gold, and menservants, and maidservants, and camels, and asses.

"And Sarah my master's wife bare a son to my master when she was old: and unto him hath he given all that he hath. And my master made me swear, saying, 'Thou shalt not take a wife to my son of the daughters of the Canaanites, in whose land I dwell: but thou shalt go unto my father's house, and to my kindred, and take a wife unto my son.' And I said unto my master, 'Peradventure the woman will not follow me.' And he said unto me, 'The Lord, before whom I walk, will send his angel with thee, and prosper thy way; and thou shalt take a wife for my son, of my kindred, and of my father's house. Then shalt thou be clear from this my oath, when thou comest to my kindred; and if they give not thee one, thou shalt be clear from my oath.'

"And I came this day unto the well, and said, 'O Lord God of my master Abraham, if now thou do prosper my way which I go: behold, I stand by the well of water, and it shall come to pass, that when the virgin cometh forth to draw water, and I say to her, "Give me, I pray thee, a little water of thy pitcher to drink"; and she say to me, "Both drink thou, and I will also draw for thy camels": let the same be the woman whom the Lord hath appointed out for my master's son.' And before I had done speaking in mine heart, behold, Rebekah came forth, with her pitcher on her shoulder; and she went down unto the well, and drew water: and I said unto her, 'Let me drink, I pray thee.' And she made haste, and let down her pitcher from her shoulder, and said, 'Drink, and I will give thy camels drink also': so I drank, and she made the camels drink also.

"And I asked her, and said, 'Whose daughter art thou?' And she said, 'The daughter of Bethuel, Nahor's son, whom Milcah bare unto him': and I put the earring upon her face, and the bracelets upon her hands. And I bowed down my head, and worshipped the Lord, and blessed the Lord God of my master Abraham, which had led me in the right way to take my master's brother's daughter unto his son. And now if ye will deal kindly and truly with my master, tell me: and if not, tell me, that I may turn to the right hand, or to the left."

Then Laban and Bethuel answered and said, "The thing proceedeth from the Lord: we cannot speak unto thee bad or good. Behold, Rebekah is before thee, take her, and go, and let her be thy master's son's wife, as the Lord hath spoken." And it came to pass, that when Abraham's servant heard their words, he worshipped the Lord, bowing himself to the earth. And the servant brought forth jewels of silver, and jewels of gold, and raiment, and gave them to Rebekah: he gave also to her brother and to her mother precious things.

And they did eat and drink, he and the men that were with him, and tarried all night; and they rose up in the morning, and he said, "Send me away unto my master." And her brother and her mother said, "Let the damsel abide with us a few days, at the least ten; after that, she shall go." And he said unto them, "Hinder me not, seeing the Lord hath prospered my way; send me away, that I may go to my master." And they said, "We will call the damsel, and inquire at her mouth." And they called Rebekah, and said unto her, "Wilt thou go with this man?" And she said, "I will go." And they sent away Rebekah their sister, and her nurse, and Abraham's servant, and his men. And they blessed Rebekah, and said unto her, "Thou art our sister, be thou the mother of thousands of millions, and let thy seed possess the gate of those which hate them."

And Rebekah arose, and her damsels, and they rode upon the camels, and followed the man: and the servant took Rebekah, and went his way. And Isaac came from the way of the well Lahai-roi, for he dwelt in the south country. And Isaac went out to meditate in the field at the eventide: and he lifted up his eyes, and saw, and behold, the camels were coming. And Rebekah lifted up her eyes, and when she saw Isaac, she lighted off the camel. For she had said unto the servant, "What man is this that walketh in the field to meet us?" And the servant had said, "It is my master": therefore she took a veil, and covered herself. And the servant told Isaac all things that he had done. And Isaac brought her into his mother Sarah's tent, and took Rebekah, and she became his wife; and he loved her: and Isaac was comforted after his mother's death.

Esau Selling His Birthright
The British Museum, London

Jacob
and
Esau

The story of Jacob and Esau opens with the supplanting of
an elder son by a younger, a theme we have seen earlier in the
stories of Cain and Abel and of Ishmael and Isaac and will see
many times again. Jacob himself sometimes seems to be two
personalities locked in struggle. In order to fulfill the mission
which God gave him through Abraham and Isaac, Jacob must use
cunning and trickery to master his physically more powerful
elder brother Esau. At other times he is reverent and contrite.
In the complexity of his characterization, Jacob introduces a new
kind of biblical figure — human, multi-dimensional, filled
with contradictions.

Genesis

Birth of Jacob and Esau

Twenty-five . . . And Isaac was forty years old when he took Rebekah to wife, the daughter of Bethuel the Syrian of Padanaram, the sister to Laban the Syrian. And Isaac entreated the Lord for his wife, because she was barren: and the Lord was entreated of him, and Rebekah his wife conceived. And the children struggled together within her; and she said, "If it be so, why am I thus?" and she went to inquire of the Lord. And the Lord said unto her, "Two nations are in thy womb, and two manner of people shall be separated from thy bowels; and the one people shall be stronger than the other people; and the elder shall serve the younger."

And when her days to be delivered were fulfilled, behold, there were twins in her womb. And the first came out red, all over like an hairy garment; and they called his name Esau. And after that came his brother out, and his hand took hold on Esau's heel; and his name was called Jacob: and Isaac was threescore years old when she bare them. And the boys grew: and Esau was a cunning hunter, a man of the field; and Jacob was a plain man, dwelling in tents. And Isaac loved Esau, because he did eat of his venison: but Rebekah loved Jacob.

Esau Sells His Birthright

And Jacob sod pottage:[1] and Esau came from the field, and he was faint. And Esau said to Jacob, "Feed me, I pray thee, with that same red pottage; for I am faint": therefore was his name called Edom. And Jacob said, "Sell me this day thy birthright." And Esau said, "Behold, I am at the point to die: and what profit shall this birthright do to me?" And Jacob said, "Swear to me this day"; and he sware unto him: and he sold his birthright unto Jacob. Then Jacob gave Esau bread and pottage of lentils; and he did eat and drink, and rose up, and went his way: thus Esau despised his birthright.

A Stolen Blessing

Twenty-seven And it came to pass that when Isaac was old, and his eyes were dim, so that he could not see, he called Esau his eldest son, and said unto him, "My son." And he said unto him, "Behold, here am I." And he said, "Behold now, I am old, I know not the day of my death. Now therefore take, I pray thee, thy weapons, thy quiver and thy bow, and go out to the field, and take me some venison; and make me savoury meat, such as I love, and bring it to me, that I may eat, that my soul may bless thee before I die." And Rebekah heard when Isaac spake to Esau his son. And Esau went to the field to hunt for venison, and to bring it.

And Rebekah spake unto Jacob her son, saying, "Behold, I heard thy father speak unto Esau thy brother, saying, 'Bring me venison, and make me savoury meat, that I may eat, and bless thee before the Lord, before my death.' Now therefore, my son, obey my voice according to that which I command thee. Go now to the flock, and fetch me from thence two good kids of the goats, and I will make them savoury meat for thy father, such as he loveth. And thou shalt bring it to thy father, that he may eat, and that he may bless thee before his death."

---

[1] *sod pottage:* boiled a stew made of lentils, onions, and other ingredients.

And Jacob said to Rebekah his mother, "Behold, Esau my brother is a hairy man, and I am a smooth man. My father peradventure will feel me, and I shall seem to him as a deceiver; and I shall bring a curse upon me, and not a blessing." And his mother said unto him, "Upon me be thy curse, my son: only obey my voice, and go fetch me them." And he went, and fetched, and brought them to his mother, and his mother made savoury meat, such as his father loved. And Rebekah took goodly raiment of her eldest son Esau, which were with her in the house, and put them upon Jacob her younger son: and she put the skins of the kids of the goats upon his hands, and upon the smooth of his neck. And she gave the savoury meat and the bread, which she had prepared, into the hand of her son Jacob.

And he came unto his father, and said, "My father": and he said, "Here am I: who art thou, my son?" And Jacob said unto his father, "I am Esau, thy firstborn; I have done according as thou badest me: arise, I pray thee, sit, and eat of my venison, that thy soul may bless me." And Isaac said unto his son, "How is it that thou hast found it so quickly, my son?" And he said, "Because the Lord thy God brought it to me." And Isaac said unto Jacob, "Come near, I pray thee, that I may feel thee, my son, whether thou be my very son Esau, or not."

And Jacob went near unto Isaac his father; and he felt him, and said, "The voice is Jacob's voice, but the hands are the hands of Esau." And he discerned him not, because his hands were hairy, as his brother Esau's hands: so he blessed him. And he said, "Art thou my very son Esau?" And he said, "I am." And he said, "Bring it near to me, and I will eat of my son's venison, that my soul may bless thee." And he brought it near to him, and he did eat: and he brought him wine, and he drank.

And his father Isaac said unto him, "Come near now, and kiss me, my son." And he came near, and kissed him: and he smelled the smell of his raiment, and blessed him, and said, "See, the smell of my son is as the smell of a field which the Lord hath blessed. Therefore God give thee of the dew of heaven, and the fatness of the earth, and plenty of corn and wine. Let people serve thee, and nations bow down to thee: be lord over thy brethren, and let thy mother's sons bow down to thee: cursed be every one that curseth thee, and blessed be he that blesseth thee."

And it came to pass, as soon as Isaac had made an end of blessing Jacob, and Jacob was yet scarce gone out from the presence of Isaac his father, that Esau his brother came in from his hunting. And he also had made savoury meat, and brought it unto his father, and said unto his father, "Let my father arise, and eat of his son's venison, that thy soul may bless me." And Isaac his father said unto him, "Who art thou?" And he said, "I am thy son, thy firstborn Esau." And Isaac trembled very exceedingly, and said, "Who? where is he that hath taken venison, and brought it to me, and I have eaten of all before thou camest, and have blessed him? yea and he shall be blessed."

And when Esau heard the words of his father, he cried with a great and exceeding bitter cry, and said unto his father, "Bless me, even me also, O my father." And he said, "Thy brother came with subtlety, and hath taken away thy blessing." And he said, "Is not he rightly named Jacob? for he hath supplanted me these two times: he took away my birthright, and behold, now he hath taken away my blessing." And he said, "Hast thou not reserved a blessing for me?" And Isaac answered and said unto Esau, "Behold, I have made him thy lord, and all his brethren have I given to him for servants; and with corn and wine have I sustained him: and what shall I do now unto thee, my son?"

And Esau said unto his father, "Hast thou but one blessing, my father? bless me, even me also, O my father." And Esau lifted up his voice, and wept. And Isaac his father answered, and said unto him, "Behold, thy dwelling shall be the fatness of the earth, and of the dew of heaven from above. And by thy sword shalt thou live, and shalt serve thy brother; and it shall come to pass when thou shalt have the dominion, that thou shalt break his yoke from off thy neck."

And Esau hated Jacob because of the blessing wherewith his father blessed him: and Esau said in his heart, "The days of mourning for my father are at hand; then will I slay my brother Jacob." And these words of Esau her elder son were told to Rebekah: and she sent and called Jacob her younger son, and said unto him, "Behold, thy brother Esau, as touching thee, doth comfort himself, purposing to kill thee. Now therefore, my son, obey my voice; and arise, flee thou to Laban my brother, to Haran. And tarry with him a few days, until thy brother's fury turn away; until thy brother's anger turn away from thee, and he forget that which thou hast done to him. Then I will send, and fetch thee from thence: why should I be deprived also of you both in one day?"

And Rebekah said to Isaac, "I am weary of my life because of the daughters of Heth: if Jacob take a wife of the daughters of Heth, such as these which are of the daughters of the land, what good shall my life do me?"

Twenty-eight And Isaac called Jacob, and blessed him, and charged him, and said unto him, "Thou shalt not take a wife of the daughters of Canaan. Arise, go to Padan-aram, to the house of Bethuel thy mother's father; and take thee a wife from thence of the daughters of Laban thy mother's brother. And God Almighty bless thee, and make thee fruitful, and multiply thee, that thou mayest be a multitude of people; and give thee the blessing of Abraham, to thee, and to thy seed with thee, that thou mayest inherit the land wherein thou art a stranger, which God gave unto Abraham." And Isaac sent away Jacob: and he went to Padan-aram unto Laban, son of Bethuel the Syrian, the brother of Rebekah, Jacob's and Esau's mother.

When Esau saw that Isaac had blessed Jacob, and sent him away to Padan-aram, to take him a wife from thence; and that as he blessed him, he gave him a charge, saying, "Thou shalt not take a wife of the daughters of Canaan"; and that Jacob obeyed his father and his mother, and was gone to Padan-aram; and Esau seeing that the daughters of Canaan pleased not Isaac his father; then went Esau unto Ishmael, and took unto the wives which he had, Mahalath the daughter of Ishmael, Abraham's son, the sister of Nebajoth, to be his wife.

Jacob's Ladder

And Jacob went out from Beer-sheba, and went toward Haran. And he lighted upon a certain place, and tarried there all night, because the sun was set; and he took of the stones of that place, and put them for his pillows, and lay down in that place to sleep. And he dreamed, and behold, a ladder set up on the earth, and the top of it·reached to heaven: and behold, the angels of God ascending and descending on it. And behold, the Lord stood above it, and said, "I am the Lord God of Abraham thy father, and the God of Isaac: the land whereon thou liest, to thee will I give it, and to thy seed. And thy seed shall be as the dust of the earth, and thou shalt spread abroad to the west, and to the east, and to the north, and to the south: and in thee, and in thy seed, shall all the families of the earth be blessed. And behold, I am with thee, and will keep thee in all places whither thou goest, and will bring thee again into this land: for I will not leave thee until I have done that which I have spoken to thee of."

And Jacob awaked out of his sleep, and he said, "Surely the Lord is in this place, and I knew it not." And he was afraid, and said, "How dreadful is this place! this is none other but the house of God, and this is the gate of heaven." And Jacob rose up early in the morning, and took the stone that he had put for his pillows, and set it up for a pillar, and poured oil upon the top of it. And he called the name of that place Bethel: but the name of that city was called Luz at the first. And Jacob vowed a vow saying, "If God will be with me, and will keep me in this way that I go, and will give me bread to eat, and raiment to put on, so that I come again to my father's house in peace: then shall the Lord be my God. And this stone, which I have set for a pillar, shall be God's house: and of all that thou shalt give me I will surely give the tenth unto thee."

The Winning of Rachel

Twenty-nine Then Jacob went on his journey, and came into the land of the people of the east. And he looked, and behold, a well in the field, and lo, there were three flocks of sheep lying by it; for out of that well they watered the flocks: and a great stone was upon the well's mouth. And thither were all the flocks gathered: and they rolled the stone from the well's mouth, and watered the sheep, and put the stone again upon the well's mouth in his place. And Jacob said unto them, "My brethren, whence be ye?" And they said, "Of Haran are we." And he said unto them,

"Know ye Laban the son of Nahor?" And they said, "We know him." And he said unto them, "Is he well?" And they said, "He is well: and behold, Rachel his daughter cometh with the sheep." And he said, "Lo, it is yet high day, neither is it time that the cattle should be gathered together: water ye the sheep, and go and feed them." And they said, "We cannot, until all the flocks be gathered together, and till they roll the stone from the well's mouth; then we water the sheep."

And while he yet spake with them, Rachel came with her father's sheep: for she kept them. And it came to pass, when Jacob saw Rachel the daughter of Laban his mother's brother, and the sheep of Laban his mother's brother, that Jacob went near, and rolled the stone from the well's mouth, and watered the flock of Laban his mother's brother. And Jacob kissed Rachel, and lifted up his voice and wept. And Jacob told Rachel that he was her father's brother,[2] and that he was Rebekah's son: and she ran and told her father.

And it came to pass, when Laban heard the tidings of Jacob his sister's son, that he ran to meet him, and embraced him, and kissed him, and brought him to his house. And he told Laban all these things. And Laban said to him, "Surely thou art my bone and my flesh." And he abode with him the space of a month.

And Laban said unto Jacob, "Because thou art my brother, shouldest thou therefore serve me for nought? tell me, what shall thy wages be?" And Laban had two daughters: the name of the elder was Leah, and the name of the younger was Rachel. Leah was tender eyed;[3] but Rachel was beautiful and well-favoured. And Jacob loved Rachel, and said, "I will serve thee seven years for Rachel thy younger daughter." And Laban said, "It is better that I give her to thee, than that I should give her to another man: abide with me." And Jacob served seven years for Rachel; and they seemed unto him but a few days, for the love he had to her.

And Jacob said unto Laban, "Give me my wife, for my days are fulfilled, that I may go in unto her." And Laban gathered together all the men of the place, and made a feast. And it came to pass in the evening, that he took Leah his daughter, and brought

[2] *father's brother:* here, nephew.
[3] *was tender eyed: i.e.,* had weak eyes.

her to him; and he went in unto her. And Laban gave unto his daughter Leah, Zilpah his maid for a handmaid.

And it came to pass, that in the morning, behold, it was Leah: and he said to Laban, "What is this thou hast done unto me? did not I serve with thee for Rachel? wherefore then hast thou beguiled me?" And Laban said, "It must not be so done in our country, to give the younger before the firstborn. Fulfill her week,[4] and we will give thee this also, for the service which thou shalt serve with me yet seven other years." And Jacob did so, and fulfilled her week: and he gave him Rachel his daughter to wife also. And Laban gave to Rachel his daughter Bilhah his handmaid to be her maid. And he went in also unto Rachel, and he loved also Rachel more than Leah, and served with him yet seven other years. . . .

Jacob and the Spotted Cattle

Thirty . . . And it came to pass, when Rachel had borne Joseph, that Jacob said unto Laban, "Send me away, that I may go unto mine own place, and to my country. Give me my wives and my children, for whom I have served thee, and let me go: for thou knowest my service which I have done thee."

And Laban said unto him, "I pray thee, if I have found favour in thine eyes, tarry: for I have learned by experience that the Lord hath blessed me for thy sake." And he said, "Appoint me thy wages, and I will give it." And he said unto him, "Thou knowest how I have served thee, and how thy cattle was with me. For it was little which thou hadst before I came, and it is now increased unto a multitude; and the Lord hath blessed thee since my coming: and now when shall I provide for mine own house also?" And he said, "What shall I give thee?"

And Jacob said, "Thou shalt not give me anything; if thou wilt do this thing for me, I will again feed and keep thy flock. I will pass through all thy flock today, removing from thence all the speckled and spotted cattle, and all the brown cattle among the sheep, and the spotted and speckled among the goats, and of such

---

[4] *her week:* The marriage feast lasted seven days.

shall be my hire. So shall my righteousness answer for me in time to come, when it shall come for my hire before thy face: every one that is not speckled and spotted amongst the goats, and brown amongst the sheep, that shall be counted stolen with me."

And Laban said, "Behold, I would it might be according to thy word." And he removed that day the he-goats that were ring-streaked and spotted, and all the she-goats that were speckled and spotted, and every one that had some white in it, and all the brown amongst the sheep, and gave them into the hand of his sons. And he set three days' journey betwixt himself and Jacob: and Jacob fed the rest of Laban's flocks.

And Jacob took him rods of green poplar, and of the hazel and chestnut tree, and pilled[5] white streaks in them, and made the white appear which was in the rods. And he set the rods which he had pilled before the flocks in the gutters in the watering troughs when the flocks came to drink, that they should conceive when they came to drink. And the flocks conceived before the rods, and brought forth cattle ring-streaked, speckled, and spotted.

And Jacob did separate the lambs, and set the faces of the flocks toward the ring-streaked, and all the brown in the flock of Laban; and he put his own flocks by themselves, and put them not unto Laban's cattle. And it came to pass whensoever the stronger cattle did conceive, that Jacob laid the rods before the eyes of the cattle in the gutters, that they might conceive among the rods. But when the cattle were feeble, he put them not in; so the feebler were Laban's, and the stronger Jacob's. And the man increased exceedingly, and had much cattle, and maidservants, and menservants, and camels, and asses.

Jacob Returns Home

Thirty-one And he heard the words of Laban's sons, saying "Jacob hath taken away all that was our father's; and of that which was our father's hath he gotten all this glory." And Jacob beheld the countenance of Laban, and behold, it was not toward

---

5 *pilled:* peeled.

him as before. And the Lord said unto Jacob, "Return unto the land of thy fathers, and to thy kindred; and I will be with thee."

And Jacob sent and called Rachel and Leah to the field unto his flock, and said unto them, "I see your father's countenance, that it is not toward me as before; but the God of my father hath been with me. And ye know that with all my power I have served your father. And your father hath deceived me, and changed my wages ten times; but God suffered him not to hurt me. If he said thus, 'The speckled shall be thy wages,' then all the cattle bare speckled: and if he said thus, 'The ring-streaked shall be thy hire,' then bare all the cattle ring-streaked. Thus God hath taken away the cattle of your father, and given them to me.

"And it came to pass at the time that the cattle conceived, that I lifted up mine eyes and saw in a dream, and, behold, the rams which leaped upon the cattle were ring-streaked, speckled, and grisled.[6] And the angel of God spake unto me in a dream, saying, 'Jacob.' And I said, 'Here am I.' And he said, 'Lift up now thine eyes and see, all the rams which leap upon the cattle are ring-streaked, speckled, and grisled: for I have seen all that Laban doeth unto thee. I am the God of Bethel, where thou anointedst the pillar, and where thou vowedst a vow unto me: now arise, get thee out from this land, and return unto the land of thy kindred.' "

And Rachel and Leah answered, and said unto him, "Is there yet any portion or inheritance for us in our father's house? Are we not counted of him strangers? for he hath sold us, and hath quite devoured also our money. For all the riches which God hath taken from our father, that is ours, and our children's: now then, whatsoever God hath said unto thee, do."

Then Jacob rose up, and set his sons and his wives upon camels. And he carried away all his cattle, and all his goods which he had gotten, the cattle of his getting, which he had gotten in Padan-aram, for to go to Isaac his father in the land of Canaan. And Laban went to shear his sheep: and Rachel had stolen the images[7] that were her father's. And Jacob stole away unawares to Laban

---

6 *grisled:* black with white spots.

7 *images:* household gods, probably clay figures. According to the custom of the time, Jacob's possession of Laban's gods insured his title to Laban's property.

the Syrian, in that he told him not that he fled. So he fled with all that he had, and he rose up and passed over the river, and set his face toward the mount Gilead.

And it was told Laban on the third day, that Jacob was fled. And he took his brethren with him, and pursued after him seven days' journey; and they overtook him in the mount Gilead. And God came to Laban the Syrian in a dream by night, and said unto him, "Take heed that thou speak not to Jacob either good or bad."

Then Laban overtook Jacob. Now Jacob had pitched his tent in the mount: and Laban with his brethren pitched in the mount of Gilead. And Laban said to Jacob, "What hast thou done, that thou hast stolen away unawares to me, and carried away my daughters, as captives taken with the sword? Wherefore didst thou flee away secretly, and steal away from me, and didst not tell me, that I might have sent thee away with mirth, and with songs, with tabret,[8] and with harp, and hast not suffered me to kiss my sons and my daughters? thou hast now done foolishly in so doing. It is in the power of my hand to do you hurt: but the God of your father spake unto me yesternight, saying, 'Take thou heed that thou speak not to Jacob either good or bad.' And now though thou wouldest needs be gone, because thou sore longedst after thy father's house, yet wherefore hast thou stolen my gods?"

And Jacob answered and said to Laban, "Because I was afraid: for I said, peradventure thou wouldest take by force thy daughters from me. With whomsoever thou findest thy gods, let him not live: before our brethren, discern thou what is thine with me, and take it to thee": for Jacob knew not that Rachel had stolen them.

And Laban went into Jacob's tent, and into Leah's tent, and into the two maidservants tents; but he found them not. Then went he out of Leah's tent, and entered into Rachel's tent. Now Rachel had taken the images, and put them in the camel's furniture, and sat upon them. And Laban searched all the tent, but found them not. And she said to her father, "Let it not displease my lord that I cannot rise up before thee; for the custom of women is upon me." And he searched but found not the images.

And Jacob was wroth, and chode with Laban: and Jacob answered and said to Laban, "What is my trespass? what is my sin,

---

[8] *tabret:* a small hand drum or tambourine.

that thou hast so hotly pursued after me? Whereas thou hast searched all my stuff, what hast thou found of all thy household stuff? set it here before my brethren, and thy brethren, that they may judge betwixt us both. This twenty years have I been with thee: thy ewes and thy she-goats have not cast their young,[9] and the rams of thy flocks have I not eaten. That which was torn of beasts I brought not unto thee; I bare the loss of it; of my hand didst thou require it, whether stolen by day, or stolen by night. Thus I was; in the day the drought consumed me, and the frost by night; and my sleep departed from mine eyes. Thus I have been twenty years in thy house; I served thee fourteen years for thy two daughters, and six years for thy cattle: and thou hast changed my wages ten times. Except the God of my father, the God of Abraham, and the fear of Isaac had been with me, surely thou hadst sent me away now empty. God hath seen mine affliction and the labour of my hands, and rebuked thee yesternight."

And Laban answered and said unto Jacob. "These daughters are my daughters, and these children are my children, and these cattle are my cattle, and all that thou seest is mine: and what can I do this day unto these my daughters, or unto their children which they have borne? Now therefore come thou, let us make a covenant, I and thou; and let it be for a witness between me and thee."

And Jacob took a stone, and set it up for a pillar. And Jacob said unto his brethren, "Gather stones"; and they took stones, and made an heap: and they did eat there upon the heap. And Laban called it Jegar-sahadutha: but Jacob called it Galeed. And Laban said, "This heap is a witness between me and thee this day." Therefore was the name of it called Galeed, and Mizpah; for he said, "The Lord watch between me and thee when we are absent one from another. If thou shalt afflict my daughters, or if thou shalt take other wives besides my daughters, no man is with us; see, God is witness betwixt me and thee." And Laban said to Jacob, "Behold this heap, and behold this pillar, which I have cast betwixt me and thee. This heap be witness, and this pillar be witness, that I will not pass over this heap to thee, and that thou shalt not pass over this heap and this pillar unto me, for harm.

9 *cast their young:* miscarried.

The God of Abraham, and the God of Nahor, the God of their father, judge betwixt us."

And Jacob sware by the fear of his father Isaac. Then Jacob offered sacrifice upon the mount, and called his brethren to eat bread, and they did eat bread, and tarried all night in the mount. And early in the morning Laban rose up and kissed his sons, and his daughters, and blessed them: and Laban departed, and returned unto his place.

Jacob's Fear of Esau

Thirty-two And Jacob went on his way, and the angels of God met him. And when Jacob saw them, he said, "This is God's host": and he called the name of that place Mahanaim. And Jacob sent messengers before him to Esau his brother, unto the land of Seir, the country of Edom. And he commanded them, saying, "Thus shall ye speak unto my lord Esau, 'Thy servant Jacob saith thus, I have sojourned with Laban, and stayed there until now. And I have oxen, and asses, flocks, and menservants, and womenservants: and I have sent to tell my lord, that I may find grace in thy sight.' "

And the messengers returned to Jacob, saying, "We came to thy brother Esau, and also he cometh to meet thee, and four hundred men with him." Then Jacob was greatly afraid, and distressed, and he divided the people that was with him, and the flocks, and herds, and the camels, into two bands, and said, "If Esau come to the one company, and smite it, then the other company which is left shall escape."

And Jacob said, "O God of my father Abraham, and God of my father Isaac, the Lord which saidst unto me, 'Return unto thy country, and to thy kindred, and I will deal well with thee': I am not worthy of the least of all the mercies, and of all the truth, which thou hast showed unto thy servant; for with my staff I passed over this Jordan, and now I am become two bands. Deliver me, I pray thee, from the hand of my brother, from the hand of Esau: for I fear him, lest he will come and smite me, and the mother with the children. And thou saidst, 'I will surely do thee good, and make thy seed as the sand of the sea, which cannot be numbered for multitude.' "

And he lodged there that same night, and took of that which came to his hand a present for Esau his brother: two hundred she-goats, and twenty he-goats, two hundred ewes, and twenty rams, thirty milch camels with their colts, forty kine, and ten bulls, twenty she-asses, and ten foals. And he delivered them into the hand of his servants, every drove by themselves, and said unto his servants, "Pass over before me, and put a space betwixt drove and drove." And he commanded the foremost, saying, "When Esau my brother meeteth thee, and asketh thee, saying, 'Whose art thou? and whither goest thou? and whose are these before thee?' then thou shalt say, 'They be thy servant Jacob's: it is a present sent unto my lord Esau: and behold, also he is behind us.' " And so commanded he the second, and the third, and all that followed the droves, saying, "On this manner shall ye speak unto Esau, when ye find him. And say ye moreover, 'Behold, thy servant Jacob is behind us' ": for he said, "I will appease him with the present that goeth before me, and afterward I will see his face; peradventure he will accept of me."

So went the present over before him: and himself lodged that night in the company. And he rose up that night, and took his two wives, and his two womenservants, and his eleven sons, and passed over the ford Jabbok. And he took them, and sent them over the brook, and sent over that he had.

The Wrestle with an Angel

And Jacob was left alone: and there wrestled a man with him until the breaking of the day. And when he saw that he prevailed not against him, he touched the hollow of his thigh; and the hollow of Jacob's thigh was out of joint, as he wrestled with him. And he said, "Let me go, for the day breaketh." And he said, "I will not let thee go, except thou bless me." And he said unto him, "What is thy name?" And he said, "Jacob." And he said, "Thy name shall be called no more Jacob, but Israel: for as a prince hast thou power with God, and with men, and hast prevailed." And

Jacob asked him, and said, "Tell me, I pray thee, thy name." And he said, "Wherefore is it that thou dost ask after my name?" And he blessed him there. And Jacob called the name of the place Peniel: "for I have seen God face to face, and my life is preserved." And as he passed over Penuel, the sun rose upon him, and he halted upon his thigh.[10] Therefore the children of Israel eat not of the sinew which shrank, which is upon the hollow of the thigh, unto this day: because he touched the hollow of Jacob's thigh in the sinew that shrank.

Reconciliation of Jacob and Esau

Thirty-three And Jacob lifted up his eyes, and looked, and behold, Esau came, and with him four hundred men. And he divided the children unto Leah, and unto Rachel, and unto the two handmaids. And he put the handmaids and their children foremost, and Leah and her children after, and Rachel and Joseph hindermost. And he passed over before them, and bowed himself to the ground seven times, until he came near to his brother.

And Esau ran to meet him, and embraced him, and fell on his neck, and kissed him: and they wept. And he lifted up his eyes, and saw the women and the children, and said, "Who are those with thee?" And he said, "The children which God hath graciously given thy servant." Then the handmaidens came near, they and their children, and they bowed themselves. And Leah also with her children came near, and bowed themselves: and after came Joseph near and Rachel, and they bowed themselves.

HATRED STIRRETH UP STRIFES: BUT LOVE COVERETH ALL SINS.

PROVERBS 10:12

And he said, "What meanest thou by all this drove which I met?" And he said, "These are to find grace in the sight of my lord." And Esau said, "I have enough, my brother; keep that

10 *halted upon his thigh:* limped.

thou hast unto thyself." And Jacob said, "Nay, I pray thee, if now I have found grace in thy sight, then receive my present at my hand: for therefore I have seen thy face, as though I had seen the face of God, and thou wast pleased with me. Take, I pray thee, my blessing that is brought to thee; because God hath dealt graciously with me, and because I have enough." And he urged him, and he took it.

And he said, "Let us take our journey, and let us go, and I will go before thee." And he said unto him, "My lord knoweth that the children are tender, and the flocks and herds with young are with me: and if men should overdrive them one day, all the flock will die. Let my lord, I pray thee, pass over before his servant, and I will lead on softly, according as the cattle that goeth before me, and the children, be able to endure, until I come unto my lord Seir." And Esau said, "Let me now leave with thee some of the folk that are with me." And he said, "What needeth it? let me find grace in the sight of my lord."

So Esau returned that day, on his way unto Seir. And Jacob journeyed to Succoth, and built him a house, and made booths for his cattle: therefore the name of the place is called Succoth.

And Jacob came to Shalem, a city of Shechem, which is in the land of Canaan, when he came from Padan-aram, and pitched his tent before the city. And he bought a parcel of a field where he had spread his tent, at the hand of the children of Hamor, Shechem's father, for an hundred pieces of money. And he erected there an altar, and called it El-Elohe-Israel.

The Altar at Bethel

Thirty-five And God said unto Jacob, "Arise, go up to Bethel, and dwell there: and make there an altar unto God, that appeared unto thee when thou fleddest from the face of Esau thy brother." Then Jacob said unto his household, and to all that were with him, "Put away the strange gods that are among you, and be clean, and change your garments. And let us arise, and go up to Bethel; and I will make there an altar unto God, who answered me in the day of my distress, and was with me in the way which I went."

And they gave unto Jacob all the strange gods which were in their hand, and all their earrings which were in their ears, and Jacob hid them under the oak which was by Shechem. And they journeyed: and the terror of God was upon the cities that were round about them, and they did not pursue after the sons of Jacob.

So Jacob came to Luz, which is in the land of Canaan, that is, Bethel, he and all the people that were with him. And he built there an altar, and called the place El-beth-el, because there God appeared unto him, when he fled from the face of his brother. But Deborah, Rebekah's nurse, died, and she was buried beneath Bethel under an oak: and the name of it was called Allon-bachuth.

And God appeared unto Jacob again, when he came out of Padan-aram, and blessed him. And God said unto him, "Thy name is Jacob: thy name shall not be called any more Jacob, but Israel shall be thy name"; and he called his name Israel. And God said unto him, "I am God Almighty: be fruitful and multiply; a nation and a company of nations shall be of thee, and kings shall come out of thy loins. And the land which I gave Abraham, and Isaac, to thee I will give it, and to thy seed after thee will I give the land." And God went up from him in the place where he talked with him. And Jacob set up a pillar in the place where he talked with him, even a pillar of stone: and he poured a drink offering thereon, and he poured oil thereon. And Jacob called the name of the place where God spake with him Bethel.

Death of Rachel and Isaac

And they journeyed from Bethel; and there was but a little way to come to Ephrath: and Rachel travailed, and she had hard labour. And it came to pass when she was in hard labour, that the midwife said unto her, "Fear not: thou shalt have this son also." And it came to pass, as her soul was in departing (for she died), that she called his name Ben-oni: but his father called him Benjamin. And Rachel died, and was buried in the way to Ephrath, which is Bethlehem. And Jacob set a pillar upon her grave: that is the pillar of Rachel's grave unto this day.

And Israel journeyed, and spread his tent beyond the tower of Edar. And it came to pass when Israel dwelt in that land, that Reuben went and lay with Bilhah his father's concubine: and Israel heard it. Now the sons of Jacob were twelve. The sons of Leah: Reuben, Jacob's firstborn, and Simeon, and Levi, and Judah, and Issachar, and Zebulun. The sons of Rachel: Joseph, and Benjamin. And the sons of Bilhah, Rachel's handmaid: Dan, and Naphtali. And the sons of Zilpah, Leah's handmaid: Gad, and Asher. These are the sons of Jacob, which were born to him in Padan-aram.

And Jacob came unto Isaac his father unto Mamre, unto the city of Arbah, which is Hebron, where Abraham and Isaac sojourned. And the days of Isaac were an hundred and fourscore years. And Isaac gave up the ghost, and died, and was gathered unto his people, being old and full of days: and his sons Esau and Jacob buried him.

Joseph Cast into the Pit by His Brothers
Formerly in the Collection of Friedrick August II,
Dresden, the drawing was destroyed in World War II.

Joseph

The story of Joseph and his coat of many colors is a familiar
one to most people. On one level it is a short novel, telling a
rather conventional success story of a young Hebrew who rises
from slavery to a position of power in Egypt in about 1700 B.C.
On another level it is a continuation of the development of the
Hebrew people from a small nomadic group of Bedouin tribesmen
to a powerful nation.

Joseph's story opens with a flashback to events before the death
of Rachel, his mother, and before the birth of Benjamin, the last
of the sons of Jacob. More than any of the previous stories, it is
man-centered, with God playing less of a role than in the accounts
of Abraham or of Jacob. Nevertheless, from Joseph's dream to
the final blessing of Jacob, we are aware of the presence of God
and of the inexorable working out of God's plan for the children
of Israel, the Hebrew people.

Genesis

The Envy of Joseph's Brothers

Thirty-seven And Jacob dwelt in the land wherein his father was a stranger, in the land of Canaan. These are the generations of Jacob: Joseph, being seventeen years old, was feeding the flock with his brethren, and the lad was with the sons of Bilhah, and with the sons of Zilpah, his father's wives: and Joseph brought unto his father their evil report.[1] Now Israel loved Joseph more than all his children, because he was the son of his old age: and he made him a coat of many colours. And when his brethren saw that their father loved him more than all his brethren, they hated him, and could not speak peaceably unto him.

And Joseph dreamed a dream, and he told it his brethren: and they hated him yet the more. And he said unto them, "Hear, I pray you, this dream which I have dreamed. For behold, we were binding sheaves in the field, and lo, my sheaf arose, and also stood upright; and behold, your sheaves stood round about, and made obeisance to my sheaf." And his brethren said to him, "Shalt thou indeed reign over us? or shalt thou indeed have dominion over us?" And they hated him yet the more, for his dreams, and for his words.

And he dreamed yet another dream, and told it his brethren, and said, "Behold, I have dreamed a dream more; and, behold, the sun and the moon, and the eleven stars made obeisance to me."

1 *their evil report:* a bad report about them.

And he told it to his father, and to his brethren: and his father rebuked him, and said unto him, "What is this dream that thou hast dreamed? Shall I and thy mother and thy brethren indeed come to bow down ourselves to thee to the earth?" And his brethren envied him; but his father observed[2] the saying.

Joseph Is Sold

And his brethren went to feed their father's flock in Shechem. And Israel said unto Joseph, "Do not thy brethren feed the flock in Shechem? Come, and I will send thee unto them." And he said to him, "Here am I." And he said to him, "Go, I pray thee, see whether it be well with thy brethren, and well with the flocks, and bring me word again." So he sent him out of the vale of Hebron, and he came to Shechem.

And a certain man found him, and, behold, he was wandering in the field: and the man asked him, saying, "What seekest thou?" And he said, "I seek my brethren: tell me, I pray thee, where they feed their flocks." And the man said, "They are departed hence; for I heard them say, 'Let us go to Dothan.'" And Joseph went after his brethren, and found them in Dothan. And when they saw him afar off, even before he came near unto them, they conspired against him, to slay him. And they said one to another, "Behold, this dreamer cometh. Come now therefore, and let us slay him, and cast him into some pit, and we will say, 'Some evil beast hath devoured him': and we shall see what will become of his dreams."

And Reuben heard it, and he delivered him out of their hands, and said, "Let us not kill him." And Reuben said unto them, "Shed no blood, but cast him into this pit that is in the wilderness, and lay no hand upon him"; that he might rid him out of their hands, to deliver him to his father again.

And it came to pass when Joseph was come unto his brethren, that they stripped Joseph out of his coat, his coat of many colours that was on him. And they took him, and cast him into a pit: and

2 *observed:* remembered.

the pit was empty, there was no water in it. And they sat down to eat bread: and they lifted up their eyes and looked, and, behold, a company of Ishmaelites came from Gilead, with their camels, bearing spicery and balm and myrrh, going to carry it down to Egypt.

And Judah said unto his brethren, "What profit is it if we slay our brother, and conceal his blood? Come, and let us sell him to the Ishmaelites, and let not our hand be upon him; for he is our brother, and our flesh." And his brethren were content. Then there passed by Midianites merchantmen; and they drew and lifted up Joseph out of the pit, and sold Joseph to the Ishmaelites for twenty pieces of silver: and they brought Joseph into Egypt.

And Reuben returned unto the pit; and behold, Joseph was not in the pit; and he rent his clothes. And he returned unto his brethren and said, "The child is not; and I, whither shall I go?"

And they took Joseph's coat, and killed a kid of the goats, and dipped the coat in the blood. And they sent the coat of many colours, and they brought it to their father, and said, "This have we found: know now whether it be thy son's coat or no." And he knew it, and said, "It is my son's coat; an evil beast hath devoured him; Joseph is without doubt rent in pieces."

And Jacob rent his clothes, and put sackcloth upon his loins, and mourned for his son many days. And all his sons and all his daughters rose up to comfort him; but he refused to be comforted; and he said, "For I will go down into the grave unto my son, mourning." Thus his father wept for him. And the Midianites sold him into Egypt unto Potiphar, an officer of Pharaoh's, and captain of the guard.

The Wife of Potiphar

Thirty-nine And Joseph was brought down to Egypt; and Potiphar, an officer of Pharaoh, captain of the guard, an Egyptian, bought him of the hand of the Ishmaelites, which had brought him down thither. And the Lord was with Joseph, and he was a prosperous man; and he was in the house of his master the Egyptian. And his master saw that the Lord was with him, and that the Lord made all that he did to prosper in his hand. And Joseph found grace in his sight, and he served him; and he made him overseer over his house, and all that he had he put into his hand.

And it came to pass from the time that he had made him overseer in his house, and over all that he had, that the Lord blessed the Egyptian's house for Joseph's sake; and the blessing of the Lord was upon all that he had in the house, and in the field. And he left all that he had in Joseph's hand; and he knew not aught he had, save the bread which he did eat. And Joseph was a goodly person, and well-favoured.

And it came to pass after these things, that his master's wife cast her eyes upon Joseph, and she said, "Lie with me." But he refused, and said unto his master's wife, "Behold, my master wotteth not what is with me in the house, and he hath committed all that he hath to my hand. There is none greater in this house than I; neither hath he kept back any thing from me but thee, because thou art his wife: how then can I do this great wickedness, and sin against God?" And it came to pass, as she spake to Joseph day by day, that he hearkened not unto her, to lie by her, or to be with her.

And it came to pass about this time, that Joseph went into the house to do his business, and there was none of the men of the house there within. And she caught him by his garment, saying, "Lie with me": and he left his garment in her hand, and fled, and got him out. And it came to pass, when she saw that he had left his garment in her hand, and was fled forth, that she called unto the men of her house, and spake unto them, saying, "See, he hath brought in an Hebrew unto us, to mock us; he came in unto me to lie with me, and I cried with a loud voice. And it came to pass when he heard that I lifted up my voice and cried, that he left his garment with me, and fled, and got him out."

And she laid up his garment by her, until her lord came home. And she spake unto him according to these words, saying, "The Hebrew servant which thou hast brought unto us came in unto me to mock me. And it came to pass as I lifted up my voice and cried, that he left his garment with me, and fled out."

And it came to pass when his master heard the words of his wife, which she spake unto him, saying, "After this manner did thy servant to me," that his wrath was kindled. And Joseph's master took him, and put him into the prison, a place where the king's prisoners were bound: and he was there in the prison.

But the Lord was with Joseph, and showed him mercy, and gave him favour in the sight of the keeper of the prison. And the keeper of the prison committed to Joseph's hand all the prisoners that were in the prison, and whatsoever they did there, he was the doer of it. The keeper of the prison looked not to any thing that was under his hand, because the Lord was with him: and that which he did, the Lord made it to prosper.

The Prisoners' Dreams

Forty And it came to pass after these things, that the butler of the king of Egypt, and his baker, had offended their lord the king of Egypt. And Pharaoh was wroth against two of his officers, against the chief of the butlers, and against the chief of the bakers. And he put them in ward in the house of the captain of the guard, into the prison, the place where Joseph was bound. And the captain of the guard charged Joseph with them, and he served them, and they continued a season in ward.

And they dreamed a dream both of them, each man his dream in one night, each man according to the interpretation of his dream, the butler and the baker of the king of Egypt, which were bound in the prison. And Joseph came in unto them in the morning, and looked upon them, and behold, they were sad. And he asked Pharaoh's officers that were with him in the ward of his lord's house, saying, "Wherefore look ye so sadly today?" And they said unto him, "We have dreamed a dream, and there is no interpreter of it." And Joseph said unto them, "Do not interpretations belong to God? tell me them, I pray you."

And the chief butler told his dream to Joseph, and said to him, "In my dream, behold, a vine was before me; and in the vine were three branches: and it was as though it budded, and her blossoms shot forth; and the clusters thereof brought forth ripe grapes. And Pharaoh's cup was in my hand, and I took the grapes and pressed them into Pharaoh's cup: and I gave the cup into Pharaoh's hand."

And Joseph said unto him, "This is the interpretation of it: the three branches are three days. Yet within three days shall Pharaoh lift up thine head, and restore thee unto thy place, and thou shalt deliver Pharaoh's cup into his hand, after the former manner when thou wast his butler. But think on me when it shall be well with thee, and show kindness, I pray thee, unto me, and make mention of me unto Pharaoh, and bring me out of this house. For indeed I was stolen away out of the land of the Hebrews: and here also have I done nothing that they should put me into the dungeon."

When the chief baker saw that the interpretation was good, he said unto Joseph, "I also was in my dream, and behold, I had three white baskets on my head. And in the uppermost basket there was of all manner of bake-meats for Pharaoh, and the birds did eat them out of the basket upon my head." And Joseph answered and said, "This is the interpretation thereof: the three baskets are three days. Yet within three days shall Pharaoh lift up thy head from off thee, and shall hang thee on a tree, and the birds shall eat thy flesh from off thee."

And it came to pass the third day, which was Pharaoh's birthday, that he made a feast unto all his servants: and he lifted up the head of the chief butler and of the chief baker among his servants. And he restored the chief butler unto his butlership again, and he gave the cup into Pharaoh's hand. But he hanged the chief baker, as Joseph had interpreted to them. Yet did not the chief butler remember Joseph, but forgot him.

Pharaoh's Dreams

Forty-one And it came to pass at the end of two full years, that Pharaoh dreamed: and behold, he stood by the river. And behold, there came up out of the river seven well-favoured kine[3] and fat-fleshed, and they fed in a meadow. And behold, seven other kine came up after them out of the river, ill-favoured and lean-fleshed, and stood by the other kine, upon the brink of the river.

3 *kine:* cows.

And the ill-favoured and lean-fleshed kine did eat up the seven well-favoured and fat kine: so Pharaoh awoke.

And he slept and dreamed the second time: and behold, seven ears of corn came up upon one stalk, rank[4] and good. And behold, seven thin ears and blasted with the east wind sprang up after them. And the seven thin ears devoured the seven rank and full ears. And Pharaoh awoke, and behold, it was a dream.

And it came to pass in the morning, that his spirit was troubled, and he sent and called for all the magicians of Egypt, and all the wise men thereof: and Pharaoh told them his dream; but there was none that could interpret them unto Pharaoh.

Then spake the chief butler unto Pharaoh, saying, "I do remember my faults this day. Pharaoh was wroth with his servants, and put me in ward, in the captain of the guard's house, both me and the chief baker. And we dreamed a dream in one night, I and he; we dreamed each man according to the interpretation of his dream. And there was there with us a young man, an Hebrew, servant to the captain of the guard; and we told him, and he interpreted to us our dreams; to each man according to his dream he did interpret. And it came to pass, as he interpreted to us, so it was; me he restored unto mine office, and him he hanged."

Then Pharaoh sent and called Joseph, and they brought him hastily out of the dungeon: and he shaved himself, and changed his raiment, and came in unto Pharaoh. And Pharaoh said unto Joseph, "I have dreamed a dream, and there is none that can interpret it: and I have heard say of thee that thou canst understand a dream to interpret it." And Joseph answered Pharaoh, saying, "It is not in me: God shall give Pharaoh an answer of peace."

And Pharaoh said unto Joseph, "In my dream, behold, I stood upon the bank of the river. And behold, there came up out of the river seven kine, fat-fleshed and well-favoured, and they fed in a meadow. And behold, seven other kine came up after them, poor and very ill-favoured and lean-fleshed, such as I never saw in all the land of Egypt for badness. And the lean and the ill-favoured kine did eat up the first seven fat kine. And when they had eaten them up, it could not be known that they had eaten

4 *rank:* luxuriant.

them, but they were still ill-favoured, as at the beginning. So I awoke. And I saw in my dream, and, behold, seven ears came up in one stalk, full and good. And behold, seven ears, withered, thin, and blasted with the east wind, sprang up after them. And the thin ears devoured the seven good ears: and I told this unto the magicians; but there was none that could declare it to me."

And Joseph said unto Pharaoh, "The dream of Pharaoh is one; God hath showed Pharaoh what he is about to do. The seven good kine are seven years; and the seven good ears are seven years: the dream is one. And the seven thin and ill-favoured kine that came up after them are seven years; and the seven empty ears blasted with the east wind shall be seven years of famine. This is the thing which I have spoken unto Pharaoh: what God is about to do he showeth unto Pharaoh. Behold, there come seven years of great plenty throughout all the land of Egypt. And there shall arise after them seven years of famine; and all the plenty shall be forgotten in the land of Egypt; and the famine shall consume the land. And the plenty shall not be known in the land by reason of that famine following; for it shall be very grievous. And for that the dream was doubled unto Pharaoh twice, it is because the thing is established by God: and God will shortly bring it to pass.

Now therefore let Pharaoh look out a man discreet and wise, and set him over the land of Egypt. Let Pharaoh do this, and let him appoint officers over the land, and take up the fifth part of the land of Egypt in the seven plenteous years. And let them gather all the food of those good years that come, and lay up corn under the hand of Pharaoh, and let them keep food in the cities. And that food shall be for store to the land against the seven years of famine, which shall be in the land of Egypt, that the land perish not through the famine."

Joseph Rules in Egypt

And the thing was good in the eyes of Pharaoh, and in the eyes of all his servants. And Pharaoh said unto his servants, "Can we find such a one as this is, a man in whom the spirit of God is?" And Pharaoh said unto Joseph, "Forasmuch as God hath showed thee all this, there is none so discreet and wise as thou art. Thou shalt be over my house, and according unto thy word shall all my people be ruled: only in the throne will I be greater than thou." And Pharaoh said unto Joseph, "See, I have set thee over all the land of Egypt." And Pharaoh took off his ring from his hand, and put it upon Joseph's hand, and arrayed him in vestures of fine linen, and put a gold chain about his neck. And he made him to ride in the second chariot which he had; and they cried before him, "Bow the knee": and he made him ruler over all the land of Egypt.

And Pharaoh said unto Joseph, "I am Pharaoh, and without thee shall no man lift up his hand or foot in all the land of Egypt." And Pharaoh called Joseph's name Zaphnath-paaneah, and he gave him to wife Asenath the daughter of Poti-pherah, priest of On. And Joseph went out over all the land of Egypt.

And Joseph was thirty years old when he stood before Pharaoh king of Egypt. And Joseph went out from the presence of Pharaoh, and went throughout all the land of Egypt. And in the seven plenteous years the earth brought forth by handfuls. And he gathered up all the food of the seven years, which were in the land of Egypt, and laid up the food in the cities: the food of the field, which was round about every city, laid he up in the same. And Joseph gathered corn as the sand of the sea, very much, until he left numbering; for it was without number.

And unto Joseph were born two sons, before the years of famine came, which Asenath the daughter of Poti-pherah, priest of On, bare unto him. And Joseph called the name of the first-born Manasseh: "For God," said he, "hath made me forget all my toil, and all my father's house." And the name of the second called he Ephraim: "For God hath caused me to be fruitful in the land of my affliction."

And the seven years of plenteousness, that was in the land of Egypt, were ended. And the seven years of dearth began to come according as Joseph had said, and the dearth was in all lands; but in all the land of Egypt there was bread. And when all the land of Egypt was famished, the people cried to Pharaoh for bread: and Pharaoh said unto all the Egyptians, "Go unto Joseph; what he saith to you, do." And the famine was over all the face of the earth; and Joseph opened all the storehouses, and sold unto the Egyptians; and the famine waxed sore in the land of Egypt. And all countries came into Egypt to Joseph, for to buy corn, because that the famine was so sore in all lands.

Joseph's Brothers Come to Egypt

Forty-two Now when Jacob saw that there was corn in Egypt, Jacob said unto his sons, "Why do ye look one upon another?" And he said, "Behold, I have heard that there is corn in Egypt: get you down thither and buy for us from thence, that we may live, and not die."

And Joseph's ten brethren went down to buy corn in Egypt. But Benjamin, Joseph's brother, Jacob sent not with his brethren; for he said, "Lest peradventure mischief befall him." And the sons of Israel came to buy corn among those that came: for the famine was in the land of Canaan. And Joseph was the governor over the land, and he it was that sold to all the people of the land: and Joseph's brethren came, and bowed down themselves before him with their faces to the earth.

And Joseph saw his brethren, and he knew them, but made himself strange unto them, and spake roughly unto them; and he said unto them, "Whence come ye?" And they said, "From the land of Canaan, to buy food." And Joseph knew his brethren, but they knew not him. And Joseph remembered the dreams which he dreamed of them, and said unto them, "Ye are spies; to see the nakedness of the land ye are come." And they said unto him, "Nay, my lord, but to buy food are thy servants come. We are all one man's sons; we are true men; thy servants are no spies." And he said unto them, "Nay: but to see the nakedness of the land you are come." And they said, "Thy servants are twelve brethren, the sons of one man in the land of Canaan; and behold, the youngest is this day with our father, and one is not."

And Joseph said unto them, "That is it that I spake unto you, saying, 'Ye are spies.' Hereby ye shall be proved: by the life of Pharaoh ye shall not go forth hence, except your youngest brother come hither. Send one of you, and let him fetch your brother, and ye shall be kept in prison, that your words may be proved, whether there be any truth in you: or else by the life of Pharaoh surely ye are spies." And he put them all together into ward three days.

And Joseph said unto them the third day, "This do, and live; for I fear God. If ye be true men, let one of your brethren be bound in the house of your prison: go ye, carry corn for the famine of your houses. But bring your youngest brother unto me, so shall your words be verified, and ye shall not die": and they did so.

And they said one to another, "We are verily guilty concerning our brother, in that we saw the anguish of his soul, when he besought us, and we would not hear; therefore is this distress come upon us." And Reuben answered them, saying, "Spake I not unto you, saying, 'Do not sin against the child,' and ye would not hear? therefore behold also, his blood is required."[5] And they knew not that Joseph understood them; for he spake unto them by an interpreter. And he turned himself about from them, and wept, and returned to them again, and communed with them, and took from them Simeon, and bound him before their eyes.

Then Joseph commanded to fill their sacks with corn, and to restore every man's money into his sack, and to give them provision for the way: and thus did he unto them. And they laded their asses with the corn, and departed thence. And as one of them opened his sack to give his ass provender in the inn, he espied his money; for behold, it was in his sack's mouth. And he said unto his brethren, "My money is restored; and lo, it is even in my sack": and their heart failed them, and they were afraid, saying one to another, "What is this that God hath done unto us?"

And they came unto Jacob their father, unto the land of Canaan, and told him all that befell unto them, saying, "The man who is the lord of the land spake roughly to us, and took us for spies of the country. And we said unto him, 'We are true men; we are no spies. We be twelve brethren, sons of our father: one is not, and the youngest is this day with our father in the land of Canaan.' And the man the lord of the country said unto us, 'Hereby shall I know that ye are true men: leave one of your brethren here with me, and take food for the famine of your

---

[5] *his blood is required:* i.e., now we have to pay for killing him.

households, and be gone. And bring your youngest brother unto me; then shall I know that you are no spies, but that you are true men: so will I deliver you your brother, and ye shall traffic in the land.' "

And it came to pass as they emptied their sacks, that behold, every man's bundle of money was in his sack: and when both they and their father saw the bundles of money, they were afraid. And Jacob their father said unto them, "Me have ye bereaved of my children: Joseph is not, and Simeon is not, and ye will take Benjamin away: all these things are against me."

And Reuben spake unto his father, saying, "Slay my two sons, if I bring him not to thee: deliver him into my hand, and I will bring him to thee again." And he said, "My son shall not go down with you, for his brother is dead, and he is left alone: if mischief befall him by the way in the which ye go, then shall ye bring down my gray hairs with sorrow to the grave."

The Second Journey of Joseph's Brothers

Forty-three And the famine was sore in the land. And it came to pass, when they had eaten up the corn which they had brought out of Egypt, their father said unto them, "Go again, buy us a little food." And Judah spake unto him, saying, "The man did solemnly protest unto us, saying, 'Ye shall not see my face, except your brother be with you.' If thou wilt send our brother with us, we will go down and buy thee food. But if thou wilt not send him, we will not go down: for the man said unto us, 'Ye shall not see my face, except your brother be with you.' "

And Israel said, "Wherefore dealt ye so ill with me, as to tell the man whether ye had yet a brother?" And they said, "The man asked us straitly of our state, and of our kindred, saying, 'Is your father yet alive? have ye another brother?' and we told him according to the tenor of these words: could we certainly know that he would say, 'Bring your brother down'?"

And Judah said unto Israel his father, "Send the lad with me, and we will arise and go, that we may live, and not die, both we, and thou, and also our little ones. I will be surety for him; of my hand shalt thou require him: if I bring him not unto thee, and set him before thee, then let me bear the blame for ever. For except we had lingered, surely now we had returned this second time."

And their father Israel said unto them, "If it must be so now, do this: take of the best fruits in the land in your vessels, and carry down the man a present, a little balm, and a little honey, spices, and myrrh, nuts, and almonds. And take double money in your hand, and the money that was brought again in the mouth of your sacks, carry it again in your hand; peradventure it was an oversight. Take also your brother, and arise, go again unto the man. And God Almighty give you mercy before the man, that he may send away your other brother, and Benjamin. If I be bereaved of my children, I am bereaved."

And the men took that present, and they took double money in their hand, and Benjamin; and rose up, and went down to Egypt, and stood before Joseph. And when Joseph saw Benjamin with them, he said to the ruler of his house, "Bring these men home, and slay, and make ready: for these men shall dine with me at noon." And the man did as Joseph bade; and the man brought the men into Joseph's house.

And the men were afraid, because they were brought into Joseph's house; and they said, "Because of the money that was returned in our sacks at the first time are we brought in, that he may seek occasion against us, and fall upon us, and take us for bondmen, and our asses."

And they came near to the steward of Joseph's house, and they communed with him at the door of the house, and said, "O sir, we came indeed down at the first time to buy food. And it came to pass, when we came to the inn, that we opened our sacks, and behold, every man's money was in the mouth of his sack, our money in full weight: and we have brought it again in our hand. And other money have we brought down in our hands to buy food: we cannot tell who put our money in our sacks."

And he said, "Peace be to you, fear not: your God, and the God of your father, hath given you treasure in your sacks: I had your money." And he brought Simeon out unto them. And the man brought the men into Joseph's house, and gave them water, and they washed their feet, and he gave their asses provender. And they made ready the present against Joseph came at noon: for they heard that they should eat bread there.

And when Joseph came home, they brought him the present which was in their hand into the house, and bowed themselves to him to the earth. And he asked them of their welfare, and said, "Is your father well, the old man of whom ye spake? Is he yet alive?" And they answered, "Thy servant our father is in good health, he is yet alive." And they bowed down their heads, and made obeisance.

And he lifted up his eyes, and saw his brother Benjamin, his mother's son, and said, "Is this your younger brother, of whom ye spake unto me?" And he said, "God be gracious unto thee, my son." And Joseph made haste; for his bowels did yearn upon his brother: and he sought where to weep; and he entered into his chamber, and wept there. And he washed his face, and went out, and refrained himself, and said, "Set on bread."

And they set on for him by himself, and for them by themselves, and for the Egyptians which did eat with him by themselves: because the Egyptians might not eat bread with the Hebrews; for that is an abomination unto the Egyptians. And they sat before him, the firstborn according to his birthright, and the youngest according to his youth: and the men marvelled one at another. And he took and sent messes unto them from before him: but Benjamin's mess was five times so much as any of theirs. And they drunk, and were merry with him.

Forty-four   And he commanded the steward of his house, saying, "Fill the men's sacks with food, as much as they can carry, and put every man's money in his sack's mouth. And put my cup, the silver cup, in the sack's mouth of the youngest, and his corn money." And he did according to the word that Joseph had spoken.

As soon as the morning was light, the men were sent away, they, and their asses. And when they were gone out of the city, and not yet far off, Joseph said unto his steward, "Up, follow after the men; and when thou dost overtake them, say unto them, 'Wherefore have ye rewarded evil for good? Is not this it in which my lord drinketh? and whereby indeed he divineth? ye have done evil in so doing.' "

And he overtook them, and he spake unto them these same words. And they said unto him, "Wherefore saith my lord these words? God forbid that thy servants should do according to this thing. Behold, the money which we found in our sacks' mouths we brought again unto thee out of the land of Canaan: how then should we steal out of thy lord's house silver or gold? With whomsoever of thy servants it be found, both let him die, and we also will be my lord's bondmen." And he said, "Now also let it be according unto your words: he with whom it is found shall be my servant; and ye shall be blameless."

Then they speedily took down every man his sack to the ground, and opened every man his sack. And he searched, and began at the eldest, and left at the youngest: and the cup was found in Benjamin's sack. Then they rent their clothes, and laded every man his ass, and returned to the city.

And Judah and his brethren came to Joseph's house, for he was yet there: and they fell before him on the ground. And Joseph said unto them, "What deed is this that ye have done? wot ye not that such a man as I can certainly divine?" And Judah said, "What shall we say unto my lord? what shall we speak? or how shall we clear ourselves? God hath found out the iniquity of thy servants: behold, we are my lord's servants, both we, and he also with whom the cup is found." And he said, "God forbid that I should do so: but the man in whose hand the cup is found, he shall be my servant; and as for you, get you up in peace unto your father."

Then Judah came near unto him, and said, "Oh my lord, let thy servant, I pray thee, speak a word in my lord's ears, and let not thine anger burn against thy servant: for thou art even as Pharaoh. My lord asked his servants, saying. 'Have ye a father, or a brother?' And we said unto my lord, 'We have a father, an old man, and a child of his old age, a little one; and his brother is dead, and he alone is left of his mother, and his father loveth him.' And thou saidst unto thy servants, 'Bring him down unto me, that I may set mine eyes upon him.' And we said unto my lord, 'The lad cannot leave his father: for if he should leave his father, his father would die.' And thou saidst unto thy servants, 'Except your youngest brother come down with you, ye shall see my face no more.'

"And it came to pass when we came up unto thy servant my father, we told him the words of my lord. And our father said, 'Go again, and buy us a little food.' And we said, 'We cannot go down: if our youngest brother be with us, then will we go down: for we may not see the man's face, except our youngest brother be with us.' And thy servant my father said unto us, 'Ye know that my wife bare me two sons. And the one went out from me, and I said, "Surely he is torn in pieces"; and I saw him not since. And if ye take this also from me, and mischief befall him, ye shall bring down my gray hairs with sorrow to the grave.'

"Now therefore when I come to thy servant my father, and the lad be not with us, seeing that his life is bound up in the lad's life, it shall come to pass, when he seeth that the lad is not with us, that he will die: and thy servants shall bring down the gray hairs of thy servant our father with sorrow to the grave. For thy servant became surety for the lad unto my father, saying, 'If I bring him not unto thee, then I shall bear the blame to my father for ever.' Now therefore, I pray thee, let thy servant abide instead of the lad a bondman to my lord; and let the lad go up with his brethren. For how shall I go up to my father, and the lad be not with me, lest peradventure I see the evil that shall come on my father?"

Joseph Reveals Himself to His Brothers

Forty-five Then Joseph could not refrain himself before all them that stood by him: and he cried, "Cause every man to go out from me"; and there stood no man with him, while Joseph made himself known unto his brethren. And he wept aloud: and the Egyptians and the house of Pharaoh heard. And Joseph said unto his brethren, "I am Joseph; doth my father yet live?" and his brethren could not answer him: for they were troubled at his presence.

And Joseph said unto his brethren, "Come near to me, I pray you." And they came near. And he said, "I am Joseph your brother, whom ye sold into Egypt. Now therefore be not grieved, nor angry with yourselves, that ye sold me hither: for God did send me before you to preserve life. For these two years hath the famine been in the land: and yet there are five years in the which there shall neither be earing[6] nor harvest. And God sent me before you to preserve you a posterity in the earth, and to save your lives by a great deliverance. So now it was not you that sent me hither, but God: and he hath made me a father to Pharaoh, and lord of all his house, and a ruler throughout all the land of Egypt.

"Haste you, and go up to my father, and say unto him, 'Thus saith thy son Joseph, "God hath made me lord of all Egypt: come down unto me, tarry not. And thou shalt dwell in the land of Goshen, and thou shalt be near unto me, thou, and thy children, and thy children's children, and thy flocks, and thy herds, and all that thou hast. And there will I nourish thee, for yet there are five years of famine, lest thou, and thy household, and all that thou hast, come to poverty." '

"And behold, your eyes see, and the eyes of my brother Benjamin, that it is my mouth that speaketh unto you. And you shall tell my father of all my glory in Egypt, and of all that you have seen, and ye shall haste and bring down my father hither." And he fell upon his brother Benjamin's neck, and wept; and Benjamin wept upon his neck. Moreover he kissed all his brethren, and wept upon them: and after that his brethren talked with him.

And the fame thereof was heard in Pharaoh's house, saying, "Joseph's brethren are come": and it pleased Pharaoh well, and his servants. And Pharaoh said unto Joseph, "Say unto thy brethren, 'This do ye, lade your beasts and go, get you unto the land of Canaan. And take your father, and your households, and come unto me; and I will give you the good of the land of Egypt, and ye shall eat the fat of the land.' Now thou art commanded, this do ye; take you wagons out of the land of Egypt for your little ones, and for your wives, and bring your father, and come.

---

[6] *earing:* ploughing.

Also regard not your stuff; for the good of all the land of Egypt is yours."

And the children of Israel did so: and Joseph gave them wagons, according to the commandment of Pharaoh, and gave them provision for the way. To all of them he gave each man changes of raiment; but to Benjamin he gave three hundred pieces of silver, and five changes of raiment. And to his father he sent after this manner: ten asses laden with the good things of Egypt, and ten she-asses laden with corn and bread and meat for his father by the way. So he sent his brethren away, and they departed: and he said unto them, "See that ye fall not out by the way."

And they went up out of Egypt, and came into the land of Canaan unto Jacob their father, and told him, saying, "Joseph is yet alive, and he is governor over all the land of Egypt." And Jacob's heart fainted, for he believed them not. And they told him all the words of Joseph, which he had said unto them: and when he saw the wagons which Joseph had sent to carry him, the spirit of Jacob their father revived. And Israel said, "It is enough; Joseph my son is yet alive: I will go and see him before I die."

Jacob Comes to Egypt

Forty-six And Israel took his journey with all that he had, and came to Beer-sheba, and offered sacrifices unto the God of his father Isaac. And God spake unto Israel in the visions of the night, and said, "Jacob, Jacob." And he said, "Here am I." And he said, "I am God, the God of thy father, fear not to go down into Egypt; for I will there make of thee a great nation. I will go down with thee into Egypt; and I will also surely bring thee up again: and Joseph shall put his hand upon thine eyes."

And Jacob rose up from Beer-sheba: and the sons of Israel carried Jacob their father, and their little ones, and their wives, in the wagons which Pharaoh had sent to carry him. And they took their cattle, and their goods, which they had gotten in the land of Canaan, and came into Egypt, Jacob, and all his seed with him: his sons, and his sons' sons with him, his daughters, and his sons' daughters, and all his seed brought he with him into Egypt.

. . . And he sent Judah before him unto Joseph, to direct his face unto Goshen, and they came into the land of Goshen. And Joseph made ready his chariot, and went up to meet Israel his father, to Goshen, and presented himself unto him; and he fell on his neck, and wept on his neck a good while. And Israel said unto Joseph, "Now let me die, since I have seen thy face, because thou art yet alive."

And Joseph said unto his brethren, and unto his father's house, "I will go up, and show Pharaoh, and say unto him, 'My brethren, and my father's house, which were in the land of Canaan, are come unto me. And the men are shepherds, for their trade hath been to feed cattle; and they have brought their flocks, and their herds, and all that they have.' And it shall come to pass when Pharaoh shall call you, and shall say, 'What is your occupation?' that ye shall say, 'Thy servants' trade hath been about cattle, from our youth even until now, both we, and also our fathers': that ye may dwell in the land of Goshen; for every shepherd is an abomination unto the Egyptians."

Forty-seven Then Joseph came and told Pharaoh, and said, "My father and my brethren, and their flocks, and their herds, and all that they have, are come out of the land of Canaan; and behold, they are in the land of Goshen." And he took some of his brethren, even five men, and presented them unto Pharaoh. And Pharaoh said unto his brethren, "What is your occupation?" And they said unto Pharaoh, "Thy servants are shepherds, both we and also our fathers." They said moreover unto Pharaoh, "For to sojourn in the land are we come; for thy servants have no pasture for their flocks, for the famine is sore in the land of Canaan: now therefore, we pray thee, let thy servants dwell in the land of Goshen."

And Pharaoh spake unto Joseph, saying, "Thy father and thy brethren are come unto thee. The land of Egypt is before thee; in the best of the land make thy father and brethren to dwell; in the land of Goshen let them dwell: and if thou knowest any man of activity amongst them, then make them rulers over my cattle."

And Joseph brought in Jacob his father, and set him before Pharaoh: and Jacob blessed Pharaoh. And Pharaoh said unto

Jacob, "How old art thou?" And Jacob said unto Pharaoh, "The days of the years of my pilgrimage are an hundred and thirty years: few and evil have the days of the years of my life been, and have not attained unto the days of the years of the life of my fathers, in the days of their pilgrimage." And Jacob blessed Pharaoh, and went out from before Pharaoh.

And Joseph placed his father, and his brethren, and gave them a possession in the land of Egypt, in the best of the land, in the land of Rameses, as Pharaoh had commanded. And Joseph nourished his father and his brethren, and all his father's household, with bread, according to their families.

And there was no bread in all the land; for the famine was very sore, so that the land of Egypt and all the land of Canaan fainted by reason of the famine. And Joseph gathered up all the money that was found in the land of Egypt, and in the land of Canaan, for the corn which they bought: and Joseph brought the money into Pharaoh's house.

And when money failed in the land of Egypt, and in the land of Canaan, all the Egyptians came unto Joseph, and said, "Give us bread: for why should we die in thy presence? for the money faileth." And Joseph said, "Give your cattle; and I will give you for your cattle, if money fail." And they brought their cattle unto Joseph: and Joseph gave them bread in exchange for horses, and for the flocks, and for the cattle of the herds, and for the asses, and he fed them with bread for all their cattle for that year.

When that year was ended, they came unto him the second year, and said unto him, "We will not hide it from my lord, how that our money is spent; my lord also had our herds of cattle; there is not aught left in the sight of my lord, but our bodies, and our lands. Wherefore shall we die before thine eyes, both we and our land? buy us and our land for bread, and we and our land will be servants unto Pharaoh: and give us seed that we may live and not die, that the land be not desolate."

And Joseph bought all the land of Egypt for Pharaoh: for the Egyptians sold every man his field, because the famine prevailed over them: so the land became Pharaoh's. And as for the people, he removed them to cities from one end of the borders of Egypt, even to the other end thereof. Only the land of the priests bought he not; for the priests had a portion assigned them of Pharaoh, and did eat their portion which Pharaoh gave them: wherefore they sold not their lands.

Then Joseph said unto the people, "Behold, I have bought you this day, and your land for Pharaoh: lo, here is seed for you, and ye shall sow the land. And it shall come to pass in the increase, that ye shall give the fifth part unto Pharaoh, and four parts shall be your own, for seed of the field, and for your food, and for them of your households, and for food for your little ones." And they said, "Thou hast saved our lives: let us find grace in the sight of my lord, and we will be Pharaoh's servants." And Joseph made it a law over the land of Egypt unto this day, that Pharaoh should have the fifth part; except the land of the priests only, which became not Pharaoh's.

And Israel dwelt in the land of Egypt, in the country of Goshen, and they had possessions therein, and grew, and multiplied exceedingly. And Jacob lived in the land of Egypt seventeen years: so the whole age of Jacob was an hundred forty and seven years. And the time drew nigh that Israel must die, and he called his son Joseph, and said unto him, "If now I have found grace in thy sight, put, I pray thee, thy hand under my thigh, and deal kindly and truly with me, bury me not, I pray thee, in Egypt. But I will lie with my fathers, and thou shalt carry me out of Egypt, and bury me in their burying place." And he said, "I will do as thou hast said." And he said, "Swear unto me." And he sware unto him. And Israel bowed himself upon the bed's head.

Death of Jacob

Forty-eight   And it came to pass after these things, that one told Joseph, "Behold, thy father is sick": and he took with him his two sons, Manasseh and Ephraim. And one told Jacob, and said, "Behold, thy son Joseph cometh unto thee": and Israel strengthened himself, and sat upon the bed. And Jacob said unto Joseph, "God Almighty appeared unto me at Luz in the land of Canaan, and blessed me, and said unto me, 'Behold, I will make thee fruitful, and multiply thee, and I will make of thee a multitude of people, and will give this land to thy seed after thee, for an everlasting possession.' And now thy two sons, Ephraim and Manasseh, which were born unto thee in the land of Egypt, before I came unto thee into Egypt, are mine, as Reuben and Simeon, they shall be mine. And thy issue, which thou begettest after them, shall be thine, and shall be called after the name of their brethren in their inheritance. And as for me, when I came from Padan, Rachel died by me in the land of Canaan, in the way, when yet there was but a little way to come unto Ephrath: and I buried her there in the way of Ephrath; the same is Bethlehem."

And Israel beheld Joseph's sons, and said, "Who are these?" And Joseph said unto his father, "They are my sons, whom God hath given me in this place." And he said, "Bring them, I pray thee, unto me, and I will bless them." Now the eyes of Israel were dim for age, so that he could not see. And he brought them near unto him, and he kissed them, and embraced them. And Israel said unto Joseph, "I had not thought to see thy face: and lo, God hath showed me also thy seed." And Joseph brought them out from between his knees, and he bowed himself with his face to the earth.

> CHILDREN'S CHILDREN ARE THE CROWN OF OLD MEN; AND
> THE GLORY OF CHILDREN ARE THEIR FATHERS.
>
> PROVERBS 17:6

And Joseph took them both, Ephraim in his right hand toward Israel's left hand, and Manasseh in his left hand toward Israel's right hand, and brought them near unto him. And Israel stretched out his right hand, and laid it upon Ephraim's head who was the younger, and his left hand upon Manasseh's head, guiding his hands wittingly: for Manasseh was the firstborn.

And he blessed Joseph and said, "God before whom my fathers Abraham and Isaac did walk, the God which fed me all my life long unto this day, the Angel which redeemed me from all evil, bless the lads, and let my name be named on them, and the name of my fathers Abraham and Isaac, and let them grow into a multitude in the midst of the earth."

And when Joseph saw that his father laid his right hand upon the head of Ephraim, it displeased him: and he held up his father's hand, to remove it from Ephraim's head unto Manasseh's head. And Joseph said unto his father, "Not so, my father: for this is the firstborn; put thy right hand upon his head."

And his father refused, and said, "I know it, my son, I know it: he also shall become a people, and he also shall be great: but truly his younger brother shall be greater than he, and his seed shall become a multitude of nations." And he blessed them that day, saying, "In thee shall Israel bless, saying, 'God make thee as Ephraim, and as Manasseh'": and he set Ephraim before Manasseh.

And Israel said unto Joseph, "Behold, I die: but God shall be with you, and bring you again unto the land of your fathers. Moreover I have given to thee one portion above thy brethren, which I took out of the hand of the Amorite with my sword, and with my bow."

Fifty And Joseph fell upon his father's face, and wept upon him, and kissed him. And Joseph commanded his servants the physicians to embalm his father: and the physicians embalmed Israel. And forty days were fulfilled for him, for so are fulfilled the days of those which are embalmed: and the Egyptians mourned for him threescore and ten days.

And when the days of his mourning were past, Joseph spake unto the house of Pharaoh, saying, "If now I have found grace in your eyes, speak, I pray you, in the ears of Pharaoh, saying, 'My father made me swear, saying, "Lo, I die: in my grave which I have digged for me, in the land of Canaan, there shalt thou bury me." Now therefore let me go up, I pray thee, and bury my father, and I will come again.'" And Pharaoh said, "Go up, and bury thy father, according as he made thee swear."

And Joseph went up to bury his father: and with him went up all the servants of Pharaoh, the elders of his house, and all the elders of the land of Egypt, and all the house of Joseph, and his brethren, and his father's house: only their little ones, and their flocks, and their herds, they left in the land of Goshen. And there went up with him both chariots and horsemen: and it was a very great company. And they came to the threshing floor of Atad, which is beyond Jordan, and there they mourned with a great and very sore lamentation: and he made a mourning for his father seven days. And when the inhabitants of the land, the Canaanites, saw the mourning in the floor of Atad, they said, "This is a grievous mourning to the Egyptians": wherefore the name of it was called, Abel-mizraim, which is beyond Jordan.

And his sons did unto him according as he commanded them: for his sons carried him into the land of Canaan, and buried him in the cave of the field of Machpelah, which Abraham bought with the field for a possession of a burying place of Ephron the Hittite, before Mamre.

And Joseph returned into Egypt, he, and his brethren, and all that went up with him to bury his father, after he had buried his father.

And when Joseph's brethren saw that their father was dead, they said, "Joseph will peradventure hate us, and will certainly requite us all the evil which we did unto him." And they sent a messenger unto Joseph, saying, "Thy father did command before he died, saying, 'So shall ye say unto Joseph, "Forgive, I pray thee now, the trespass of thy brethren, and their sin; for they did unto thee evil" ': and now we pray thee, forgive the trespass of the servants of the God of thy father."

And Joseph wept when they spake unto him. And his brethren also went and fell down before his face, and they said, "Behold, we be thy servants." And Joseph said unto them, "Fear not: for am I in the place of God? But as for you, ye thought evil against me; but God meant it unto good, to bring to pass, as it is this day, to save much people alive. Now therefore fear ye not: I will nourish you, and your little ones." And he comforted them, and spake kindly unto them.

And Joseph dwelt in Egypt, he, and his father's house: and Joseph lived an hundred and ten years. And Joseph saw Ephraim's children, of the third generation: the children also of Machir, the son of Manasseh, were brought up upon Joseph's knees.

And Joseph said unto his brethren, "I die: and God will surely visit you, and bring you out of this land, unto the land which he sware to Abraham, to Isaac, and to Jacob." And Joseph took an oath of the children of Israel, saying, "God will surely visit you, and ye shall carry up my bones from hence." So Joseph died, being an hundred and ten years old: and they embalmed him, and he was put in a coffin, in Egypt.

The Finding of Moses
Rijksmuseum, Amsterdam

Moses

*Moses, "the God-intoxicated man," is the dominant figure of
the Old Testament. It was long believed that Moses himself was
the author of the first five books of the Old Testament, the
Torah or Pentateuch. He was the liberator of the Hebrew
people from Egyptian bondage, their leader in the wilderness,
their judge, their provider, and general of their armies in the
hostile territories of Canaan. Most important, he was the greatest
prophet and lawgiver of the Hebrews. He was an intermediary
between the people and God, with whom he spoke often and from
whom he received the Ten Commandments. At the same time,
like the patriarchs before him, Moses is very human — capable
of anger, capable of error, capable even of fear and doubt, in
the face of the impossible tasks he was called on almost daily
to accomplish.*

*By the time of Moses almost four centuries had passed since
the death of Joseph, and the status of the Hebrew people had
changed from that of welcome guests to that of slaves. According
to most scholars the exodus under Moses took place sometime in
the 13th century, probably around 1290 B.C. There is uncertainty
about the exact date because this event so crucial in the history
of the Hebrews and so vividly retold in the book of Exodus is
not mentioned in the Egyptian records.*

Exodus

The Hebrews Are Enslaved

One Now these are the names of the children of Israel, which came into Egypt, every man and his household came with Jacob. Reuben, Simeon, Levi, and Judah, Issachar, Zebulun, and Benjamin, Dan, and Naphtali, Gad, and Asher. And all the souls that came out of the loins of Jacob were seventy souls: for Joseph was in Egypt already. And Joseph died, and all his brethren, and all that generation.

And the children of Israel were fruitful, and increased abundantly, and multiplied, and waxed exceeding mighty, and the land was filled with them. Now there arose up a new king over Egypt, which knew not Joseph. And he said unto his people, "Behold, the people of the children of Israel are more and mightier than we. Come on, let us deal wisely with them, lest they multiply, and it come to pass that, when there falleth out any war, they join also unto our enemies, and fight against us, and so get them up out of the land."

Therefore they did set over them taskmasters to afflict them with their burdens. And they built for Pharaoh treasure cities, Pithom and Raamses. But the more they afflicted them, the more they multiplied and grew. And they were grieved because of the children of Israel. And the Egyptians made the children of Israel to serve with rigour. And they made their lives bitter with hard bondage, in mortar, and in brick, and in all manner of service in the field: all their service wherein they made them serve was with rigour.

And the king of Egypt spake to the Hebrew midwives, of which the name of the one was Shiphrah, and the name of the other Puah, and he said, "When ye do the office of a midwife to the Hebrew women, and see them upon the stools, if it be a son, then ye shall kill him: but if it be a daughter, then she shall live."

But the midwives feared God, and did not as the king of Egypt commanded them, but saved the men children alive. And the king of Egypt called for the midwives, and said unto them, "Why have ye done this thing, and have saved the men children alive?" And the midwives said unto Pharaoh, "Because the Hebrew women are not as the Egyptian women: for they are lively, and are delivered ere the midwives come in unto them." Therefore God dealt well with the midwives: and the people multiplied and waxed very mighty. And it came to pass, because the midwives feared God, that he made them houses. And Pharaoh charged all his people, saying, "Every son that is born, ye shall cast into the river, and every daughter ye shall save alive."

Moses in the Ark of Bulrushes

Two And there went a man of the house of Levi, and took to wife a daughter of Levi. And the woman conceived, and bare a son: and when she saw him that he was a goodly child, she hid him three months. And when she could not longer hide him, she took for him an ark of bulrushes, and daubed it with slime and with pitch, and put the child therein; and she laid it in the flags[1] by the river's brink. And his sister stood afar off, to wit what would be done to him.

And the daughter of Pharaoh came down to wash herself at the river, and her maidens walked along by the river side; and when she saw the ark among the flags, she sent her maid to fetch it. And when she had opened it, she saw the child: and behold, the babe

[1] *flags:* reeds or marsh grass.

wept. And she had compassion on him, and said, "This is one of the Hebrews' children."

Then said his sister to Pharaoh's daughter, "Shall I go and call to thee a nurse of the Hebrew women, that she may nurse the child for thee?" And Pharaoh's daughter said to her, "Go." And the maid went and called the child's mother. And Pharaoh's daughter said unto her, "Take this child away, and nurse it for me, and I will give thee thy wages." And the woman took the child, and nursed it. And the child grew, and she brought him unto Pharaoh's daughter, and he became her son. And she called his name Moses: and she said, "Because I drew him out of the water."

The Flight of Moses

And it came to pass in those days, when Moses was grown, that he went out unto his brethren, and looked on their burdens, and he spied an Egyptian smiting an Hebrew, one of his brethren. And he looked this way and that way, and when he saw that there was no man, he slew the Egyptian, and hid him in the sand. And when he went out the second day, behold, two men of the Hebrews strove together: and he said to him that did the wrong, "Wherefore smitest thou thy fellow?" And he said, "Who made thee a prince and a judge over us? intendest thou to kill me, as thou killedst the Egyptian?" And Moses feared, and said, "Surely this thing is known."

Now when Pharaoh heard this thing, he sought to slay Moses. But Moses fled from the face of Pharaoh, and dwelt in the land of Midian: and he sat down by a well. Now the priest of Midian had seven daughters, and they came and drew water, and filled the troughs to water their father's flock. And the shepherds came and drove them away: but Moses stood up and helped them, and watered their flock. And when they came to Reuel their father, he said, "How is it that ye are come so soon today?" And they said, "An Egyptian delivered us out of the hand of the shepherds, and also drew water enough for us, and watered the flock." And he said unto his daughters, "And where is he? why is it that ye have left the man? Call him, that he may eat bread."

And Moses was content to dwell with the man, and he gave Moses Zipporah his daughter. And she bare him a son, and he called his name Gershom: for he said, "I have been a stranger in a strange land."

And it came to pass in process of time, that the king of Egypt died: and the children of Israel sighed by reason of the bondage, and they cried, and their cry came up unto God, by reason of the bondage. And God heard their groaning, and God remembered his covenant with Abraham, with Isaac, and with Jacob. And God looked upon the children of Israel, and God had respect unto them.

The Burning Bush

Three Now Moses kept the flock of Jethro his father-in-law, the priest of Midian: and he led the flock to the backside of the desert, and came to the mountain of God, even to Horeb. And the angel of the Lord appeared unto him, in a flame of fire out of the midst of a bush: and he looked, and behold, the bush burned with fire, and the bush was not consumed. And Moses said, "I will now turn aside, and see this great sight, why the bush is not burning."

And when the Lord saw that he turned aside to see, God called unto him out of the midst of the bush, and said, "Moses, Moses." And he said, "Here am I." And he said, "Draw not nigh hither: put off thy shoes from off thy feet, for the place whereon thou standest is holy ground." Moreover he said, "I am the God of thy father, the God of Abraham, the God of Isaac, and the God of Jacob." And Moses hid his face; for he was afraid to look upon God.

And the Lord said, "I have surely seen the affliction of my people which are in Egypt, and have heard their cry by reason of their taskmasters; for I know their sorrows, and I am come down to deliver them out of the hand of the Egyptians, and to bring them up out of that land unto a good land and a large, unto a land flowing with milk and honey, unto the place of the Canaanites, and the Hittites, and the Amorites, and the Perizzites, and the Hivites, and the Jebusites. Now therefore behold, the cry of the children of Israel is come unto me: and I have also seen the oppression wherewith the Egyptians oppress them. Come now therefore, and I will send thee unto Pharaoh, that thou mayest bring forth my people the children of Israel out of Egypt."

And Moses said unto God, "Who am I, that I should go unto Pharaoh, and that I should bring forth the children of Israel out of Egypt?" And he said, "Certainly I will be with thee, and this shall be a token unto thee, that I have sent thee. When thou hast brought forth the people out of Egypt, ye shall serve God upon this mountain."

And Moses said unto God, "Behold, when I come unto the children of Israel, and shall say unto them, 'The God of your fathers hath sent me unto you'; and they shall say to me, 'What is his name?' what shall I say unto them?" And God said unto Moses, "I AM THAT I AM": and he said, "Thus shalt thou say unto the children of Israel, 'I AM hath sent me unto you.' "

And God said moreover unto Moses, "Thus shalt thou say unto the children of Israel, 'The Lord God of your fathers, the God of Abraham, the God of Isaac, and the God of Jacob, hath sent me unto you: this is my name for ever, and this is my memorial unto all generations.' Go and gather the elders of Israel together, and say unto them, 'The Lord God of your fathers, the God of Abraham, of Isaac, and of Jacob, appeared unto me, saying, I have surely visited you, and seen that which is done to you in Egypt. And I have said, I will bring you up out of the affliction of Egypt unto the land of the Canaanites, and the Hittites, and the Amorites, and the Perizzites, and the Hivites, and the Jebusites, unto a land flowing with milk and honey.' And they shall hearken to thy voice: and thou shalt come, thou and the elders of Israel, unto the king of Egypt, and ye shall say unto him, 'The Lord God of the Hebrews hath met with us: and now let us go, we beseech thee, three days' journey into the wilderness, that we may sacrifice to the Lord our God.'

"And I am sure that the king of Egypt will not let you go, no, not by a mighty hand. And I will stretch out my hand, and smite

Egypt with all my wonders which I will do in the midst thereof: and after that he will let you go. And I will give this people favour in the sight of the Egyptians, and it shall come to pass that when ye go, ye shall not go empty: but every woman shall borrow of her neighbour, and of her that sojourneth in her house, jewels of silver, and jewels of gold, and raiment: and ye shall put them upon your sons, and upon your daughters, and ye shall spoil the Egyptians."

Four And Moses answered, and said, "But behold, they will not believe me, nor hearken unto my voice: for they will say, 'The Lord hath not appeared unto thee.'" And the Lord said unto him, "What is that in thine hand?" And he said, "A rod." And he said, "Cast it on the ground." And he cast it on the ground, and it became a serpent; and Moses fled from before it. And the Lord said unto Moses, "Put forth thine hand, and take it by the tail." And he put forth his hand, and caught it, and it became a rod in his hand: "That they may believe that the Lord God of their fathers, the God of Abraham, the God of Isaac, and the God of Jacob, hath appeared unto thee."

And the Lord said furthermore unto him, "Put now thine hand into thy bosom." And he put his hand into his bosom: and when he took it out, behold, his hand was leprous as snow. And he said, "Put thine hand into thy bosom again." And he put his hand into his bosom again, and plucked it out of his bosom, and behold, it was turned again as his other flesh. "And it shall come to pass, if they will not believe thee, neither hearken to the voice of the first sign, that they will believe the voice of the latter sign. And it shall come to pass, if they will not believe also these two signs, neither hearken unto thy voice, that thou shalt take of the water of the river, and pour it upon the dry land: and the water which thou takest out of the river shall become blood upon the dry land."

And Moses said unto the Lord, "O my Lord, I am not eloquent, neither heretofore, nor since thou hast spoken unto thy servant: but I am slow of speech, and of a slow tongue." And the Lord said unto him, "Who hath made man's mouth? or who maketh the dumb or deaf, or the seeing, or the blind? have not I the Lord?

Now therefore go, and I will be with thy mouth, and teach thee what thou shalt say." And he said, "O my Lord, send I pray thee, by the hand of him whom thou wilt send."[2] And the anger of the Lord was kindled against Moses, and he said, "Is not Aaron the Levite thy brother? I know that he can speak well. And also behold, he cometh forth to meet thee: and when he seeth thee, he will be glad in his heart. And thou shalt speak unto him, and put words in his mouth, and I will be with thy mouth, and with his mouth, and will teach you what ye shall do. And he shall be thy spokesman unto the people: and he shall be, even he shall be to thee instead of a mouth, and thou shalt be to him instead of God. And thou shalt take this rod in thine hand, wherewith thou shalt do signs."

Moses Returns to Egypt

And Moses went and returned to Jethro his father-in-law, and said unto him, "Let me go, I pray thee, and return unto my brethren which are in Egypt, and see whether they be yet alive." And Jethro said to Moses, "Go in peace." And the Lord said unto Moses in Midian, "Go, return into Egypt: for all the men are dead which sought thy life."

And Moses took his wife, and his sons, and set them upon an ass, and he returned to the land of Egypt: and Moses took the rod of God in his hand. And the Lord said unto Moses, "When thou goest to return into Egypt, see that thou do all those wonders before Pharaoh, which I have put in thine hand: but I will harden his heart, that he shall not let the people go. And thou shalt say unto Pharaoh, 'Thus saith the Lord: Israel is my son, even my firstborn. And I say unto thee, Let my son go, that he may serve me: and if thou refuse to let him go, behold, I will slay thy son, even thy firstborn.' "

And it came to pass by the way in the inn, that the Lord met him, and sought to kill him. Then Zipporah took a sharp stone, and cut off the foreskin of her son, and cast it at his feet, and said, "Surely a bloody husband art thou to me." So he let him

[2] *send . . . send: i.e.,* send somebody else.

go: then she said, "A bloody husband thou art, because of the circumcision."

And the Lord said to Aaron, "Go into the wilderness to meet Moses." And he went, and met him in the mount of God, and kissed him. And Moses told Aaron all the words of the Lord, who had sent him, and all the signs which he had commanded him.

And Moses and Aaron went, and gathered together all the elders of the children of Israel. And Aaron spake all the words which the Lord had spoken unto Moses, and did the signs in the sight of the people. And the people believed: and when they heard that the Lord had visited the children of Israel, and that he had looked upon their affliction, then they bowed their heads and worshipped.

"Let My People Go"

Five And afterward Moses and Aaron went in, and told Pharaoh, "Thus saith the Lord God of Israel, 'Let my people go, that they may hold a feast unto me in the wilderness.' " And Pharaoh said, "Who is the Lord, that I should obey his voice to let Israel go? I know not the Lord, neither will I let Israel go." And they said, "The God of the Hebrews hath met with us: let us go, we pray thee, three days' journey into the desert, and sacrifice unto the Lord our God, lest he fall upon us with pestilence, or with the sword."

And the king of Egypt said unto them, "Wherefore do ye, Moses and Aaron, let³ the people from their works? get you unto your burdens." And Pharaoh said, "Behold, the people of the land now are many, and ye make them rest from their burdens.

And Pharaoh commanded the same day the taskmasters of the people, and their officers, saying, "Ye shall no more give the people straw to make brick, as heretofore: let them go and gather straw for themselves. And the tale⁴ of the bricks, which they did make heretofore, you shall lay upon them; ye shall not diminish aught thereof: for they be idle; therefore they cry, saying, 'Let us go and sacrifice to our God.' Let there more work be laid upon the men,

---

³ *let:* hinder.
⁴ *tale:* number.

that they may labour therein, and let them not regard vain words."

And the taskmasters of the people went out, and their officers, and they spake to the people, saying, "Thus saith Pharaoh, 'I will not give you straw. Go ye, get you straw where ye can find it: yet not aught of your work shall be diminished.'" So the people were scattered abroad throughout all the land of Egypt to gather stubble instead of straw. And the taskmasters hasted them, saying, "Fulfill your works, your daily tasks, as when there was straw." And the officers of the children of Israel, which Pharaoh's taskmasters had set over them, were beaten, and demanded, "Wherefore have ye not fulfilled your task, in making brick both yesterday and today, as heretofore?"

Then the officers of the children of Israel came and cried unto Pharaoh, saying, "Wherefore dealest thou thus with thy servants? There is no straw given unto thy servants, and they say to us, 'Make brick': and behold, thy servants are beaten; but the fault is in thine own people." But he said, "Ye are idle, ye are idle: therefore ye say, 'Let us go and do sacrifice to the Lord.' Go therefore now and work; for there shall no straw be given you, yet shall ye deliver the tale of bricks." And the officers of the children of Israel did see that they were in evil case, after it was said, "Ye shall not minish aught from your bricks of your daily task."

And they met Moses and Aaron, who stood in the way, as they came forth from Pharaoh. And they said unto them, "The Lord look upon you, and judge, because ye have made our savour to be abhorred in the eyes of Pharaoh, and in the eyes of his servants, to put a sword in their hands to slay us."

And Moses returned unto the Lord, and said, "Lord, wherefore hast thou so evil entreated this people? why is it that thou hast sent me? For since I came to Pharaoh to speak in thy name, he hath done evil to this people, neither hast thou delivered thy people at all."

Six Then the Lord said unto Moses, "Now shalt thou see what I will do to Pharaoh: for with a strong hand shall he let them go, and with a strong hand shall he drive them out of his land." And God spake unto Moses, and said unto him, "I am the Lord. And I appeared unto Abraham, unto Isaac, and unto Jacob, by the name of God Almighty, but by my name JEHOVAH was I not known to them. And I have also established my covenant with them, to give them the land of Canaan, the land of their pilgrimage, wherein they were strangers. And I have also heard the groaning of the children of Israel, whom the Egyptians keep in bondage; and I have remembered my covenant. Wherefore say unto the children of Israel: I am the Lord, and I will bring you out from under the burdens of the Egyptians, and I will rid you out of their bondage, and I will redeem you with a stretched-out arm, and with great judgments. And I will take you to me for a people, and I will be to you a God: and ye shall know that I am the Lord your God, which bringeth you out from under the burdens of the Egyptians. And I will bring you in unto the land concerning the which I did swear to give it, to Abraham, to Isaac, and to Jacob, and I will give it you for an heritage: I am the Lord."

And Moses spake so unto the children of Israel: but they hearkened not unto Moses, for anguish of spirit, and for cruel bondage. And the Lord spake unto Moses, saying, "Go in, speak unto Pharaoh king of Egypt, that he let the children of Israel go out of his land." And Moses spake before the Lord, saying, "Behold, the children of Israel have not hearkened unto me: how then shall Pharaoh hear me, who am of uncircumcised lips?" And the Lord spake unto Moses and unto Aaron, and gave them a charge unto the children of Israel, and unto Pharaoh king of Egypt, to bring the children of Israel out of the land of Egypt. . . .

Seven   And the Lord said unto Moses, "See, I have made thee a god to Pharaoh, and Aaron thy brother shall be thy prophet. Thou shalt speak all that I command thee, and Aaron thy brother shall speak unto Pharaoh, that he send the children of Israel out of his land. And I will harden Pharaoh's heart, and multiply my signs and my wonders in the land of Egypt. But Pharaoh shall not hearken unto you, that I may lay my hand upon Egypt, and bring forth mine armies, and my people the children of Israel, out of the land of Egypt, by great judgments. And the Egyptians shall know that I am the Lord, when I stretch forth mine hand upon Egypt, and bring out the children of Israel from among them." And Moses and Aaron did as the Lord commanded them, so did

they. And Moses was fourscore years old, and Aaron fourscore
and three years old, when they spake unto Pharaoh.

Miracle of the Rods

And the Lord spake unto Moses, and unto Aaron, saying,
"When Pharaoh shall speak unto you, saying, 'Show a miracle
for you': then thou shalt say unto Aaron, 'Take thy rod and
cast it before Pharaoh, and it shall become a serpent.' "

And Moses and Aaron went in unto Pharaoh, and they did so as
the Lord had commanded: and Aaron cast down his rod before
Pharaoh, and before his servants, and it became a serpent. Then
Pharaoh also called the wise men and the sorcerers: now the magicians of Egypt, they also did in like manner with their enchantments. For they cast down every man his rod, and they became
serpents: but Aaron's rod swallowed up their rods. And he
hardened Pharaoh's heart, that he hearkened not unto them, as
the Lord had said.

River of Blood

And the Lord said unto Moses, "Pharaoh's heart is hardened:
he refuseth to let the people go. Get thee unto Pharaoh in the
morning, lo, he goeth out unto the water, and thou shalt stand
by the river's brink against[5] he come: and the rod which was
turned to a serpent shalt thou take in thine hand. And thou shalt
say unto him, 'The Lord God of the Hebrews hath sent me unto
thee, saying, Let my people go, that they may serve me in the
wilderness: and behold, hitherto thou wouldest not hear. Thus
saith the Lord: In this thou shalt know that I am the Lord: behold, I will smite with the rod that is in my hand upon the waters
which are in the river, and they shall be turned to blood. And
the fish that is in the river shall die, and the river shall stink, and
the Egyptians shall loathe to drink of the water of the river.' "

---

[5] *against:* until.

And the Lord spake unto Moses, "Say unto Aaron, 'Take thy rod, and stretch out thine hand upon the waters of Egypt, upon their streams, upon their rivers, and upon their ponds, and upon all their pools of water, that they may become blood, and that there may be blood throughout all the land of Egypt, both in vessels of wood, and in vessels of stone.' "

And Moses and Aaron did so, as the Lord commanded: and he lifted up the rod and smote the waters that were in the river, in the sight of Pharaoh, and in the sight of his servants; and all the waters that were in the river were turned to blood. And the fish that was in the river died; and the river stank, and the Egyptians could not drink of the water of the river; and there was blood throughout all the land of Egypt. And the magicians of Egypt did so with their enchantments: and Pharaoh's heart was hardened, neither did he hearken unto them, as the Lord had said. And Pharaoh turned and went into his house, neither did he set his heart to this also. And all the Egyptians digged round about the river for water to drink; for they could not drink of the water of the river. And seven days were fulfilled after that the Lord had smitten the river.

The Plague of Frogs

Eight   And the Lord spake unto Moses, "Go unto Pharaoh, and say unto him, 'Thus saith the Lord: Let my people go, that they may serve me. And if thou refuse to let them go, behold, I will smite all thy borders with frogs. And the river shall bring forth frogs abundantly, which shall go up and come into thine house, and into thy bedchamber, and upon thy bed, and into the house of thy servants, and upon thy people, and into thine ovens, and into thy kneading troughs. And the frogs shall come up both on thee, and upon thy people, and upon all thy servants.' "

And the Lord spake unto Moses, "Say unto Aaron, 'Stretch forth thine hand with thy rod over the streams, over the rivers, and over the ponds, and cause frogs to come up upon the land of Egypt.' " And Aaron stretched out his hand over the waters of Egypt; and the frogs came up, and covered the land of Egypt.

And the magicians did so with their enchantments, and brought up frogs upon the land of Egypt.

Then Pharaoh called for Moses, and Aaron, and said, "Entreat the Lord, that he may take away the frogs from me, and from my people; and I will let the people go, that they may do sacrifice unto the Lord." And Moses said unto Pharaoh, "Glory over me: when shall I entreat for thee, and for thy servants, and for thy people, to destroy the frogs from thee and thy houses, that they may remain in the river only?" And he said, "Tomorrow." And he said, "Be it according to thy word: that thou mayest know that there is none like unto the Lord our God. And the frogs shall depart from thee, and from thy houses, and from thy servants, and from thy people; they shall remain in the river only."

And Moses and Aaron went out from Pharaoh, and Moses cried unto the Lord because of the frogs which he had brought against Pharaoh. And the Lord did according to the word of Moses; and the frogs died out of the houses, out of the villages, and out of the fields. And they gathered them together upon heaps, and the land stank. But when Pharaoh saw that there was respite, he hardened his heart, and hearkened not unto them, as the Lord had said.

The Plague of Lice and Flies

And the Lord said unto Moses, "Say unto Aaron, 'Stretch out thy rod, and smite the dust of the land, that it may become lice throughout all the land of Egypt.'" And they did so: for Aaron stretched out his hand with his rod, and smote the dust of the earth, and it became lice, in man and in beast; all the dust of the land became lice throughout all the land of Egypt. And the magicians did so with their enchantments to bring forth lice, but they could not: so there were lice upon man and upon beast. Then the magicians said unto Pharaoh, "This is the finger of God." And Pharaoh's heart was hardened, and he hearkened not unto them, as the Lord had said.

And the Lord said unto Moses, "Rise up early in the morning, and stand before Pharaoh; lo, he cometh forth to the water, and say unto him, 'Thus saith the Lord: Let my people go, that they may serve me. Else, if thou wilt not let my people go, behold, I will send swarms of flies upon thee, and upon thy servants, and upon thy people, and into thy houses: and the houses of the Egyptians shall be full of swarms of flies, and also the ground whereon they are. And I will sever in that day the land of Goshen in which my people dwell, that no swarms of flies shall be there, to the end thou mayest know that I am the Lord in the midst of the earth. And I will put a division between my people and thy people: tomorrow shall this sign be.' "

And the Lord did so; and there came a grievous swarm of flies into the house of Pharaoh, and into his servants' houses, and into all the land of Egypt: the land was corrupted by reason of the swarm of flies.

And Pharaoh called for Moses and for Aaron, and said, "Go ye, sacrifice to your God in the land." And Moses said, "It is not meet so to do; for we shall sacrifice the abomination of the Egyptians to the Lord our God: lo, shall we sacrifice the abomination of the Egyptians before their eyes, and will they not stone us? We will go three days' journey into the wilderness, and sacrifice to the Lord our God, as he shall command us."

And the Pharaoh said, "I will let you go that ye may sacrifice to the Lord your God in the wilderness: only you shall not go very far away: entreat for me." And Moses said, "Behold, I go out from thee, and I will entreat the Lord that the swarms of flies may depart from Pharaoh, from his servants, and from his people tomorrow: but let not Pharaoh deal deceitfully any more in not letting the people go to sacrifice to the Lord."

And Moses went out from Pharaoh, and entreated the Lord: and the Lord did according to the word of Moses; and he removed the swarms of flies from Pharaoh, from his servants, and from his people; there remained not one. And Pharaoh hardened his heart at this time also, neither would he let the people go.

The Plague of Locusts

Ten And the Lord said unto Moses, "Go in unto Pharaoh: for I have hardened his heart, and the heart of his servants, that I might show these my signs before him: and that thou mayest tell in the ears of thy son, and of thy son's son, what things I have wrought in Egypt, and my signs which I have done among them, that ye may know how that I am the Lord."

And Moses and Aaron came in unto Pharaoh, and said unto him, "Thus saith the Lord God of the Hebrews: How long wilt thou refuse to humble thyself before me? Let my people go, that they may serve me. Else, if thou refuse to let my people go, behold, tomorrow will I bring the locusts into thy coast. And they shall cover the face of the earth, that one cannot be able to see the earth: and they shall eat the residue of that which is escaped, which remaineth unto you from the hail, and shall eat every tree which groweth for you out of the field. And they shall fill thy houses, and the houses of all thy servants, and the houses of all the Egyptians, which neither thy fathers, nor thy fathers' fathers have seen, since the day that they were upon the earth unto this day." And he turned himself, and went out from Pharaoh.

And Pharaoh's servants said unto him, "How long shall this man be a snare unto us? Let the men go, that they may serve the Lord their God: knowest thou not yet that Egypt is destroyed?" And Moses and Aaron were brought again unto Pharaoh: and he said unto them, "Go, serve the Lord your God: but who are they that shall go?"

And Moses said, "We will go with our young and with our old, with our sons and with our daughters, with our flocks and with our herds will we go; for we must hold a feast unto the Lord." And he said unto them, "Let the Lord be so with you, as I will let you go, and your little ones. Look to it, for evil is before you. Not so: go now ye that are men, and serve the Lord, for that you did desire." And they were driven out from Pharaoh's presence.

And the Lord said unto Moses, "Stretch out thine hand over the land of Egypt for the locusts, that they may come up upon the land of Egypt, and eat every herb of the land, even all that the hail hath left." And Moses stretched forth his rod over the land of Egypt, and the Lord brought an east wind upon the land all that day, and all that night; and when it was morning, the east wind brought the locusts. And the locusts went up over all the land of Egypt, and rested in all the coasts of Egypt: very grievous were they; before them there were no such locusts as they, neither after them shall be such. For they covered the face of the whole earth, so that the land was darkened; and they did eat every herb of the land, and all the fruit of the trees which the hail had left: and there remained not any green thing in the trees, or in the herbs of the field, through all the land of Egypt.

Then Pharaoh called for Moses and Aaron in haste; and he said, "I have sinned against the Lord your God, and against you. Now therefore forgive, I pray thee, my sin only this once, and entreat the Lord your God, that he may take away from me this death only." And he went out from Pharaoh, and entreated the Lord. And the Lord turned a mighty strong west wind, which took away the locusts, and cast them into the Red Sea; there remained not one locust in all the coasts of Egypt. But the Lord hardened Pharaoh's heart, so that he would not let the children of Israel go.

The Plague of Darkness

And the Lord said unto Moses, "Stretch out thine hand toward heaven, that there may be darkness over the land of Egypt, even darkness which may be felt." And Moses stretched forth his hand toward heaven; and there was a thick darkness in all the land of Egypt three days. They saw not one another, neither rose any from his place for three days: but all the children of Israel had light in their dwellings.

And Pharaoh called unto Moses, and said, "Go ye, serve the Lord; only let your flocks and your herds be stayed: let your little ones also go with you." And Moses said, "Thou must give us also sacrifices, and burnt offerings, that we may sacrifice unto the Lord our God. Our cattle also shall go with us: there shall not an hoof be left behind; for thereof must we take to serve the Lord our God; and we know not with what we must serve the Lord, until we come thither."

But the Lord hardened Pharaoh's heart, and he would not let them go. And Pharaoh said unto him, "Get thee from me, take heed to thyself, see my face no more; for in that day thou seest my face, thou shalt die." And Moses said, "Thou hast spoken well, I will see thy face again no more."

The Passover

Eleven And the Lord said unto Moses, "Yet will I bring one plague more upon Pharaoh, and upon Egypt; afterwards he will let you go hence: when he shall let you go, he shall surely thrust you out hence altogether. Speak now in the ears of the people, and let every man borrow of his neighbour, and every woman of her neighbour, jewels of silver, and jewels of gold." And the Lord gave the people favour in the sight of the Egyptians. Moreover the man Moses was very great in the land of Egypt, in the sight of Pharaoh's servants, and in the sight of the people.

And Moses said, "Thus saith the Lord: About midnight will I go out into the midst of Egypt. And all the firstborn in the land of Egypt shall die, from the firstborn of Pharaoh that sitteth upon his throne, even unto the firstborn of the maidservant that is behind the mill, and all the firstborn of beasts. And there shall be a great cry throughout all the land of Egypt, such as there was none like it, nor shall be like it any more. But against any of the children of Israel shall not a dog move his tongue, against man or beast: that ye may know how that the Lord doth put a difference between the Egyptians and Israel. And all these thy servants shall come down unto me, and bow down themselves unto me, saying, 'Get thee out, and all the people that follow thee': and after that I will go out." And he went out from Pharaoh in a great anger.

And the Lord said unto Moses, "Pharaoh shall not hearken unto you, that my wonders may be multiplied in the land of Egypt." And Moses and Aaron did all these wonders before Pharaoh: and the Lord hardened Pharaoh's heart, so that he would not let the children of Israel go out of his land.

Twelve And the Lord spake unto Moses and Aaron in the land of Egypt, saying, "This month shall be unto you the beginning of months: it shall be the first month of the year to you.

"Speak ye unto all the congregation of Israel, saying, In the tenth day of this month they shall take to them every man a lamb, according to the house of their fathers, a lamb for an house. And if the household be too little for the lamb, let him and his neighbour next unto his house take it according to the number of the souls; every man according to his eating shall make your count for the lamb. Your lamb shall be without blemish, a male of the first year: ye shall take it out from the sheep or from the goats. And ye shall keep it up until the fourteenth day of the same month: and the whole assembly of the congregation of Israel shall kill it in the evening. And they shall take of the blood and strike it on the two side posts and on the upper door post of the houses wherein they shall eat it.

"And they shall eat the flesh in that night, roast with fire, and unleavened bread; and with bitter herbs they shall eat it. Eat not of it raw, nor sodden at all with water, but roast with fire; his head with his legs, and with the purtenance thereof. And ye shall let nothing of it remain until the morning; and that which remaineth of it until the morning ye shall burn with fire.

"And thus shall ye eat it; with your loins girded, your shoes on your feet, and your staff in your hand; and ye shall eat it in haste: it is the Lord's Passover. For I will pass through the land of Egypt this night, and will smite all the firstborn in the land of Egypt, both man and beast; and against all the gods of Egypt I will execute judgment: I am the Lord. And the blood shall be to you for a token upon the houses where ye are: and when I see the blood, I will pass over you, and the plague shall not be upon you to destroy you, when I smite the land of Egypt.

"And this day shall be unto you for a memorial; and ye shall keep it a feast to the Lord throughout your generations; you shall keep it a feast by an ordinance for ever. Seven days shall ye eat unleavened bread; even the first day ye shall put away leaven out of your houses: for whosoever eateth leavened bread from the first day until the seventh day, that soul shall be cut off from Israel. And in the first day there shall be an holy convocation, and in the seventh day there shall be an holy convocation to you; no manner of work shall be done in them, save that which every man must eat, that only may be done of you. And ye shall observe the feast of unleavened bread; for in this selfsame day have I brought your armies out of the land of Egypt: therefore shall ye observe this day in your generations by an ordinance for ever.

"In the first month, on the fourteenth day of the month at even, ye shall eat unleavened bread, until the one and twentieth day of the month at even. Seven days shall there be no leaven found in your houses: for whosoever eateth that which is leavened, even that soul shall be cut off from the congregation of Israel, whether he be a stranger, or born in the land. Ye shall eat nothing leavened: in all your habitations shall ye eat unleavened bread."

Then Moses called for all the elders of Israel, and said unto them, "Draw out and take you a lamb, according to your families, and kill the Passover.[6] And ye shall take a bunch of hyssop,[7] and dip it in the blood that is in the basin, and strike the lintel and the two side posts with the blood that is in the basin; and none of you shall go out at the door of his house until the morning. For the Lord will pass through to smite the Egyptians; and when he seeth the blood upon the lintel, and on the two side posts, the Lord will pass over the door, and will not suffer the destroyer to come in unto your houses to smite you.

"And ye shall observe this thing for an ordinance to thee and to thy sons for ever. And it shall come to pass when ye be come to the land which the Lord will give you, according as he hath promised, that ye shall keep this service. And it shall come to pass, when your children shall say unto you, 'What mean ye by this service?' that ye shall say, 'It is the sacrifice of the Lord's Passover, who passed over the houses of the children of Israel in Egypt, when he smote the Egyptians, and delivered our houses.' " And the people bowed the head, and worshipped. And the children of Israel went away, and did as the Lord had commanded Moses and Aaron, so did they.

And it came to pass, that at midnight the Lord smote all the firstborn in the land of Egypt, from the firstborn of Pharaoh that sat on his throne unto the firstborn of the captive that was in the dungeon, and all the firstborn of cattle. And Pharaoh rose up in the night, he, and all his servants, and all the Egyptians; and

---

6 *the Passover: i.e.,* the lamb used for Passover.
7 *hyssop:* a plant.

there was a great cry in Egypt; for there was not a house where there was not one dead.

"Get You Forth"

And he called for Moses and Aaron by night, and said, "Rise up, and get you forth from amongst my people, both ye and the children of Israel; and go, serve the Lord, as ye have said. Also take your flocks and your herds, as ye have said, and be gone, and bless me also." And the Egyptians were urgent upon the people, that they might send them out of the land in haste; for they said, "We be all dead men." And the people took their dough before it was leavened, their kneading troughs being bound up in their clothes upon their shoulders. And the children of Israel did according to the word of Moses; and they borrowed of the Egyptians jewels of silver, and jewels of gold, and raiment. And the Lord gave the people favour in the sight of the Egyptians, so that they lent unto them such things as they required: and they spoiled the Egyptians.

And the children of Israel journeyed from Rameses to Succoth, about six hundred thousand on foot that were men, besides children. And a mixed multitude went up also with them, and flocks and herds, even very much cattle. And they baked unleavened cakes of the dough, which they brought forth out of Egypt; for it was not leavened; because they were thrust out of Egypt, and could not tarry, neither had they prepared for themselves any victual.

Now the sojourning of the children of Israel, who dwelt in Egypt, was four hundred and thirty years. And it came to pass at the end of the four hundred and thirty years, even the selfsame day it came to pass, that all the hosts of the Lord went out from the land of Egypt. It is a night to be much observed unto the Lord, for bringing them out from the land of Egypt: this is that night of the Lord to be observed of all the children of Israel, in their generations.

And the Lord said unto Moses and Aaron, "This is the ordinance of the Passover: there shall no stranger eat thereof. But every man's servant that is bought for money, when thou hast circumcised him, then shall he eat thereof. A foreigner and an hired servant shall not eat thereof. In one house shall it be eaten; thou shalt not carry forth aught of the flesh abroad out of the house; neither shall ye break a bone thereof. All the congregation of Israel shall keep it. And when a stranger shall sojourn with thee, and will keep the Passover to the Lord, let all his males be circumcised, and then let him come near, and keep it; and he shall be as one that is born in the land: for no uncircumcised person shall eat thereof. One law shall be to him that is homeborn, and unto the stranger that sojourneth among you."

Thus did all the children of Israel; as the Lord commanded Moses and Aaron, so did they. And it came to pass the selfsame day, that the Lord did bring the children of Israel out of the land of Egypt by their armies.[8]

Thirteen And the Lord spake unto Moses, saying, "Sanctify unto me all the firstborn, whatsoever openeth the womb among the children of Israel, both of man and of beast: it is mine."

And Moses said unto the people, "Remember this day, in which ye came out from Egypt, out of the house of bondage; for by strength of hand the Lord brought you out from this place: there shall no leavened bread be eaten. This day came ye out, in the month Abib.[9]

"And it shall be when the Lord shall bring thee into the land of the Canaanites, and the Hittites, and the Amorites, and the Hivites, and the Jebusites, which he sware unto thy fathers to give thee, a land flowing with milk and honey, that thou shalt keep this service in this month. Seven days thou shalt eat unleavened bread, and in the seventh day shall be a feast to the Lord. Unleavened bread shall be eaten seven days; and there shall no leavened bread be seen with thee, neither shall there be leaven seen with thee in all thy quarters.

"And thou shalt show thy son in that day, saying, 'This is done because of that which the Lord did unto me, when I came forth out of Egypt. And it shall be for a sign unto thee, upon thine hand, and for a memorial between thine eyes, that the Lord's law

8 *by their armies:* in large numbers.
9 *Abib:* the Hebrew month of Nisan, about the same time as April.

may be in thy mouth: for with a strong hand hath the Lord brought thee out of Egypt. Thou shalt therefore keep this ordinance in his season from year to year.'

"And it shall be when the Lord shall bring thee into the land of the Canaanites as he sware unto thee and to thy fathers, and shall give it thee, that thou shalt set apart unto the Lord all that openeth the matrix, and every firstling that cometh of a beast which thou hast; the males shall be the Lord's. And every firstling of an ass thou shalt redeem with a lamb; and if thou wilt not redeem it, then thou shalt break his neck, and all the firstborn of man among thy children shalt thou redeem.

"And it shall be when thy son asketh thee in time to come, saying, 'What is this?' that thou shalt say unto him, 'By strength of hand the Lord brought us out from Egypt, from the house of bondage. And it came to pass when Pharaoh would hardly let us go, that the Lord slew all the firstborn in the land of Egypt, both the firstborn of man, and the firstborn of beast: therefore I sacrifice to the Lord all that openeth the matrix, being males; but all the firstborn of my children I redeem. And it shall be for a token upon thine hand, and for frontlets between thine eyes: for by strength of hand the Lord brought us forth out of Egypt.' "

And it came to pass when Pharaoh had let the people go, that God led them not through the way of the land of the Philistines, although that was near; for God said, "Lest peradventure the people repent when they see war, and they return to Egypt." But God led the people about, through the way of the wilderness of the Red Sea: and the children of Israel went up harnessed[10] out of the land of Egypt. And Moses took the bones of Joseph with him: for he had straitly sworn the children of Israel, saying, "God will surely visit you, and ye shall carry up my bones away hence with you."

And they took their journey from Succoth, and encamped in Etham, in the edge of the wilderness. And the Lord went before them by day in a pillar of cloud to lead them the way; and by night in a pillar of fire, to give them light; to go by day and night. He took not away the pillar of the cloud by day, nor the pillar of fire by night, from before the people.

---

10 *harnessed:* armed or equipped for battle.

The Pursuit

Fourteen And the Lord spake unto Moses, saying, "Speak unto the children of Israel, that they turn and encamp before Pi-hahiroth, between Migdol and the sea, over against Baal-zephon: before it shall ye encamp by the sea. For Pharaoh will say of the children of Israel, 'They are entangled in the land, the wilderness hath shut them in.' And I will harden Pharaoh's heart, that he shall follow after them, and I will be honoured upon Pharaoh, and upon all his host, that the Egyptians may know that I am the Lord." And they did so.

And it was told the king of Egypt, that the people fled: and the heart of Pharaoh and of his servants was turned against the people, and they said, "Why have we done this, that we have let Israel go from serving us?" And he made ready his chariot, and took his people with him. And he took six hundred chosen chariots, and all the chariots of Egypt, and captains over every one of them. And the Lord hardened the heart of Pharaoh king of Egypt, and he pursued after the children of Israel: and the children of Israel went out with an high hand. But the Egyptians pursued after them, all the horses and chariots of Pharaoh, and his horsemen, and his army, and overtook them encamping by the sea, beside Pi-hahiroth, before Baal-zephon.

And when Pharaoh drew nigh, the children of Israel lifted up their eyes, and behold, the Egyptians marched after them; and they were sore afraid: and the children of Israel cried out unto the Lord. And they said unto Moses, "Because there were no graves in Egypt, hast thou taken us away to die in the wilderness? Wherefore hast thou dealt thus with us, to carry us forth out of Egypt? Is not this the word that we did tell thee in Egypt, saying, 'Let us alone, that we may serve the Egyptians?' For it had been better for us to serve the Egyptians, than that we should die in the wilderness."

And Moses said unto the people, "Fear ye not, stand still, and see the salvation of the Lord, which he will show to you today: for the Egyptians whom ye have seen today, ye shall see them again no more for ever. The Lord shall fight for you, and ye shall hold your peace."

And the Lord said unto Moses, "Wherefore criest thou unto me? Speak unto the children of Israel, that they go forward: but lift thou up thy rod, and stretch out thine hand over the sea, and divide it: and the children of Israel shall go on dry ground through the midst of the sea. And I, behold, I will harden the hearts of the Egyptians, and they shall follow them: and I will get me honour upon Pharaoh, and upon all his host, upon his chariots, and upon his horsemen. And the Egyptians shall know that I am the Lord, when I have gotten me honour upon Pharaoh, upon his chariots, and upon his horsemen."

The Divided Waters

And the angel of God, which went before the camp of Israel, removed and went behind them; and the pillar of the cloud went from before their face, and stood behind them. And it came between the camp of the Egyptians and the camp of Israel; and it was a cloud and darkness to them, but it gave light by night to these: so that the one came not near the other all the night.

And Moses stretched out his hand over the sea, and the Lord caused the sea to go back by a strong east wind all that night, and made the sea dry land, and the waters were divided. And the children of Israel went into the midst of the sea upon the dry ground: and the waters were a wall unto them on their right hand, and on their left.

And the Egyptians pursued, and went in after them, to the midst of the sea, even all Pharaoh's horses, his chariots, and his horsemen. And it came to pass, that in the morning watch the Lord looked unto the host of the Egyptians, through the pillar of fire and of the cloud, and troubled the host of the Egyptians, and took off their chariot wheels, that they drave them heavily: so that the Egyptians said, "Let us flee from the face of Israel; for the Lord fighteth for them against the Egyptians."

And the Lord said unto Moses, "Stretch out thine hand over the sea, that the waters may come again upon the Egyptians, upon their chariots, and upon their horsemen." And Moses stretched forth his hand over the sea, and the sea returned to his strength when the morning appeared; and the Egyptians fled against it; and the Lord overthrew the Egyptians in the midst of the sea. And the waters returned, and covered the chariots, and the horsemen, and all the host of Pharaoh that came into the sea after them; there remained not so much as one of them. But the children of Israel walked upon dry land, in the midst of the sea; and the waters were a wall unto them on their right hand, and on their left. Thus the Lord saved Israel that day out of the hand of the Egyptians; and Israel saw the Egyptians dead upon the sea shore. And Israel saw that great work which the Lord did upon the Egyptians: and the people feared the Lord, and believed the Lord, and his servant Moses.

"I Will Sing unto the Lord"

Fifteen   Then sang Moses and the children of Israel this song unto the Lord, and spake, saying,

> "I will sing unto the Lord: for he hath triumphed gloriously, the horse and his rider hath he thrown into the sea.
> The Lord is my strength and song, and he is become my salvation: he is my God, and I will prepare him an habitation; my father's God, and I will exalt him.
> The Lord is a man of war: the Lord is his name.
> Pharaoh's chariots and his host hath he cast into the sea: his chosen captains also are drowned in the Red Sea.
> The depths have covered them: they sank into the bottom as a stone.
> Thy right hand, O Lord, is become glorious in power: thy right hand, O Lord, hath dashed in pieces the enemy.
> And in the greatness of thine excellency thou hast overthrown them that rose up against thee: thou sentest forth thy wrath, which consumed them as stubble.

And with the blast of thy nostrils the waters were
gathered together, the floods stood upright as
an heap, and the depths were congealed in the
heart of the sea.

The enemy said, 'I will pursue, I will overtake, I
will divide the spoil; my lust shall be satisfied
upon them; I will draw my sword, mine hand
shall destroy them.'

Thou didst blow with thy wind, the sea covered
them: they sank as lead in the mighty waters.

Who is like unto thee, O Lord, among the gods?
who is like thee, glorious in holiness, fearful
in praises, doing wonders?

Thou stretchedst out thy right hand, the earth
swallowed them.

Thou in thy mercy has led forth the people which
thou hast redeemed: thou hast guided them
in thy strength unto thy holy habitation.

The people shall hear, and be afraid: sorrow shall
take hold on the inhabitants of Palestina,

Then the dukes of Edom shall be amazed; the
mighty men of Moab, trembling shall take hold
upon them; all the inhabitants of Canaan shall
melt away.

Fear and dread shall fall upon them, by the greatness of thine arm they shall be as still as a stone,
till thy people pass over, O Lord, till the people
pass over, which thou hast purchased.

Thou shalt bring them in, and plant them in the
mountain of thine inheritance, in the place,
O Lord, which thou hast made for thee to dwell
in, in the sanctuary, O Lord, which thy hands
have established.

The Lord shall reign for ever and ever.

For the horse of Pharaoh went in with his chariots
and with his horsemen into the sea, and the
Lord brought again the waters of the sea upon
them; but the children of Israel went on dry
land in the midst of the sea."

And Miriam the prophetess, the sister of Aaron, took a timbrel in her hand; and all the women went out after her with timbrels and with dances. And Miriam answered them, "Sing ye to the Lord, for he hath triumphed gloriously; the horse and his rider hath he thrown into the sea." So Moses brought Israel from the Red Sea, and they went out into the wilderness of Shur; and they went three days in the wilderness, and found no water.

And when they came to Marah, they could not drink of the waters of Marah, for they were bitter: therefore the name of it was called Marah. And the people murmured against Moses, saying, "What shall we drink?" And he cried unto the Lord; and the Lord showed him a tree, which when he had cast into the waters, the waters were made sweet: there he made for them a statute and an ordinance, and there he proved them,[11] and said, "If thou wilt diligently hearken to the voice of the Lord thy God, and wilt do that which is right in his sight, and wilt give ear to his commandments, and keep all his statutes, I will put none of these diseases upon thee, which I have brought upon the Egyptians: for I am the Lord that healeth thee."

And they came to Elim, where were twelve wells of water, and threescore and ten palm trees, and they encamped there by the waters.

Wandering in the Wilderness

Sixteen And they took their journey from Elim, and all the congregation of the children of Israel came unto the wilderness of Sin, which is between Elim and Sinai, on the fifteenth day of the second month after their departing out of the land of Egypt.

And the whole congregation of the children of Israel murmured against Moses and Aaron in the wilderness. And the children of Israel said unto them, "Would to God we had died by the hand of the Lord in the land of Egypt, when we sat by the flesh pots, and when we did eat bread to the full; for ye have brought us forth into this wilderness, to kill this whole assembly with hunger."

11 *proved them:* put them to a test.

Then said the Lord unto Moses, "Behold, I will rain bread from heaven for you; and the people shall go out, and gather a certain rate every day, that I may prove them, whether they will walk in my law, or no. And it shall come to pass, that on the sixth day they shall prepare that which they bring in, and it shall be twice as much as they gather daily."

And Moses and Aaron said unto all the children of Israel, "At even, then ye shall know that the Lord hath brought you out from the land of Egypt. And in the morning, then ye shall see the glory of the Lord, for that he heareth your murmurings against the Lord: and what are we, that ye murmur against us?" And Moses said, "This shall be when the Lord shall give you in the evening flesh to eat, and in the morning bread to the full; for that the Lord heareth your murmurings which ye murmur against him: and what are we? your murmurings are not against us, but against the Lord."

And Moses spake unto Aaron, "Say unto all the congregation of the children of Israel, 'Come near before the Lord: for he hath heard your murmurings.' " And it came to pass as Aaron spake unto the whole congregation of the children of Israel, that they looked toward the wilderness, and behold, the glory of the Lord appeared in the cloud.

And the Lord spake unto Moses, saying, "I have heard the murmurings of the children of Israel: speak unto them, saying. 'At even ye shall eat flesh, and in the morning ye shall be filled with bread; and ye shall know that I am the Lord your God.' "

And it came to pass, that at even the quails came up, and covered the camp: and in the morning the dew lay round about the host. And when the dew that lay was gone up, behold, upon the face of the wilderness there lay a small round thing, as small as the hoar frost on the ground. And when the children of Israel saw it, they said one to another, "It is manna": for they wist not what it was.

And Moses said unto them, "This is the bread which the Lord hath given you to eat. This is the thing which the Lord hath commanded: 'Gather of it every man according to his eating: an omer[12] for every man, according to the number of your persons,

---

[12] *omer:* a little over 7 pints.

take ye every man for them which are in his tents.' " And the children of Israel did so, and gathered, some more, some less. And when they did mete it with an omer, he that gathered much had nothing over, and he that gathered little had no lack: they gathered every man according to his eating.

And Moses said, "Let no man leave of it till the morning." Notwithstanding they hearkened not unto Moses, but some of them left of it until the morning, and it bred worms, and stank: and Moses was wroth with them. And they gathered it every morning, every man according to his eating: and when the sun waxed hot it melted.

And it came to pass, that on the sixth day they gathered twice as much bread, two omers for one man: and all the rulers of the congregation came and told Moses. And he said unto them, "This is that which the Lord hath said, 'Tomorrow is the rest of the holy sabbath unto the Lord: bake that which you will bake to-day, and seethe[13] that ye will seethe; and that which remaineth over lay up for you to be kept until the morning.' " And they laid it up till the morning, as Moses bade; and it did not stink, neither was there any worm therein. And Moses said, "Eat that today, for today is a sabbath unto the Lord: today ye shall not find it in the field. Six days ye shall gather it, but on the seventh day, which is the sabbath, in it there shall be none."

And it came to pass, that there went out some of the people on the seventh day for to gather, and they found none. And the Lord said unto Moses, "How long refuse ye to keep my commandments and my laws? See, for that the Lord hath given you the sabbath, therefore he giveth you on the sixth day the bread of two days; abide ye every man in his place, let no man go out of his place on the seventh day." So the people rested on the seventh day. And the house of Israel called the name thereof manna: and it was like coriander seed, white: and the taste of it was like wafers made with honey.

And Moses said, "This is the thing which the Lord commandeth: 'Fill an omer of it to be kept for your generations, that they may see the bread wherewith I have fed you in the wilder-

---

[13] *seethe:* boil.

ness, when I brought you forth from the land of Egypt.' " And Moses said unto Aaron, "Take a pot, and put an omer full of manna therein, and lay it up before the Lord, to be kept for your generations." As the Lord commanded Moses, so Aaron laid it up before the testimony,[14] to be kept.

And the children of Israel did eat manna forty years, until they came to a land inhabited: they did eat manna, until they came unto the borders of the land of Canaan. Now an omer is the tenth part of an ephah.

Seventeen And all the congregation of the children of Israel journeyed from the wilderness of Sin, after their journeys, according to the commandment of the Lord, and pitched in Rephidim: and there was no water for the people to drink. Wherefore the people did chide with Moses and said, "Give us water that we may drink." And Moses said unto them, "Why chide ye with me? Wherefore do ye tempt the Lord?" And the people thirsted there for water; and the people murmured against Moses, and said, "Wherefore is this that thou hast brought us up out of Egypt, to kill us and our children and our cattle with thirst?"

And Moses cried unto the Lord, saying, "What shall I do unto this people? they be almost ready to stone me." And the Lord said unto Moses, "Go on before the people, and take with thee of the elders of Israel; and thy rod, wherewith thou smotest the river, take in thine hand, and go. Behold, I will stand before thee there, upon the rock in Horeb; and thou shalt smite the rock, and there shall come water out of it, that the people may drink." And Moses did so, in the sight of the elders of Israel. And he called the name of the place Massah, and Meribah, because of the chiding of the children of Israel, and because they tempted the Lord, saying, "Is the Lord among us, or not?"

Then came Amalek, and fought with Israel in Rephidim. And Moses said unto Joshua, "Choose us out men, and go out, fight with Amalek: tomorrow I will stand on the top of the hill, with the rod of God in mine hand." So Joshua did as Moses had said

[14] *testimony:* the Sacred Ark, which symbolized the personal, but invisible presence of the Lord.

to him, and fought with Amalek: and Moses, Aaron, and Hur went up to the top of the hill.

And it came to pass when Moses held up his hand, that Israel prevailed: and when he let down his hand, Amalek prevailed. But Moses' hands were heavy; and they took a stone, and put it under him, and he sat thereon; and Aaron and Hur stayed up his hands, the one on the one side, and the other on the other side; and his hands were steady until the going down of the sun. And Joshua discomfited Amalek and his people with the edge of the sword.

And the Lord said unto Moses, "Write this for a memorial in a book, and rehearse it in the ears of Joshua: for I will utterly put out the remembrance of Amalek from under heaven." And Moses built an altar, and called the name of it Jehovah-nissi: for he said, "Because the Lord hath sworn that the Lord will have war with Amalek from generation to generation."

The Covenant

Nineteen In the third month when the children of Israel were gone forth out of the land of Egypt, the same day came they into the wilderness of Sinai. For they were departed from Rephidim, and were come to the desert of Sinai, and had pitched in the wilderness; and there Israel camped before the mount.

And Moses went up unto God: and the Lord called unto him out of the mountain, saying, "Thus shalt thou say to the house of Jacob, and tell the children of Israel: 'Ye have seen what I did unto the Egyptians, and how I bare you on eagles' wings, and brought you unto myself. Now therefore, if ye will obey my voice indeed, and keep my covenant, then ye shall be a peculiar treasure unto me above all people: for all the earth is mine. And ye shall be unto me a kingdom of priests, and an holy nation.' These are the words which thou shalt speak unto the children of Israel."

And Moses came and called for the elders of the people, and laid before their faces all these words which the Lord commanded him. And all the people answered together, and said, "All that the Lord hath spoken we will do." And Moses returned the words of the people unto the Lord. And the Lord said unto

Moses, "Lo, I come unto thee in a thick cloud, that the people may hear when I speak with thee, and believe thee for ever." And Moses told the words of the people unto the Lord.

And the Lord said unto Moses, "Go unto the people, and sanctify them today and tomorrow, and let them wash their clothes. And be ready against the third day: for the third day the Lord will come down in the sight of all the people, upon mount Sinai. And thou shalt set bounds unto the people round about, saying, 'Take heed to yourselves, that ye go not up into the mount, or touch the border of it: whosoever toucheth the mount shall be surely put to death. There shall not a hand touch it, but he shall surely be stoned, or shot through; whether it be beast or man, it shall not live': when the trumpet soundeth long, they shall come up to the mount."

And Moses went down from the mount unto the people, and sanctified the people; and they washed their clothes. And he said unto the people, "Be ready against the third day: come not at your wives."

And it came to pass on the third day in the morning, that there were thunders and lightnings, and a thick cloud upon the mount, and the voice of the trumpet exceeding loud, so that all the people that was in the camp trembled. And Moses brought forth the people out of the camp to meet with God; and they stood at the nether part of the mount. And mount Sinai was altogether on a smoke, because the Lord descended upon it in fire: and the smoke thereof ascended as the smoke of a furnace, and the whole mount quaked greatly.

And when the voice of the trumpet sounded long, and waxed louder and louder, Moses spake, and God answered him by a voice. And the Lord came down upon mount Sinai, on the top of the mount: and the Lord called Moses up to the top of the mount, and Moses went up. And the Lord said unto Moses, "Go down, charge the people, lest they break through unto the Lord to gaze, and many of them perish. And let the priests also, which come near to the Lord, sanctify themselves, lest the Lord break forth upon them."

And Moses said unto the Lord, "The people cannot come up to mount Sinai: for thou chargedst us, saying, 'Set bounds about the mount, and sanctify it.' " And the Lord said unto him, "Away, get thee down, and thou shalt come up, thou, and Aaron with thee: but let not the priests and the people break through, to come up unto the Lord lest he break forth upon them." So Moses went down unto the people, and spake unto them.

The Commandments

Twenty And God spake all these words, saying, "I am the Lord thy God, which have brought thee out of the land of Egypt, out of the house of bondage.

Thou shalt have no other gods before me.

Thou shalt not make unto thee any graven image, or any likeness of any thing that is in heaven above, or that is in the earth beneath, or that is in the water under the earth. Thou shalt not bow down thyself to them, nor serve them: for I the Lord thy God am a jealous God, visiting the iniquity of the fathers upon the children unto the third and fourth generation of them that hate me: and showing mercy unto thousands of them that love me, and keep my commandments.

Thou shalt not take the name of the Lord thy God in vain; for the Lord will not hold him guiltless that taketh his name in vain.

Remember the sabbath day, to keep it holy. Six days shalt thou labour, and do all thy work: but the seventh day is the sabbath of the Lord thy God: in it thou shalt not do any work, thou, nor thy son, nor thy daughter, thy manservant, nor thy maidservant, nor thy cattle, nor thy stranger that is within thy gates. For in six days the Lord made heaven and earth, the sea, and all that in them is, and rested the seventh day: wherefore the Lord blessed the sabbath day, and hallowed it.

Honour thy father and thy mother: that thy days may be long upon the land, which the Lord thy God giveth thee.

Thou shalt not kill.

Thou shalt not commit adultery.

Thou shalt not steal.

Thou shalt not bear false witness against thy neighbour.

Thou shalt not covet thy neighbour's house, thou shalt not covet thy neighbour's wife, nor his manservant, nor his maidservant, nor his ox, nor his ass, nor any thing that is thy neighbour's."

MY SON, FORGET NOT MY LAW; BUT LET THINE HEART KEEP MY COMMANDMENTS.

PROVERBS 3:1

And all the people saw the thunderings, and the lightnings, and the noise of the trumpet, and the mountain smoking: and when the people saw it, they removed, and stood afar off. And they said unto Moses, "Speak thou with us, and we will hear: but let not God speak with us, lest we die." And Moses said unto the people, "Fear not: for God is come to prove you, and that his fear may be before your faces, that ye sin not." And the people stood afar off, and Moses drew near unto the thick darkness where God was.

And the Lord said unto Moses, "Thus thou shalt say unto the children of Israel, 'Ye have seen that I have talked with you from heaven. Ye shall not make with me gods of silver, neither shall ye make unto you gods of gold. An altar of earth thou shalt make unto me, and shalt sacrifice thereon thy burnt offerings, and thy peace offerings, thy sheep, and thine oxen: in all places where I record my name I will come unto thee, and I will bless thee. And if thou wilt make me an altar of stone, thou shalt not build it of hewn stone: for if thou lift up thy tool upon it, thou hast polluted it. Neither shalt thou go up by steps unto mine altar, that thy nakedness be not discovered thereon.' "

Deuteronomy

Death of Moses

Thirty-four   And Moses went up from the plains of Moab, unto the mountain of Nebo, to the top of Pisgah, that is over against Jericho: and the Lord showed him all the land of Gilead, unto Dan, and all Naphtali, and the land of Ephraim, and Manasseh, and all the land of Judah, unto the utmost sea, and the south, and the plain of the valley of Jericho, the city of palm trees, unto Zoar. And the Lord said unto him. "This is the land which I sware unto Abraham, unto Isaac, and unto Jacob, saying, 'I will give it unto thy seed': I have caused thee to see it with thine eyes, but thou shalt not go over thither."

So Moses the servant of the Lord died there in the land of Moab, according to the word of the Lord. And he buried him in a valley in the land of Moab, over against Beth-peor: but no man knoweth of his sepulchre unto this day.

And Moses was an hundred and twenty years old when he died: his eye was not dim, nor his natural force abated.

And the children of Israel wept for Moses in the plains of Moab thirty days: so the days of weeping and mourning for Moses were ended.

And Joshua the son of Nun was full of the spirit of wisdom: for Moses had laid his hands upon him, and the children of Israel hearkened unto him, and did as the Lord commanded Moses.

And there arose not a prophet since in Israel like unto Moses, whom the Lord knew face to face in all the signs and the wonders which the Lord sent him to do in the land of Egypt to Pharaoh, and to all his servants, and to all his land, and in all that mighty hand, and in all the great terror, which Moses showed in the sight of all Israel.

Samson and Delilah
Coll. Groningen Museum, Groningen, Netherlands

Samson

On one level Samson resembles a combination of Hercules, Till Eulenspiegel, and Paul Bunyan — huge, fun-loving, powerful. Dedicated at birth to God, he seems the very opposite of a judge (leader) of Israel in his love of practical jokes and his pursuit of Philistine women. Yet in his final moments Samson becomes one of the great tragic figures in biblical literature, redeeming his mission to Israel with his own life.

The time is in the period during the dark ages of Israel's past, the chaotic era between the Hebrews' entrance into Canaan (about 1250 B.C.) and their establishment of a kingdom (1025 B.C.). Before they could establish their kingdom, the Hebrews had first to conquer the native Canaanites and then defend their conquests from the Philistines, new invaders from the Aegean who occupied land and cities along the coast. Among the Hebrews who led uprisings against the Philistines was Samson, who lived around 1100 B.C.

Judges

The Story of Samson

Thirteen   And the children of Israel did evil again in the sight of the Lord, and the Lord delivered them into the hand of the Philistines forty years.

And there was a certain man of Zorah, of the family of the Danites, whose name was Manoah, and his wife was barren, and bare not. And the angel of the Lord appeared unto the woman, and said unto her, "Behold now, thou are barren, and bearest not: but thou shalt conceive, and bear a son. Now therefore beware, I pray thee, and drink not wine nor strong drink, and eat not any unclean thing. For lo, thou shalt conceive, and bear a son, and no razor shall come on his head: for the child shall be a Nazarite[1] unto God from the womb: and he shall begin to deliver Israel out of the hand of the Philistines."

Then the woman came, and told her husband, saying, "A man of God came unto me, and his countenance was like the countenance of an angel of God, very terrible: but I asked him not whence he was, neither told he me his name: but he said unto me, 'Behold, thou shalt conceive, and bear a son; and now, drink no wine nor strong drink, neither eat any unclean thing: for the child shall be a Nazarite to God from the womb to the day of his death.'"

Then Manoah entreated the Lord, and said, "O my Lord, let

[1] *Nazarite:* a class of persons devoted by a special vow to the Lord. Among other things, they were not allowed to cut their hair.

the man of God which thou didst send come again unto us, and teach us what we shall do unto the child that shall be born." And God hearkened to the voice of Manoah; and the angel of God came again unto the woman as she sat in the field: but Manoah her husband was not with her. And the woman made haste, and showed her husband, and said unto him, "Behold, the man hath appeared unto me that came unto me the other day." And Manoah arose, and went after his wife, and came to the man, and said unto him, "Art thou the man that spakest unto the woman?" And he said, "I am." And Manoah said, "Now let thy words come to pass. How shall we order the child, and how shall we do unto him?" And the angel of the Lord said unto Manoah, "Of all that I said unto the woman, let her beware. She may not eat of any thing that cometh of the vine, neither let her drink wine or strong drink, nor eat any unclean thing: all that I commanded her, let her observe."

And Manoah said unto the angel of the Lord. "I pray thee, let us detain thee, until we shall have made ready a kid for thee." And the angel of the Lord said unto Manoah, "Though thou detain me, I will not eat of thy bread: and if thou wilt offer a burnt offering, thou must offer it unto the Lord": for Manoah knew not that he was an angel of the Lord. And Manoah said unto the angel of the Lord, "What is thy name, that when thy sayings come to pass we may do thee honour?" And the angel of the Lord said unto him, "Why askest thou thus after my name, seeing it is secret?" So Manoah took a kid, with a meat offering, and offered it upon a rock unto the Lord: and the angel did wondrously, and Manoah and his wife looked on. For it came to pass, when the flame went up toward heaven from off the altar, that the angel of the Lord ascended in the flame of the altar: and Manoah and his wife looked on it, and fell on their faces to the ground. (But the angel of the Lord did no more appear to Manoah and to his wife.) Then Manoah knew that he was an angel of the Lord. And Manoah said unto his wife, "We shall surely die, because we have seen God." But his wife said unto him, "If the Lord were pleased to kill us, he would not have received a burnt offering and a meat offering at our hands, neither would he have showed us all these things, nor would as at this time have told us such things as these."

And the woman bare a son, and called his name Samson: and the child grew, and the Lord blessed him. And the spirit of the Lord began to move him at times in the camp of Dan, between Zorah and Eshtaol.

Fourteen And Samson went down to Timnath, and saw a woman in Timnath, of the daughters of the Philistines. And he came up, and told his father and his mother, and said, "I have seen a woman in Timnath of the daughters of the Philistines: now therefore get her for me to wife." Then his father and his mother said unto him, "Is there never a woman among the daughters of thy brethren, or among all my people, that thou goest to take a wife of the uncircumcised Philistines?" And Samson said unto his father, "Get her for me, for she pleaseth me well." But his father and mother knew not that it was of the Lord, that he sought an occasion against the Philistines: for at that time the Philistines had dominion over Israel.

Then went Samson down, and his father and his mother, to Timnath, and came to the vineyards of Timnath: and behold, a young lion roared against him. And the Spirit of the Lord came mightily upon him, and he rent him as he would have rent a kid, and he had nothing in his hand: but he told not his father or his mother what he had done. And he went down, and talked with the woman; and she pleased Samson well.

And after a time he returned to take her, and he turned aside to see the carcass of the lion: and behold, there was a swarm of bees and honey in the carcass of the lion. And he took thereof in his hands, and went on eating, and came to his father and mother, and he gave them, and they did eat: but he told not them that he had taken the honey out of the carcass of the lion.

So his father went down unto the woman: and Samson made there a feast; for so used the young men to do. And it came to pass when they saw him, that they brought thirty companions to be with him. And Samson said unto them, "I will now put forth a riddle unto you: if you can certainly declare it me within the seven days of the feast, and find it out, then I will give you thirty sheets, and thirty change of garments. But if ye cannot declare it me, then shall ye give me thirty sheets, and thirty change of garments." And they said unto him, "Put forth thy riddle, that we may hear it." And he said unto them, "Out of the eater came forth meat, and out of the strong came forth sweetness."

And they could not in three days expound the riddle. And it came to pass on the seventh day, that they said unto Samson's wife, "Entice thy husband, that he may declare unto us the riddle, lest we burn thee and thy father's house with fire: have ye called us to take that we have? is it not so?"

And Samson's wife wept before him, and said, "Thou dost but hate me, and lovest me not: thou hast put forth a riddle unto the children of my people, and hast not told it me." And he said unto her, "Behold, I have not told it my father nor my mother, and shall I tell it thee?" And she wept before him the seven days, while their feast lasted: and it came to pass on the seventh day, that he told her, because she lay sore upon him: and she told the riddle to the children of her people. And the men of the city said unto him on the seventh day before the sun went down, "What is sweeter than honey? and what is stronger than a lion?" And he said unto them, "If ye had not plowed with my heifer, ye had not found out my riddle."

And the Spirit of the Lord came upon him, and he went down to Ashkelon, and slew thirty men of them, and took their spoil, and gave change of garments unto them which expounded the riddle; and his anger was kindled, and he went up to his father's house. But Samson's wife was given to his companion, whom he had used as his friend.

Fifteen But it came to pass within a while after, in the time of wheat harvest, that Samson visited his wife with a kid, and he said, "I will go in to my wife into the chamber." But her father would not suffer him to go in. And her father said, "I verily thought that thou hadst utterly hated her; therefore I gave her to thy companion: is not her younger sister fairer than she? take her, I pray thee, instead of her."

And Samson said concerning them, "Now shall I be more blameless than the Philistines, though I do them a displeasure?" And Samson went and caught three hundred foxes, and took firebrands, and turned tail to tail, and put a firebrand in the midst between two tails. And when he had set the brands on fire, he let them go into the standing corn of the Philistines, and burnt up both the shocks, and also the standing corn, with the vineyards and olives.

Then the Philistines said, "Who hath done this?" And they answered, "Samson, the son-in-law of the Timnite, because he had taken his wife and given her to his companion." And the Philistines came up, and burnt her and her father with fire. And Samson said unto them. "Though ye have done this, yet will I be avenged of you, and after that I will cease." And he smote them hip and thigh with a great slaughter: and he went down and dwelt in the top of the rock Etam.

Then the Philistines went up, and pitched in Judah, and spread themselves in Lehi. And the men of Judah said, "Why are ye come up against us?" And they answered, "To bind Samson are we come up, to do to him as he hath done to us." Then three thousand men of Judah went to the top of the rock Etam, and said to Samson, "Knowest thou not that the Philistines are rulers over us? What is this that thou hast done unto us?" And he said unto them, "As they did unto me, so have I done unto them." And they said unto him, "We are come down to bind thee, that we may deliver thee into the hand of the Philistines." And Samson said unto them, "Swear unto me that ye will not fall upon me yourselves." And they spake unto him, saying, "No: but we will bind thee fast, and deliver thee into their hand: but surely we will not kill thee." And they bound him with two new cords, and brought him up from the rock.

And when he came unto Lehi, the Philistines shouted against him: and the spirit of the Lord came mightily upon him, and the cords that were upon his arms became as flax that was burnt with fire, and his bands loosed from off his hands. And he found a new jawbone of an ass, and put forth his hand, and took it, and slew a thousand men therewith. And Samson said, "With the jawbone of an ass, heaps upon heaps, with the jaw of an ass have I slain a thousand men." And it came to pass when he had made an end of speaking, that he cast away the jawbone out of his hand, and called that place Ramath-lehi.

And he was sore athirst, and called on the Lord, and said, "Thou hast given this great deliverance into the hand of thy servant: and now shall I die for thirst, and fall into the hand of the uncircumcised?" But God clave a hollow place that was in the jaw, and there came water thereout, and when he had drunk, his spirit came again, and he revived: wherefore he called the name thereof En-hakkore, which is in Lehi unto this day. And he judged Israel in the days of the Philistines twenty years.

Sixteen Then went Samson to Gaza, and saw there an harlot, and went in unto her. And it was told the Gazites, saying, "Samson is come hither." And they compassed him in, and laid wait for him all night in the gate of the city, and were quiet all the night, saying, "In the morning, when it is day, we shall kill him." And Samson lay till midnight, and took the doors of the gate of the city, and the two posts, and went away with them, bar and all, and put them upon his shoulders, and carried them up to the top of a hill that is before Hebron.

And it came to pass afterward, that he loved a woman in the valley of Sorek, whose name was Delilah. And the lords of the Philistines came up unto her, and said unto her, "Entice him, and see wherein his great strength lieth, and by what means we may prevail against him, that we may bind him, to afflict him: and we will give thee every one of us eleven hundred pieces of silver."

And Delilah said to Samson, "Tell me, I pray thee, wherein thy great strength lieth, and wherewith thou mightest be bound, to afflict thee." And Samson said unto her, "If they bind me with seven green withes[2] that were never dried, then shall I be weak, and be as another man." Then the lords of the Philistines brought up to her seven green withes which had not been dried, and she bound him with them. Now there were men lying in wait, abiding with her in the chamber. And she said unto him, "The Philistines be upon thee, Samson." And he brake the withes, as a thread of tow is broken when it toucheth the fire. So his strength was not known.

And Delilah said unto Samson, "Behold, thou hast mocked me, and told me lies: now tell me, I pray thee, wherewith thou mightest be bound." And he said unto her, "If they bind me fast with

---

2 *withes:* slender branches used as ropes (the original Hebrew term would be more accurately translated "bowstrings").

new ropes that never were occupied, then shall I be weak, and be as another man." Delilah therefore took new ropes, and bound him therewith, and said unto him, "The Philistines be upon thee, Samson." And there were liers in wait abiding in the chamber. And he brake them from off his arms, like a thread.

And Delilah said unto Samson, "Hitherto thou hast mocked me, and told me lies: tell me wherewith thou mightest be bound." And he said unto her, "If thou weavest the seven locks of my head with the web."³ And she fastened it with the pin, and said unto him, "The Philistines be upon thee, Samson." And he awaked out of his sleep, and went away with the pin of the beam, and with the web.

And she said unto him, "How canst thou say, 'I love thee,' when thine heart is not with me? Thou hast mocked me these three times, and hast not told me wherein thy great strength lieth." And it came to pass, when she pressed him daily with her words, and urged him, so that his soul was vexed unto death, that he told her all his heart, and said unto her, "There hath not come a razor upon mine head; for I have been a Nazarite unto God from my mother's womb: if I be shaven, then my strength will go from me, and I shall become weak, and be like any other man."

And when Delilah saw that he had told her all his heart, she sent and called for the lords of the Philistines, saying, "Come up this once, for he hath showed me all his heart." Then the lords of the Philistines came up unto her, and brought money in their hand.

And she made him sleep upon her knees, and she called for a man, and she caused him to shave off the seven locks of his head, and she began to afflict him, and his strength went from him. And she said, "The Philistines be upon thee, Samson." And he awoke out of his sleep, and said, "I will go out as at other times before, and shake myself." And he wist not that the Lord was departed from him.

But the Philistines took him, and put out his eyes, and brought him down to Gaza, and bound him with fetters of brass, and he

³ *web:* Web, pin, and beam are parts of the loom. (Delilah weaves Samson's hair into the threads on her loom. When he is startled out of his sleep, Samson wrenches the loom from the peg which fastened it to the floor.)

did grind in the prison house. Howbeit the hair of his head began to grow again, after he was shaven.

Then the lords of the Philistines gathered them together, for to offer a great sacrifice unto Dagon their god, and to rejoice: for they said, "Our god hath delivered Samson our enemy into our hand." And when the people saw him, they praised their god: for they said, "Our god hath delivered into our hands our enemy, and the destroyer of our country, which slew many of us."

REJOICE NOT WHEN THINE ENEMY FALLETH, AND LET NOT THINE HEART BE GLAD WHEN HE STUMBLETH: LEST THE LORD SEE IT, AND IT DISPLEASE HIM, AND HE TURN AWAY HIS WRATH FROM HIM.

PROVERBS 24:17–18

And it came to pass when their hearts were merry, that they said, "Call for Samson, that he may make us sport." And they called for Samson out of the prison house; and he made them sport, and they set him between the pillars. And Samson said unto the lad that held him by the hand, "Suffer me, that I may feel the pillars whereupon the house standeth, that I may lean upon them."

Now the house was full of men and women, and all the lords of the Philistines were there; and there were upon the roof about three thousand men and women, that beheld while Samson made sport. And Samson called unto the Lord, and said, "O Lord God, remember me, I pray thee, and strengthen me, I pray thee, only this once, O God, that I may be at once avenged of the Philistines for my two eyes."

And Samson took hold of the two middle pillars, upon which the house stood, and on which it was borne up, of the one with his right hand, and of the other with his left. And Samson said, "Let me die with the Philistines." And he bowed himself with all his might; and the house fell upon the lords, and upon all the people that were therein.

So the dead which he slew at his death were more than they which he slew in his life. Then his brethren, and all the house of his father, came down, and took him, and brought him up, and buried him between Zorah and Eshtaol, in the burying place of Manoah his father: and he judged Israel twenty years.

David Playing the Harp before Saul
Cabinet des Dessins, Musée du Louvre, Paris

Saul
and
David

With the reigns of Saul (1025–1005) and David (1005–970)
the Hebrew people enter a new phase in their history. The
twelve tribes are bound into a single nation, still at war with
their powerful Philistine neighbors. Summoned to lead Israel
against the Philistines and other enemies, Saul is a tragic figure,
a man who comes to kingship reluctantly and is destroyed by
the responsibilities and temptations of power. Forced to watch
a younger, more attractive hero win the acclaim of his people,
Saul's love for his country and his God is corrupted by his jealous
desire to retain the throne. David, on the other hand, at first
unconscious of his destiny, remains loyal to Saul even while a
fugitive from the king's wrath. How David, the favored of God,
will wear the mantle of power he inherits is yet to be revealed.

I Samuel

"A Choice Young Man"

Nine Now there was a man of Benjamin whose name was Kish, the son of Abiel, the son of Zeror, the son of Bechorath, the son of Aphiah, a Benjamite, a mighty man of power. And he had a son whose name was Saul, a choice young man, and a goodly: and there was not among the children of Israel a goodlier person than he: from his shoulders and upward he was higher than any of the people.

And the asses of Kish, Saul's father, were lost; and Kish said to Saul his son, "Take now one of the servants with thee, and arise, go seek the asses." And he passed through mount Ephraim, and passed through the land of Shalisha, but they found them not; then they passed through the land of Shalim, and there they were not; and he passed through the land of the Benjamites, but they found them not. And when they were come to the land of Zuph, Saul said to his servant that was with him, "Come, and let us return, lest my father leave caring for the asses and take thought for us."

And he said unto him, "Behold now, there is in this city a man of God, and he is an honourable man; all that he sayeth cometh surely to pass: now let us go thither; peradventure he can show us our way that we should go."

Then said Saul to his servant, "But behold, if we go, what shall we bring the man? for the bread is spent in our vessels, and there is not a present to bring to the man of God: what have we?" And the servant answered Saul again, and said, "Behold, I have here at hand the fourth part of a shekel of silver: that will I give to the man of God, to tell us our way." (Beforetime in Israel, when a man went to inquire of God, thus he spake: "Come, and let us go to the seer": for he that is now called a prophet was beforetime called a seer.) Then said Saul to his servant, "Well said: come, let us go." So they went unto the city where the man of God was.

And as they went up the hill to the city, they found young maidens going out to draw water, and said unto them, "Is the seer here?" And they answered them, and said, "He is: behold, he is before you, make haste now, for he came today to the city; for there is a sacrifice of the people today in the high place. As soon as ye be come into the city, ye shall straightway find him, before he go up to the high place to eat: for the people will not eat until he come, because he doth bless the sacrifice; and afterwards they eat that be bidden. Now therefore get you up, for about this time ye shall find him." And they went up into the city: and when they were come into the city, behold, Samuel came out against them, for to go up to the high place.

Now the Lord had told Samuel in his ear a day before Saul came, saying, "Tomorrow about this time I will send thee a man out of the land of Benjamin, and thou shalt anoint him to be captain over my people Israel, that he may save my people out of the hand of the Philistines: for I have looked upon my people, because their cry is come unto me." And when Samuel saw Saul, the Lord said unto him, "Behold the man whom I spake to thee of! this same shall reign over my people."

Then Saul drew near to Samuel in the gate, and said, "Tell me, I pray thee, where the seer's house is." And Samuel answered Saul, and said, "I am the seer: go up before me into the high place; for ye shall eat with me today, and tomorrow I will let thee go, and will tell thee all that is in thine heart. And as for thine asses that were lost three days ago, set not thy mind on them, for they are found. And on whom is all the desire of Israel? Is it not on thee, and on all thy father's house?"

And Saul answered, and said, "Am not I a Benjamite, of the smallest of the tribes of Israel? and my family the least of all the families of the tribe of Benjamin? Wherefore then speakest thou so to me?"

And Samuel took Saul, and his servant, and brought them into the parlor, and made them sit in the chiefest place among them that were bidden, which were about thirty persons. And Samuel said unto the cook, "Bring the portion which I gave thee, of which I said unto thee, 'Set it by thee.' " And the cook took up the shoulder, and that which was upon it, and set it before Saul. And Samuel said, "Behold, that which is left, set it before thee, and eat: for unto this time hath it been kept for thee, since I said, 'I have invited the people.' " So Saul did eat with Samuel that day.

And when they were come down from the high place into the city, Samuel communed with Saul upon the top of the house. And they arose early: and it came to pass, about the spring of the day, that Samuel called Saul to the top of the house, saying, "Up, that I may send thee away." And Saul arose, and they went out both of them, he and Samuel, abroad. And as they were going down to the end of the city, Samuel said to Saul, "Bid the servant pass on before us (and he passed on), but stand thou still a while, that I may show thee the word of God."

Samuel Anoints Saul

Ten Then Samuel took a vial of oil, and poured it upon his head, and kissed him, and said, "Is it not because the Lord hath anointed thee to be captain over his inheritance? When thou art departed from me today, then thou shalt find two men by Rachel's sepulchre in the border of Benjamin, at Zelzah: and they will say unto thee, 'The asses which thou wentest to seek are found: and lo, thy father hath left the care of the asses, and sorroweth for you, saying, "What shall I do for my son?" ' Then shalt thou go on forward from thence, and thou shalt come to the plain of Tabor, and there shall meet thee three men, going up to God to Bethel, one carrying three kids, and another carrying three loaves of bread, and another carrying a bottle of wine. And they will salute thee, and give thee two loaves of bread, which thou shalt receive of their hands.

"After that thou shalt come to the hill of God, where is the garrison of the Philistines: and it shall come to pass when thou art come thither to the city, that thou shalt meet a company of prophets coming down from the high place with a psaltery, and a tabret, and a pipe, and a harp before them, and they shall prophesy. And the spirit of the Lord will come upon thee, and thou shalt prophesy with them, and shalt be turned into another man.

"And let it be when these signs are come unto thee, that thou do as occasion serve thee, for God is with thee. And thou shalt go down before me to Gilgal, and behold, I will come down unto thee, to offer burnt offerings, and to sacrifice sacrifices of peace offerings: seven days shalt thou tarry, till I come to thee, and show thee what thou shalt do."

And it was so that when he turned his back to go from Samuel, God gave him another heart: and all those signs came to pass that day. And when they came thither to the hill, behold a company of the prophets met him, and the spirit of God came upon him, and he prophesied among them. And it came to pass when all that knew him beforetime saw that, behold, he prophesied among the prophets, then the people said one to another, "What is this that is come unto the son of Kish? Is Saul also among the prophets?" And one of the same place answered, and said, "But who is their father?" Therefore it became a proverb: "Is Saul also among the prophets?" And when he had made an end of prophesying, he came to the high place.

And Saul's uncle said unto him, and to his servant, "Whither went ye?" And he said, "To seek the asses: and when we saw that they were nowhere, we came to Samuel." And Saul's uncle said, "Tell me, I pray thee, what Samuel said unto you." And Saul said unto his uncle, "He told us plainly that the asses were found." But of the matter of the kingdom, whereof Samuel spake, he told him not.

And Samuel called the people together unto the Lord to Mizpeh, and said unto the children of Israel, "Thus saith the Lord God of Israel, 'I brought up Israel out of Egypt, and delivered you out of the hand of the Egyptians, and out of the hand of all kingdoms, and of them that oppressed you.' And ye have this day rejected your God, who himself saved you out of all your adversities and your tribulations: and ye have said unto him, 'Nay, but set a king over us.' Now therefore present yourselves before the Lord by your tribes, and by your thousands."

And when Samuel had caused all the tribes of Israel to come near, the tribe of Benjamin was taken. When he had caused the tribe of Benjamin to come near by their families, the family of Matri was taken, and Saul the son of Kish was taken: and when they sought him, he could not be found. Therefore they inquired of the Lord further, if the man should yet come thither: and the Lord answered, "Behold, he hath hid himself among the stuff." And they ran, and fetched him thence: and when he stood among the people, he was higher than any of the people from his shoulders and upward. And Samuel said to all the people, "See ye him whom the Lord hath chosen, that there is none like him among all the people?" And all the people shouted, and said, "God save the king." Then Samuel told the people the manner of the kingdom, and wrote it in a book, and laid it up before the Lord. And Samuel sent all the people away, every man to his house.

And Saul also went home to Gibeah, and there went with him a band of men, whose hearts God had touched. But the children of Belial said, "How shall this man save us?" And they despised him, and brought him no presents: but he held his peace.

Saul Defeats the Ammonites

Eleven   Then Nahash the Ammonite came up, and encamped against Jabesh Gilead: and all the men of Jabesh said unto Nahash, "Make a covenant with us, and we will serve thee." And Nahash the Ammonite answered them, "On this condition will I make a covenant with you, that I may thrust out all your right eyes, and lay it for a reproach upon all Israel." And the elders of Jabesh said unto him, "Give us seven days' respite, that we may send messengers unto all the coasts of Israel: and then, if there be no man to save us, we will come out to thee."

Then came the messengers to Gibeah of Saul, and told the tidings in the ears of the people: and all the people lifted up their voices, and wept. And behold, Saul came after the herd out of the field, and Saul said, "What aileth the people that they weep?" And they told him the tidings of the men of Jabesh. And the spirit of

God came upon Saul when he heard those tidings and his anger was kindled greatly. And he took a yoke of oxen, and hewed them in pieces, and sent them throughout all the coasts of Israel by the hands of messengers, saying, "Whosoever cometh not forth after Saul and after Samuel, so shall it be done unto his oxen": and the fear of the Lord fell on the people, and they came out with one consent. And when he numbered them in Bezek, the children of Israel were three hundred thousand, and the men of Judah thirty thousand.

And they said unto the messengers that came, "Thus shall ye say unto the men of Jabesh Gilead, 'Tomorrow, by that time the sun be hot, ye shall have help.' " And the messengers came, and showed it to the men of Jabesh, and they were glad. Therefore the men of Jabesh said, "Tomorrow we will come out unto you, and ye shall do with us all that seemeth good unto you." And it was so on the morrow, that Saul put the people in three companies, and they came into the midst of the host in the morning watch, and slew the Ammonites, until the heat of the day: and it came to pass, that they which remained were scattered, so that two of them were not left together.

And the people said unto Samuel, "Who is he that said, 'Shall Saul reign over us?' Bring the men, that we may put them to death." And Saul said, "There shall not a man be put to death this day: for today the Lord hath wrought salvation in Israel." Then said Samuel to the people, "Come, and let us go to Gilgal, and renew the kingdom there." And all the people went to Gilgal, and there they made Saul king before the Lord in Gilgal: and there they sacrificed sacrifices of peace offerings before the Lord: and there Saul and all the men of Israel rejoiced greatly.

Saul Disobeys the Lord

Fifteen   Samuel also said unto Saul, "The Lord sent me to anoint thee to be king over his people, over Israel: now therefore hearken thou unto the voice of the words of the Lord. Thus saith the Lord of hosts, 'I remember that which Amalek did to Israel, how he laid wait for him in the way, when he came up from Egypt. Now go and smite Amalek, and utterly destroy all that they have, and

spare them not; but slay both man and woman, infant and suck-
ling, ox and sheep, camel and ass.' "

. . . And Saul smote the Amalekites from Havilah until thou
comest to Shur, that is over against Egypt. And he took Agag the
king of the Amalekites alive, and utterly destroyed all the people
with the edge of the sword. But Saul and the people spared Agag,
and the best of the sheep, and of the oxen, and of the fatlings, and
the lambs, and all that was good and would not utterly destroy
them: but everything that was vile and refuse, that they destroyed
utterly.

Then came the word of the Lord unto Samuel, saying, "It
repenteth me that I have set up Saul to be king: for he is turned
back from following me and hath not performed my commandments." And it grieved Samuel; and he cried unto the Lord all
night. And when Samuel rose early to meet Saul in the morning,
it was told Samuel, saying, "Saul came to Carmel, and behold, he
set him up a place, and is gone about, and passed on, and gone
down to Gilgal."

And Samuel came to Saul: and Saul said unto him, "Blessed be
thou of the Lord: I have performed the commandment of the
Lord."

And Samuel said, "What meaneth then this bleating of the
sheep in mine ears, and the lowing of the oxen which I hear?"

And Saul said, "They have brought them from the Amalekites:
for the people spared the best of the sheep and of the oxen, to
sacrifice unto the Lord thy God; and the rest we have utterly
destroyed."

Then Samuel said unto Saul, "Stay, and I will tell thee what
the Lord hath said to me this night." And he said unto him, "Say
on." And Samuel said, "When thou wast little in thine own sight,
was thou not made the head of the tribes of Israel, and the Lord
anointed thee king over Israel? And the Lord sent thee on a
journey, and said, 'Go and utterly destroy the sinners the Amalekites, and fight against them until they be consumed.' Wherefore
then didst thou not obey the voice of the Lord, but didst fly upon
the spoil, and didst evil in the sight of the Lord?"

And Saul said unto Samuel, "Yea, I have obeyed the voice of the
Lord, and have gone the way which the Lord sent me, and have

brought Agag the king of Amalek, and have utterly destroyed the Amalekites. But the people took of the spoil, sheep and oxen, the chief of the things which should have been utterly destroyed, to sacrifice unto the Lord thy God in Gilgal."

And Samuel said, "Hath the Lord as great delight in burnt offerings and sacrifices, as in obeying the voice of the Lord? Behold, to obey is better than sacrifice, and to hearken than the fat of rams. For rebellion is as the sin of witchcraft, and stubbornness is as iniquity and idolatry. Because thou hast rejected the word of the Lord, he hath also rejected thee from being king."

And Saul said unto Samuel, "I have sinned: for I have transgressed the commandment of the Lord, and thy words: because I feared the people, and obeyed their voice. Now therefore, I pray thee, pardon my sin, and turn again with me, that I may worship the Lord."

And Samuel said unto Saul, "I will not return with thee: for thou hast rejected the word of the Lord, and the Lord hath rejected thee from being king over Israel." And as Samuel turned about to go away, he laid hold upon the skirt of his mantle, and it rent. And Samuel said unto him, "The Lord hath rent the kingdom of Israel from thee this day, and hath given it to a neighbor of thine, that is better than thou. And also the Strength of Israel will not lie nor repent: for he is not a man, that he should repent."

Then he said, "I have sinned: yet honor me now, I pray thee, before the elders of my people, and before Israel, and turn again with me, that I may worship the Lord thy God." So Samuel turned again after Saul; and Saul worshipped the Lord.

Then said Samuel, "Bring ye hither to me Agag the king of the Amalekites." And Agag came unto him delicately. And Agag said, "Surely the bitterness of death is past." And Samuel said, "As thy sword hath made women childless, so shall thy mother be childless among women." And Samuel hewed Agag in pieces before the Lord in Gilgal.

Then Samuel went to Ramah; and Saul went up to his house to Gibeah of Saul. And Samuel came no more to see Saul until the day of his death: nevertheless Samuel mourned for Saul: and the Lord repented that he had made Saul king over Israel.

Samuel Anoints David

Sixteen And the Lord said unto Samuel, "How long wilt thou mourn for Saul, seeing I have rejected him from reigning over Israel? Fill thine horn with oil, and go, I will send thee to Jesse the Bethlehemite: for I have provided me a king among his sons." And Samuel said "How can I go? if Saul hear it, he will kill me." And the Lord said, "Take a heifer with thee, and say, 'I am come to sacrifice to the Lord.' And call Jesse to the sacrifice, and I will show thee what thou shalt do: and thou shalt anoint unto me him whom I name unto thee."

And Samuel did that which the Lord spake, and came to Bethlehem. And the elders of the town trembled at his coming, and said, "Comest thou peaceably?" And he said, "Peaceably: I am come to sacrifice unto the Lord: sanctify yourselves, and come with me to the sacrifice." And he sanctified Jesse and his sons, and called them to the sacrifice.

And it came to pass, when they were come, that he looked on Eliab, and said, "Surely the Lord's anointed is before him." But the Lord said unto Samuel, "Look not on his countenance, or on the height of his stature; because I have refused him: for the Lord seeth not as man seeth; for man looketh on the outward appearance, but the Lord looketh on the heart." Then Jesse called Abinadab, and made him pass before Samuel. And he said, "Neither hath the Lord chosen this." Then Jesse made Shammah to pass by. And he said, "Neither hath the Lord chosen this." Again, Jesse made seven of his sons to pass before Samuel. And Samuel said unto Jesse, "The Lord hath not chosen these."

And Samuel said unto Jesse, "Are here all thy children?" And he said, "There remaineth yet the youngest, and behold, he keepeth the sheep." And Samuel said unto Jesse, "Send and fetch him: for we will not sit down till he come hither." And he sent, and brought him in. Now he was ruddy, and withal of a beautiful countenance, and goodly to look to. And the Lord said, "Arise, anoint him: for this is he." Then Samuel took the horn of oil, and anointed him in the midst of his brethren: and the Spirit of the Lord came upon David from that day forward. So Samuel rose up, and went to Ramah.

"A Cunning Player on an Harp"

But the spirit of the Lord departed from Saul, and an evil spirit from the Lord troubled him. And Saul's servants said unto him, "Behold now, an evil spirit from God troubleth thee. Let our lord now command thy servants, which are before thee, to seek out a man, who is a cunning player on an harp: and it shall come to pass when the evil spirit from God is upon thee, that he shall play with his hand, and thou shalt be well."

And Saul said unto his servants, "Provide me now a man that can play well, and bring him to me." Then answered one of the servants, and said, "Behold, I have seen a son of Jesse the Bethlehemite, that is cunning in playing, and a mighty valiant man, and a man of war, and prudent in matters, and a comely person, and the Lord is with him."

Wherefore Saul sent messengers unto Jesse, and said, "Send me David thy son, which is with the sheep." And Jesse took an ass laden with bread, and a bottle of wine, and a kid, and sent them by David his son unto Saul. And David came to Saul, and stood before him: and he loved him greatly, and he became his armour-bearer. And Saul sent to Jesse, saying, "Let David, I pray thee, stand before me: for he hath found favour in my sight." And it came to pass, when the evil spirit from God was upon Saul, that David took an harp, and played with his hand: so Saul was refreshed, and was well, and the evil spirit departed from him.

David and Goliath

Seventeen Now the Philistines gathered together their armies to battle and were gathered together at Shochoh, which belongeth to Judah, and pitched between Shochoh and Azekah, in Ephes-dammim. And Saul and the men of Israel were gathered together, and pitched by the valley of Elah, and set the battle in array against the Philistines. And the Philistines stood on a mountain on the one side, and Israel stood on a mountain on the other side: and there was a valley between them.

And there went out a champion out of the camp of the Philistines, named Goliath, of Gath: whose height was six cubits and a span. And he had an helmet of brass upon his head, and he was armed with a coat of mail: and the weight of the coat was five thousand shekels of brass. And he had greaves[1] of brass upon his legs, and a target[2] of brass between his shoulders. And the staff of his spear was like a weaver's beam; and his spear's head weighed six hundred shekels of iron: and one bearing a shield went before him.

And he stood and cried unto the armies of Israel, and said unto them, "Why are ye come out to set your battle in array? am not I a Philistine, and ye servants to Saul? choose you a man for you, and let him come down to me. If he be able to fight with me, and to kill me, then will we be your servants: but if I prevail against him, and kill him, then shall ye be our servants, and serve us." And the Philistine said, "I defy the armies of Israel this day; give me a man, that we may fight together." When Saul and all Israel heard those words of the Philistine, they were dismayed, and greatly afraid.

Now David was the son of that Ephrathite of Bethlehem-Judah whose name was Jesse, and he had eight sons: and the man went among men for an old man in the days of Saul. And the three eldest sons of Jesse went and followed Saul to the battle: and the names of his three sons that went to the battle were Eliab, the firstborn, and next unto him Abinadab, and the third, Shammah. And David was the youngest: and the three eldest followed Saul. But David went and returned from Saul to feed his father's sheep at Bethlehem. And the Philistine drew near, morning and evening, and presented himself forty days.

And Jesse said unto David his son, "Take now for thy brethren an ephah of this parched corn, and these ten loaves, and run to the camp to thy brethren. And carry these ten cheeses unto the captain of their thousand, and look how thy brethren fare, and take their pledge." Now Saul, and they, and all the men of Israel were in the valley of Elah, fighting with the Philistines.

---

[1] *greaves:* armour for the leg below the knee.
[2] *target:* a large shield.

And David rose up early in the morning, and left the sheep with a keeper, and took, and went, as Jesse had commanded him; and he came to the trench, as the host was going forth to the fight, and shouted for the battle. For Israel and the Philistines had put the battle in array, army against army. And David left his carriage in the hand of the keeper of the carriage, and ran into the army, and came and saluted his brethren.

And as he talked with them, behold, there came up the champion, the Philistine of Gath, Goliath by name, out of the armies of the Philistines, and spake according to the same words: and David heard them. And all the men of Israel, when they saw the man, fled from him, and were sore afraid. And the men of Israel said, "Have ye seen this man that is come up? Surely to defy Israel is he come up: and it shall be, that the man who killeth him, the king will enrich him with great riches, and will give him his daughter, and make his father's house free in Israel." And David spake to the men that stood by him, saying, "What shall be done to the man that killeth this Philistine, and taketh away the reproach from Israel? for who is this uncircumcised Philistine, that he should defy the armies of the living God?" And the people answered him after this manner, saying, "So shall it be done to the man that killeth him."

And Eliab his eldest brother heard when he spake unto the men; and Eliab's anger was kindled against David, and he said, "Why camest thou down hither? and with whom hast thou left those few sheep in the wilderness? I know thy pride, and the naughtiness of thine heart; for thou art come down that thou mightest see the battle." And David said, "What have I now done? Is there not a cause?" And he turned from him toward another, and spake after the same manner: and the people answered him again after the former manner. And when the words were heard which David spake, they rehearsed them before Saul: and he sent for him.

And David said to Saul, "Let no man's heart fail because of him: thy servant will go and fight with this Philistine." And Saul said to David, "Thou art not able to go against this Philistine, to fight with him: for thou art but a youth, and he a man of war from his youth." And David said unto Saul, "Thy servant kept his father's sheep, and there came a lion, and a bear, and took a lamb out of the flock: and I went after him, and smote him, and delivered it out of his mouth: and when he arose against me, I caught him by his beard, and smote him, and slew him. Thy servant slew both the lion and the bear: and this uncircumcised Philistine shall be as one of them, seeing he hath defied the armies of the living God." David said moreover, "The Lord that delivered me out of the paw of the lion, and out of the paw of the bear, he will deliver me out of the hand of this Philistine." And Saul said unto David, "Go, and the Lord be with thee."

And Saul armed David with his armour, and he put an helmet of brass upon his head, also he armed him with a coat of mail. And David girded his sword upon his armour, and he assayed to go, for he had not proved it: and David said unto Saul, "I cannot go with these: for I have not proved them." And David put them off him. And he took his staff in his hand, and chose him five smooth stones out of the brook, and put them in a shepherd's bag which he had, even in a scrip,[3] and his sling was in his hand: and he drew near to the Philistine.

And the Philistine came on and drew near unto David, and the man that bare the shield went before him. And when the Philistine looked about, and saw David, he disdained him: for he was but a youth, and ruddy, and of a fair countenance. And the Philistine said unto David, "Am I a dog, that thou comest to me with staves?" And the Philistine cursed David by his gods. And the Philistine said to David, "Come to me, and I will give thy flesh unto the fowls of the air, and to the beasts of the field."

Then said David to the Philistine, "Thou comest to me with a sword, and with a spear, and with a shield: but I come to thee in the name of the Lord of hosts, the God of the armies of Israel, whom thou hast defied. This day will the Lord deliver thee into mine hand, and I will smite thee, and take thine head from thee, and I will give the carcasses of the host of the Philistines this day unto the fowls of the air, and to the wild beasts of the earth; that all the earth may know that there is a God in Israel. And all this assembly shall know that the Lord saveth not with sword and spear: for the battle is the Lord's, and he will give you into our hands."

[3] *scrip:* a shepherd's bag used to carry provisions.

And it came to pass when the Philistine arose, and came and drew nigh to meet David, that David hasted, and ran toward the army to meet the Philistine. And David put his hand in his bag, and took thence a stone, and slang it, and smote the Philistine in his forehead, that the stone sunk into his forehead; and he fell upon his face to the earth. So David prevailed over the Philistine with a sling and with a stone, and smote the Philistine, and slew him; but there was no sword in the hand of David. Therefore David ran, and stood upon the Philistine, and took his sword, and drew it out of the sheath thereof, and slew him, and cut off his head therewith. And when the Philistines saw their champion was dead, they fled. And the men of Israel and of Judah arose, and shouted, and pursued the Philistines, until thou come to the valley, and to the gates of Ekron: and the wounded of the Philistines fell down by the way to Shaaraim, even unto Gath, and unto Ekron. And the children of Israel returned from chasing after the Philistines, and they spoiled their tents. And David took the head of the Philistine, and brought it to Jerusalem, but he put his armour in his tent. And when Saul saw David go forth against the Philistine, he said unto Abner the captain of the host, "Abner, whose son is this youth?" And Abner said, "As thy soul liveth, O king, I cannot tell." And the king said, "Inquire thou whose son the stripling is." And as David returned from the slaughter of the Philistine, Abner took him, and brought him before Saul, with the head of the Philistine in his hand. And Saul said to him, "Whose son art thou, thou young man?" And David answered, "I am the son of thy servant Jesse, the Bethlehemite."

Eighteen   And it came to pass when he had made an end of speaking unto Saul, that the soul of Jonathan was knit with the soul of David, and Jonathan loved him as his own soul. And Saul took him that day, and would let him go no more home to his father's house. Then Jonathan and David made a covenant, because he loved him as his own soul. And Jonathan stripped himself of the robe that was upon him, and gave it to David, and his garments, even to his sword, and to his bow, and to his girdle.

Saul's Jealousy of David

And David went out whithersoever Saul sent him, and behaved himself wisely: and Saul set him over the men of war, and he was accepted in the sight of all the people, and also in the sight of Saul's servants. And it came to pass as they came, when David was returned from the slaughter of the Philistine, that the women came out of all cities of Israel, singing and dancing, to meet King Saul, with tabrets, with joy, and with instruments of music. And the women answered one another as they played, and said, "Saul hath slain his thousands, and David his ten thousands." And Saul was very wroth, and the saying displeased him; and he said, "They have ascribed unto David ten thousands, and to me they have ascribed but thousands: and what can he have more but the kingdom?" And Saul eyed David from that day and forward.

And it came to pass on the morrow, that the evil spirit from God came upon Saul, and he prophesied in the midst of the house: and David played with his hand, as at other times: and there was a javelin in Saul's hand. And Saul cast the javelin; for he said, "I will smite David even to the wall with it." And David avoided out of his presence twice.

> HE THAT HATH NO RULE OVER HIS OWN SPIRIT IS LIKE A
> CITY THAT IS BROKEN DOWN, AND WITHOUT WALLS.
>
> PROVERBS 25:28

And Saul was afraid of David, because the Lord was with him, and was departed from Saul. Therefore Saul removed him from him, and made him his captain over a thousand; and he went out and came in before the people. And David behaved himself wisely in all his ways; and the Lord was with him. Wherefore when Saul saw that he behaved himself very wisely, he was afraid of him. But all Israel and Judah loved David, because he went out and came in before them.

And Saul said to David, "Behold, my elder daughter Merab, her will I give thee to wife: only be thou valiant for me, and fight the Lord's battles." For Saul said, "Let not mine hand be upon him, but let the hand of the Philistines be upon him." And David said unto Saul, "Who am I? and what is my life, or my father's family in Israel, that I should be son-in-law to the king?" But it came to pass at the time when Merab, Saul's daughter, should have been given to David, that she was given unto Adriel the Meholathite to wife. And Michal, Saul's daughter, loved David: and they told Saul, and the thing pleased him. And Saul said, "I will give him her, that she may be a snare to him, and that the hand of the Philistines may be against him." Wherefore Saul said to David, "Thou shalt this day be my son-in-law in the one of the twain."

And Saul commanded his servants, saying, "Commune with David secretly, and say, 'Behold, the king hath delight in thee, and all his servants love thee: now therefore be the king's son-in-law.' " And Saul's servants spake those words in the ears of David. And David said, "Seemeth it to you a light thing to be a king's son-in-law, seeing that I am a poor man, and lightly esteemed?" And the servants of Saul told him, saying, "On this manner spake David." And Saul said, "Thus shall ye say to David, 'The king desireth not any dowry, but an hundred foreskins of the Philistines, to be avenged of the king's enemies.' " But Saul thought to make David fall by the hand of the Philistines.

And when his servants told David these words, it pleased David well to be the king's son-in-law: and the days were not expired. Wherefore David arose and went, he and his men, and slew of the Philistines two hundred men; and David brought their foreskins, and they gave them in full tale to the king, that he might be the king's son-in-law. And Saul gave him Michal his daughter to wife.

And Saul saw and knew that the Lord was with David, and that Michal, Saul's daughter, loved him. And Saul was yet the more afraid of David; and Saul became David's enemy continually. Then the princes of the Philistines went forth: and it came to pass after they went forth, that David behaved himself more wisely than all the servants of Saul, so that his name was much set by.

Nineteen And Saul spake to Jonathan his son, and to all his servants, that they should kill David. But Jonathan Saul's son delighted much in David: and Jonathan told David, saying, "Saul my father seeketh to kill thee. Now therefore, I pray thee, take heed to thyself until the morning, and abide in a secret place, and hide thyself. And I will go out and stand beside my father in the field where thou art, and I will commune with my father of thee; and what I see, that I will tell thee."

And Jonathan spake good of David unto Saul his father, and said unto him, "Let not the king sin against his servant, against David; because he hath not sinned against thee, and because his works have been to thee-ward very good. For he did put his life in his hand, and slew the Philistine, and the Lord wrought a great salvation for all Israel: thou sawest it, and didst rejoice. Wherefore then wilt thou sin against innocent blood, to slay David without a cause?" And Saul hearkened unto the voice of Jonathan: and Saul sware, "As the Lord liveth, he shall not be slain." And Jonathan called David, and Jonathan showed him all those things. And Jonathan brought David to Saul, and he was in his presence, as in times past.

David's Escape

And there was war again: and David went out, and fought with the Philistines, and slew them with a great slaughter; and they fled from him. And the evil spirit from the Lord was upon Saul, as he sat in his house with his javelin in his hand: and David played with his hand. And Saul sought to smite David even to the wall with the javelin; but he slipped away out of Saul's presence, and he smote the javelin into the wall: and David fled, and escaped that night. Saul also sent messengers unto David's house, to watch him, and to slay him in the morning: and Michal, David's wife, told him, saying, "If thou save not thy life tonight, tomorrow thou shalt be slain."

So Michal let David down through a window: and he went, and fled, and escaped. And Michal took an image, and laid it in the bed, and put a pillow of goats' hair for his bolster,[4] and

---

4 *bolster:* head.

covered it with a cloth. And when Saul sent messengers to take David, she said, "He is sick." And Saul sent the messengers again to see David, saying, "Bring him up to me in the bed, that I may slay him." And when the messengers were come in, behold, there was an image in the bed, with a pillow of goats' hair for his bolster. And Saul said unto Michal, "Why hast thou deceived me so, and sent away mine enemy, that he is escaped?" And Michal answered Saul, "He said unto me, 'Let me go; why should I kill thee?' "

So David fled, and escaped, and came to Samuel to Ramah, and told him all that Saul had done to him. And he and Samuel went and dwelt in Naioth. And it was told Saul, saying, "Behold, David is at Naioth in Ramah." And Saul sent messengers to take David: and when they saw the company of the prophets prophesying, and Samuel standing as appointed over them, the spirit of God was upon the messengers of Saul, and they also prophesied. And when it was told Saul, he sent other messengers, and they prophesied likewise. And Saul sent messengers again the third time, and they prophesied also.

Then went he also to Ramah, and came to a great well that is in Sechu: and he asked, and said, "Where are Samuel and David?" And one said, "Behold, they be at Naioth in Ramah." And he went thither to Naioth in Ramah: and the spirit of God was upon him also, and he went on, and prophesied until he came to Naioth in Ramah. And he stripped off his clothes also, and prophesied before Samuel in like manner, and lay down naked all that day and all that night. Wherefore they say, "Is Saul also among the prophets?"

Jonathan's Devotion to David

Twenty And David fled from Naioth in Ramah, and came and said before Jonathan, "What have I done? what is mine iniquity? and what is my sin before thy father, that he seeketh my life?" And he said unto him, "God forbid, thou shalt not die: behold, my father will do nothing either great or small, but that he will show it me: and why should my father hide this thing from me? it is not so."

And David sware moreover, and said, "Thy father certainly knoweth that I have found grace in thine eyes; and he saith, 'Let not Jonathan know this, lest he be grieved': but truly, as the Lord liveth, and as thy soul liveth, there is but a step between me and death." Then said Jonathan unto David, "Whatsoever thy soul desireth, I will even do it for thee."

And David said unto Jonathan, "Behold, tomorrow is the new moon, and I should not fail to sit with the king at meat: but let me go, that I may hide myself in the field unto the third day at even. If thy father at all miss me, then say, 'David earnestly asked leave of me that he might run to Bethlehem his city: for there is a yearly sacrifice there for all the family.' If he say thus, 'It is well,' thy servant shall have peace: but if he be very wroth, then be sure that evil is determined by him. Therefore thou shalt deal kindly with thy servant, for thou hast brought thy servant into a covenant of the Lord with thee: notwithstanding, if there be in me iniquity, slay me thyself: for why shouldest thou bring me to thy father?"

And Jonathan said, "Far be it from thee: for if I knew certainly that evil were determined by my father to come upon thee, then would not I tell it thee?" Then said David to Jonathan, "Who shall tell me? or what if thy father answer thee roughly?"

And Jonathan said unto David, "Come, and let us go out into the field." And they went out both of them into the field. And Jonathan said unto David, "O Lord God of Israel, when I have sounded my father about tomorrow any time, or the third day, and behold, if there be good toward David, and I then send not unto thee, and show it thee; the Lord do so and much more to Jonathan: but if it please my father to do thee evil, then I will show it thee, and send thee away, that thou mayest go in peace, and the Lord be with thee, as he hath been with my father. And thou shalt not only while yet I live show me the kindness of the Lord, that I die not: but also thou shalt not cut off thy kindness from my house for ever: no, not when the Lord hath cut off the enemies of David, every one from the face of the earth."

So Jonathan made a covenant with the house of David, saying,

"Let the Lord even require it at the hand of David's enemies." And Jonathan caused David to swear again, because he loved him: for he loved him as he loved his own soul.

Then Jonathan said to David, "Tomorrow is the new moon: and thou shalt be missed, because thy seat will be empty. And when thou hast stayed three days, then thou shalt go down quickly, and come to the place where thou didst hide thyself when the business was in hand, and shalt remain by the stone Ezel. And I will shoot three arrows on the side thereof, as though I shot at a mark. And behold, I will send a lad, saying, 'Go, find out the arrows.' If I expressly say unto the lad, 'Behold, the arrows are on this side of thee, take them'; then come thou, for there is peace to thee, and no hurt, as the Lord liveth. But if I say thus unto the young man, 'Behold, the arrows are beyond thee'; go thy way, for the Lord hath sent thee away. And as touching the matter which thou and I have spoken of, behold, the Lord be between thee and me for ever."

So David hid himself in the field: and when the new moon was come, the king sat him down to eat meat. And the king sat upon his seat, as at other times, even upon a seat by the wall: and Jonathan arose, and Abner sat by Saul's side, and David's place was empty. Nevertheless, Saul spake not any thing that day: for he thought, "Something hath befallen him, he is not clean; surely he is not clean." And it came to pass on the morrow, which was the second day of the month, that David's place was empty: and Saul said unto Jonathan his son, "Wherefore cometh not the son of Jesse to meat, neither yesterday nor today?"

And Jonathan answered Saul, "David earnestly asked leave of me to go to Bethlehem. And he said, 'Let me go, I pray thee, for our family hath a sacrifice in the city; and my brother, he hath commanded me to be there: and now, if I have found favour in thine eyes, let me get away, I pray thee, and see my brethren.' Therefore he cometh not unto the king's table."

Then Saul's anger was kindled against Jonathan, and he said unto him, "Thou son of the perverse rebellious woman, do not I know that thou hast chosen the son of Jesse to thine own confusion, and unto the confusion of thy mother's nakedness? For as long as the son of Jesse liveth upon the ground, thou shalt not be established, nor thy kingdom. Wherefore now send and fetch him unto me, for he shall surely die."

And Jonathan answered Saul his father, and said unto him, "Wherefore shall he be slain? what hath he done?" And Saul cast a javelin at him to smite him: whereby Jonathan knew that it was determined of his father to slay David. So Jonathan arose from the table in fierce anger, and did eat no meat the second day of the month: for he was grieved for David, because his father had done him shame.

And it came to pass in the morning, that Jonathan went out into the field, at the time appointed with David, and a little lad with him. And he said unto his lad, "Run, find out now the arrows which I shoot." And as the lad ran, he shot an arrow beyond him. And when the lad was come to the place of the arrow which Jonathan had shot, Jonathan cried after the lad, and said, "Is not the arrow beyond thee?" And Jonathan cried after the lad, "Make speed, haste, stay not." And Jonathan's lad gathered up the arrows, and came to his master. But the lad knew not any thing: only Jonathan and David knew the matter. And Jonathan gave his artillery[5] unto his lad, and said unto him, "Go, carry them to the city."

And as soon as the lad was gone, David arose out of a place toward the south, and fell on his face to the ground, and bowed himself three times: and they kissed one another, and wept one with another, until David exceeded. And Jonathan said to David, "Go in peace, forasmuch as we have sworn both of us in the name of the Lord, saying, 'The Lord be between me and thee, and between my seed and thy seed for ever.' " And he arose, and departed: and Jonathan went into the city.

David the Outlaw

Twenty-one Then came David to Nob, to Ahimelech the priest: and Ahimelech was afraid at the meeting of David, and said unto him, "Why art thou alone, and no man with thee?" And David said unto Ahimelech the priest, "The king hath commanded me a

---

[5] *artillery: i.e.,* bows and arrows.

business, and hath said unto me, 'Let no man know any thing of the business whereabout I send thee, and what I have commanded thee': and I have appointed my servants to such and such a place. Now therefore what is under thine hand? give me five loaves of bread in mine hand, or what there is present."

And the priest answered David, and said, "There is no common bread under mine hand, but there is hallowed bread; if the young men have kept themselves at least from women." And David answered the priest, and said unto him, "Of a truth women have been kept from us about these three days, since I came out, and the vessels of the young men are holy, and the bread is in a manner common, yea, though it were sanctified this day in the vessel."

So the priest gave him hallowed bread; for there was no bread there but the showbread,[6] that was taken from before the Lord, to put hot bread in the day when it was taken away. Now a certain man of the servants of Saul was there that day, detained before the Lord, and his name was Doeg, an Edomite, the chiefest of the herdmen that belonged to Saul.

And David said unto Ahimelech, "And is there not here under thine hand spear or sword? for I have neither brought my sword nor my weapons with me, because the king's business required haste." And the priest said, "The sword of Goliath the Philistine, whom thou slewest in the valley of Elah, behold, it is here wrapped in a cloth behind the ephod: if thou wilt take that, take it; for there is no other save that here." And David said, "There is none like that, give it me."

And David arose, and fled that day, for fear of Saul, and went to Achish the king of Gath. And the servants of Achish said unto him, "Is not this David the king of the land? did they not sing one to another of him in dances, saying, 'Saul hath slain his thousands, and David his ten thousands'?"

And David laid up these words in his heart, and was sore afraid of Achish the king of Gath. And he changed his behaviour before them, and feigned himself mad in their hands, and scrabbled on the doors of the gate, and let his spittle fall down upon his beard. Then said Achish unto his servants, "Lo, you see the man is mad:

6 *showbread:* holy bread placed before the Lord in the shrine.

wherefore then have ye brought him to me? Have I need of mad men, that ye have brought this fellow to play the mad man in my presence? Shall this fellow come into my house?"

Twenty-two David therefore departed thence, and escaped to the cave Adullam: and when his brethren and all his father's house heard it, they went down thither to him. And every one that was in distress, and every one that was in debt, and every one that was discontented, gathered themselves unto him; and he became a captain over them: and there were with him about four hundred men.

And David went thence to Mizpeh of Moab; and he said unto the king of Moab, "Let my father and my mother, I pray thee, come forth, and be with you, till I know what God will do for me." And he brought them before the king of Moab: and they dwelt with him all the while that David was in the hold.[7] And the prophet Gad said unto David, "Abide not in the hold; depart, and get thee into the land of Judah." Then David departed, and came into the forest of Hareth.

When Saul heard that David was discovered, and the men that were with him (now Saul abode in Gibeah under a tree in Ramah, having his spear in his hand, and all his servants were standing about him); then Saul said unto his servants that stood about him, "Hear now, ye Benjamites; will the son of Jesse give every one of you fields, and vineyards, and make you all captains of thousands, and captains of hundreds: that all of you have conspired against me, and there is none that showeth me that my son hath made a league with the son of Jesse, and there is none of you that is sorry for me, or showeth unto me that my son hath stirred up my servant against me, to lie in wait, as at this day?"

Then answered Doeg the Edomite, which was set over the servants of Saul, and said, "I saw the son of Jesse coming to Nob, to Ahimelech the son of Ahitub. And he inquired of the Lord for him, and gave him victuals, and gave him the sword of Goliath the Philistine."

Then the king sent to call Ahimelech the priest, the son of Ahitub, and all his father's house, the priests that were in Nob:

---

[7] *hold:* stronghold, citadel.

and they came all of them to the king. And Saul said, "Hear now thou son of Ahitub." And he answered, "Here I am, my lord." And Saul said unto him, "Why have ye conspired against me, thou and the son of Jesse, in that thou hast given him bread, and a sword, and hast inquired of God for him, that he should rise against me, to lie in wait, as at this day?"

Then Ahimelech answered the king, and said, "And who is so faithful among all thy servants as David, which is the king's son-in-law, and goeth at thy bidding, and is honourable in thine house? Did I then begin to inquire of God for him? be it far from me: let not the king impute any thing unto his servant, nor to all the house of my father: for thy servant knew nothing of all this, less or more." And the king said, "Thou shalt surely die, Ahimelech, thou, and all thy father's house."

And the king said unto the footmen that stood about him, "Turn and slay the priests of the Lord, because their hand also is with David, and because they knew when he fled, and did not show it to me." But the servants of the king would not put forth their hand to fall upon the priests of the Lord. And the king said to Doeg, "Turn thou and fall upon the priests." And Doeg the Edomite turned, and fell upon the priests, and slew on that day fourscore and five persons that did wear a linen ephod.[8] And Nob, the city of the priests, smote he with the edge of the sword, both men and women, children and sucklings, and oxen and asses, and sheep, with the edge of the sword.

And one of the sons of Ahimelech the son of Ahitub, named Abiathar, escaped, and fled after David: and Abiathar showed David that Saul had slain the Lord's priests. And David said unto Abiathar, "I knew it that day, when Doeg the Edomite was there, that he would surely tell Saul. I have occasioned the death of all the persons of thy father's house. Abide thou with me, fear not: for he that seeketh my life seeketh thy life: but with me thou shalt be in safeguard."

Twenty-three   Then they told David, saying, "Behold, the Philistines fight against Keilah, and they rob the threshingfloors." Therefore David inquired of the Lord, saying, "Shall I go and

---

8 *ephod:* a waistcloth worn by priests.

smite these Philistines?" And the Lord said unto David, "Go, and smite the Philistines, and save Keilah." And David's men said unto him, "Behold, we be afraid here in Judah: how much more then if we come to Keilah against the armies of the Philistines?" Then David inquired of the Lord yet again. And the Lord answered him, and said, "Arise, go down to Keilah; for I will deliver the Philistines into thine hand."

So David and his men went to Keilah, and fought with the Philistines, and brought away their cattle, and smote them with a great slaughter. So David saved the inhabitants of Keilah. And it came to pass when Abiathar the son of Ahimelech fled to David to Keilah, that he came down with an ephod in his hand.

Saul's Pursuit of David

And it was told Saul that David was come to Keilah. And Saul said, "God hath delivered him into mine hand; for he is shut in, by entering into a town that hath gates and bars." And Saul called all the people together to war, to go down to Keilah, to besiege David and his men.

And David knew that Saul secretly practiced mischief against him, and he said to Abiathar the priest, "Bring hither the ephod." Then said David, "O Lord God of Israel, thy servant hath certainly heard that Saul seeketh to come to Keilah, to destroy the city for my sake. Will the men of Keilah deliver me up into his hand? will Saul come down, as thy servant hath heard? O Lord God of Israel, I beseech thee, tell thy servant." And the Lord said, "He will come down." Then said David, "Will the men of Keilah deliver me, and my men, into the hand of Saul?" And the Lord said, "They will deliver thee up."

Then David and his men, which were about six hundred, arose and departed out of Keilah, and went whithersoever they could go. And it was told Saul that David was escaped from Keilah; and he forbare to go forth. And David abode in the wilderness in strongholds, and remained in a mountain in the wilderness of Ziph. And Saul sought him every day, but God delivered him not into his hand. And David saw that Saul was come out to seek his life: and David was in the wilderness of Ziph in a wood. And Jonathan, Saul's son, arose, and went to David into the wood, and strengthened his hand in God. And he said unto him, "Fear not: for the hand of Saul my father shall not find thee; and thou shalt be king over Israel, and I shall be next unto thee; and that also Saul my father knoweth." And they two made a covenant before the Lord: and David abode in the wood, and Jonathan went to his house.

Then came up the Ziphites to Saul to Gibeah, saying, "Doth not David hide himself with us in strongholds in the wood, in the hill of Hachilah, which is on the south of Jeshimon? Now therefore, O king, come down according to all the desire of thy soul to come down, and our part shall be to deliver him into the king's hand."

And Saul said, "Blessed be ye of the Lord, for ye have compassion on me. Go, I pray you, prepare yet, and know and see his place where his haunt is, and who hath seen him there: for it is told me that he dealeth very subtly. See therefore, and take knowledge of all the lurking places where he hideth himself, and come ye again to me with the certainty, and I will go with you: and it shall come to pass, if he be in the land, that I will search him out throughout all the thousands of Judah."

And they arose, and went to Ziph before Saul: but David and his men were in the wilderness of Maon, in the plain on the south of Jeshimon. Saul also and his men went to seek him. And they told David: wherefore he came down into a rock, and abode in the wilderness of Maon: and when Saul heard that, he pursued after David in the wilderness of Maon. And Saul went on this side of the mountain, and David and his men on that side of the mountain: and David made haste to get away for fear of Saul; for Saul and his men compassed David and his men round about to take them.

But there came a messenger unto Saul, saying, "Haste thee, and come; for the Philistines have invaded the land." Wherefore Saul returned from pursuing after David, and went against the Philistines; therefore they called that place Sela-hammahlekoth. And David went up from thence, and dwelt in strongholds at En-gedi.

"I Have Not Sinned against Thee"

Twenty-four And it came to pass when Saul was returned from following the Philistines, that it was told him, saying, "Behold, David is in the wilderness of En-gedi." Then Saul took three thousand chosen men out of all Israel, and went to seek David and his men upon the rocks of the wild goats. And he came to the sheepcotes by the way, where was a cave, and Saul went in to cover his feet: and David and his men remained in the sides of the cave. And the men of David said unto him, "Behold the day of which the Lord said unto thee, 'Behold, I will deliver thine enemy into thine hand, that thou mayest do to him as it shall seem good unto thee.' " Then David arose, and cut off the skirt of Saul's robe privily.

And it came to pass afterward, that David's heart smote him, because he had cut off Saul's skirt. And he said unto his men, "The Lord forbid that I should do this thing unto my master, the Lord's anointed, to stretch forth mine hand against him, seeing he is the anointed of the Lord." So David stayed his servants with these words, and suffered them not to rise against Saul.

But Saul rose up out of the cave, and went on his way. David also arose afterward, and went out of the cave, and cried after Saul, saying, "My lord the king." And when Saul looked behind him, David stooped with his face to the earth, and bowed himself.

And David said to Saul, "Wherefore hearest thou men's words, saying, 'Behold, David seeketh thy hurt'? Behold, this day thine eyes have seen how that the Lord had delivered thee today into mine hand in the cave: and some bade me kill thee, but mine eye spared thee, and I said, 'I will not put forth mine hand against my lord, for he is the Lord's anointed.' Moreover, my father, see, yea, see the skirt of thy robe in my hand: for in that I cut off the skirt of thy robe, and killed thee not, know thou and see that there is neither evil nor transgression in mine hand, and I have not sinned against thee; yet thou huntest my soul, to take it. The Lord judge between me and thee, and the Lord avenge me of thee: but mine hand shall not be upon thee. As saith the proverb of the ancients, 'Wickedness proceedeth from the wicked': but mine hand shall not be upon thee. After whom is the king of

Israel come out? after whom dost thou pursue? after a dead dog, after a flea. The Lord therefore be judge, and judge between me and thee, and see, and plead my cause, and deliver me out of thine hand."

And it came to pass when David had made an end of speaking these words unto Saul, that Saul said, "Is this thy voice, my son David?" And Saul lifted up his voice, and wept. And he said to David, "Thou art more righteous than I: for thou hast rewarded me good, whereas I have rewarded thee evil. And thou hast showed this day how that thou has dealt well with me: forasmuch as when the Lord had delivered me into thine hand, thou killedst me not. For if a man find his enemy, will he let him go well away? wherefore the Lord reward thee good, for that thou hast done unto me this day. And now behold, I know well that thou shalt surely be king, and that the kingdom of Israel shall be established in thine hand. Swear now therefore unto me by the Lord, that thou wilt not cut off my seed after me, and that thou wilt not destroy my name out of my father's house." And David sware unto Saul, and Saul went home; but David and his men got them up into the hold.

Saul's Spear

Twenty-six And the Ziphites came unto Saul to Gibeah, saying, "Doth not David hide himself in the hill of Hachilah, which is before Jeshimon?" Then Saul arose, and went down to the wilderness of Ziph, having three thousand chosen men of Israel with him, to seek David in the wilderness of Ziph. And Saul pitched in the hill of Hachilah, which is before Jeshimon, by the way. But David abode in the wilderness, and he saw that Saul came after him into the wilderness. David therefore sent out spies, and understood that Saul was come in very deed.

And David arose, and came to the place where Saul had pitched: and David beheld the place where Saul lay, and Abner the son of Ner, the captain of his host: and Saul lay in the trench, and the people pitched round about him. Then answered David, and said to Ahimelech the Hittite, and to Abishai the son of Zeruiah brother to Joab, saying, "Who will go down with me to Saul to the camp?" And Abishai said, "I will go down with thee."

So David and Abishai came to the people by night: and behold, Saul lay sleeping within the trench, and his spear stuck in the ground at his bolster: but Abner and the people lay round about him. Then said Abishai to David, "God hath delivered thine enemy into thine hand this day: now therefore let me smite him, I pray thee, with the spear, even to the earth at once, and I will not smite him the second time."

And David said to Abishai, "Destroy him not: for who can stretch forth his hand against the Lord's anointed, and be guiltless?" David said furthermore, "As the Lord liveth, the Lord shall smite him; or his day shall come to die; or he shall descend into battle, and perish. The Lord forbid that I should stretch forth mine hand against the Lord's anointed: but I pray thee, take thou now the spear that is at his bolster, and the cruse[9] of water, and let us go." So David took the spear and the cruse of water from Saul's bolster; and they got them away, and no man saw it, nor knew it, neither awaked: for they were all asleep, because a deep sleep from the Lord was fallen upon them.

Then David went over to the other side, and stood on the top of a hill afar off, a great space being between them: and David cried to the people, and to Abner the son of Ner, saying, "Answerest thou not, Abner?" Then Abner answered, and said, "Who art thou that criest to the king?" And David said to Abner, "Art not thou a valiant man? and who is like to thee in Israel? Wherefore then hast thou not kept thy lord the king? for there came one of the people in, to destroy the king thy lord. This thing is not good that thou hast done: as the Lord liveth, ye are worthy to die, because ye have not kept your master, the Lord's anointed. And now see where the king's spear is, and the cruse of water that was at his bolster."

And Saul knew David's voice, and said, "Is this thy voice, my son David?" And David said, "It is my voice, my lord, O king." And he said, "Wherefore doth my lord thus pursue after his servant? for what have I done? or what evil is in mine hand? Now therefore, I pray thee, let my lord the king hear the words of his

---

9 *cruse:* a jar used for carrying water on journeys.

servants. If the Lord have stirred thee up against me, let him accept an offering: but if they be the children of men, cursed be they before the Lord; for they have driven me out this day from abiding in the inheritance of the Lord, saying, 'Go, serve other gods.' Now therefore, let not my blood fall to the earth before the face of the Lord: for the king of Israel is come out to seek a flea, as when one doth hunt a partridge in the mountains."

Then said Saul, "I have sinned: return, my son David, for I will no more do thee harm, because my soul was precious in thine eyes this day: behold, I have played the fool, and have erred exceedingly." And David answered, and said, "Behold the king's spear! and let one of the young men come over and fetch it. The Lord render to every man his righteousness, and his faithfulness: for the Lord delivered thee into my hand today, but I would not stretch forth mine hand against the Lord's anointed. And behold, as thy life was much set by this day in mine eyes, so let my life be much set by in the eyes of the Lord, and let him deliver me out of all tribulation." Then Saul said to David, "Blessed be thou, my son David: thou shalt both do great things, and also shalt still prevail." So David went on his way, and Saul returned to his place.

David's Escape to the Land of the Philistines

Twenty-seven And David said in his heart, "I shall now perish one day by the hand of Saul: there is nothing better for me than that I should speedily escape into the land of the Philistines; and Saul shall despair of me, to seek me any more in any coast of Israel: so shall I escape out of his hand." And David arose, and he passed over with the six hundred men that were with him, unto Achish, the son of Maoch, king of Gath. And David dwelt with Achish at Gath, he and his men, every man with his household, even David with his two wives, Ahinoam the Jezreelitess, and Abigail the Carmelitess, Nabal's wife. And it was told Saul that David was fled to Gath, and he sought no more again for him.

And David said unto Achish, "If I have now found grace in thine eyes, let them give me a place in some town in the country, that I may dwell there: for why should thy servant dwell in the royal city with thee?" Then Achish gave him Ziklag that day: wherefore Ziklag pertaineth unto the kings of Judah unto this day. And the time that David dwelt in the country of the Philistines was a full year and four months.

And David and his men went up and invaded the Geshurites, and the Gezrites, and the Amalekites: for those nations were of old the inhabitants of the land, as thou goest to Shur, even unto the land of Egypt. And David smote the land, and left neither man nor woman alive, and took away the sheep, and the oxen, and the asses, and the camels, and the apparel, and returned, and came to Achish. And Achish said, "Whither have ye made a road[10] today?" And David said, "Against the south of Judah, and against the south of the Jerahmeelites, and against the south of the Kenites." And David saved neither man nor woman alive, to bring tidings to Gath, saying, "Lest they should tell on us, saying, 'So did David, and so will be his manner all the while he dwelleth in the country of the Philistines.'" And Achish believed David, saying, "He hath made his people Israel utterly to abhor him, therefore he shall be my servant for ever."

Twenty-eight And it came to pass in those days, that the Philistines gathered their armies together for warfare, to fight with Israel: and Achish said unto David, "Know thou assuredly, that thou shalt go out with me to battle, thou, and thy men." And David said to Achish, "Surely thou shalt know what thy servant can do." And Achish said to David, "Therefore will I make thee keeper of mine head for ever."

Saul and Samuel's Ghost

Now Samuel was dead, and all Israel had lamented him, and buried him in Ramah, even in his own city. And Saul had put away those that had familiar spirits, and the wizards, out of the land. And the Philistines gathered themselves together, and came and pitched in Shunem: and Saul gathered all Israel together, and they pitched in Gilboa. And when Saul saw the host of the

---

[10] *road: i.e.,* raid.

Philistines, he was afraid, and his heart greatly trembled. And when Saul inquired of the Lord, the Lord answered him not, neither by dreams, nor by Urim,[11] nor by prophets.

Then said Saul unto his servants, "Seek me a woman that hath a familiar spirit, that I may go to her, and inquire of her." And his servants said to him, "Behold, there is a woman that hath a familiar spirit at Endor."

And Saul disguised himself, and put on other raiment, and he went, and two men with him, and they came to the woman by night: and he said, "I pray thee, divine unto me by the familiar spirit, and bring me him up, whom I shall name unto thee."

And the woman said unto him, "Behold, thou knowest what Saul hath done, how he hath cut off those that have familiar spirits, and the wizards, out of the land: wherefore then layest thou a snare for my life, to cause me to die?" And Saul sware to her by the Lord, saying, "As the Lord liveth, there shall be no punishment happen to thee for this thing." Then said the woman, "Whom shall I bring up unto thee?" And he said, "Bring me up Samuel."

And when the woman saw Samuel, she cried with a loud voice: and the woman spake to Saul, saying, "Why hast thou deceived me? for thou art Saul." And the king said unto her, "Be not afraid: for what sawest thou?" And the woman said unto Saul, "I saw gods ascending out of the earth." And he said unto her, "What form is he of?" And she said, "An old man cometh up, and he is covered with a mantle." And Saul perceived that it was Samuel, and he stooped with his face to the ground, and bowed himself.

And Samuel said to Saul, "Why hast thou disquieted me, to bring me up?" And Saul answered, "I am sore distressed; for the Philistines make war against me, and God is departed from me, and answereth me no more, neither by prophets, nor by dreams: therefore I have called thee, that thou mayest make known unto me what I shall do."

Then said Samuel, "Wherefore then dost thou ask of me, seeing the Lord is departed from thee, and is become thine enemy? And the Lord hath done to him, as he spake by me: for the Lord hath

11 *Urim:* a sacred lot used to ascertain the will of the Lord.

rent the kingdom out of thine hand, and given it to thy neighbour, even to David. Because thou obeyedst not the voice of the Lord, nor executedst his fierce wrath upon Amalek, therefore hath the Lord done this thing unto thee this day. Moreover, the Lord will also deliver Israel with thee into the hand of the Philistines: and tomorrow shalt thou and thy sons be with me: the Lord also shall deliver the host of Israel into the hand of the Philistines."

Then Saul fell straightway all along on the earth, and was sore afraid, because of the words of Samuel, and there was no strength in him: for he had eaten no bread all the day, nor all the night.

And the woman came unto Saul, and saw that he was sore troubled, and said unto him, "Behold, thine handmaid hath obeyed thy voice, and I have put my life in my hand, and have hearkened unto thy words which thou spakest unto me. Now therefore, I pray thee, hearken thou also unto the voice of thine handmaid, and let me set a morsel of bread before thee; and eat, that thou mayest have strength, when thou goest on thy way."

But he refused, and said, "I will not eat." But his servants together with the woman compelled him; and he hearkened unto their voice: so he arose from the earth, and sat upon the bed. And the woman had a fat calf in the house, and she hasted, and killed it, and took flour and kneaded it, and did bake unleavened bread thereof. And she brought it before Saul, and before his servants, and they did eat: then they arose up, and went away that night.

Death of Saul and His Sons

Thirty-one Now the Philistines fought against Israel: and the men of Israel fled from before the Philistines, and fell down slain in mount Gilboa. And the Philistines followed hard upon Saul, and upon his sons, and the Philistines slew Jonathan, and Abinadab, and Malchishua, Saul's sons. And the battle went sore against Saul, and the archers hit him, and he was sore wounded of the archers.

Then said Saul unto his armour-bearer, "Draw thy sword, and thrust me through therewith, lest these uncircumcised come and thrust me through, and abuse me." But his armour-bearer would not, for he was sore afraid. Therefore Saul took a sword, and fell upon it. And when his armour-bearer saw that Saul was dead, he fell likewise upon his sword, and died with him. So Saul died, and his three sons, and his armour-bearer, and all his men, that same day together.

And when the men of Israel that were on the other side of the valley, and they that were on the other side Jordan, saw that the men of Israel fled, and that Saul and his sons were dead, they forsook the cities and fled, and the Philistines came and dwelt in them.

And it came to pass on the morrow when the Philistines came to strip the slain, that they found Saul and his three sons fallen in mount Gilboa. And they cut off his head, and stripped off his armour, and sent into the land of the Philistines round about, to publish it in the house of their idols, and among the people. And they put his armour in the house of Ashtaroth: and they fastened his body to the wall of Beth-shan.

And when the inhabitants of Jabesh-gilead heard of that which the Philistines had done to Saul, all the valiant men arose, and went all night, and took the body of Saul and the bodies of his sons from the wall of Beth-shan, and came to Jabesh, and burnt them there. And they took their bones, and buried them under a tree at Jabesh, and fasted seven days.

Nathan before David
Staedelsches Kunstinstitut, Frankfurt

David
the
King

The curse of power that begins with Saul continues during the reign of David. Saul, who cannot give up his throne even to please the God he loves, suffers terribly for his sins. David is a hero of a different mold. Although he suffers for his sins of sensuality and murder, his story is not a tragedy as is Saul's — it is a heroic story of epic proportions. Like the Iliad, the prose epic of David has the scope, the deeds of individual heroism, the divine intervention, the objective statement, and the lofty style that mark all great epic stories. Most important, its hero David the King is an attractive, vigorous leader who is recreated in all of his grandeur and complexity.

II Samuel

David's Lament for Jonathan and Saul

One Now it came to pass after the death of Saul, when David was returned from the slaughter of the Amalekites, and David had abode two days in Ziklag, it came even to pass on the third day, that behold, a man came out of the camp from Saul with his clothes rent, and earth upon his head: and so it was when he came to David, that he fell to the earth, and did obeisance.

And David said unto him, "From whence comest thou?" And he said unto him, "Out of the camp of Israel am I escaped." And David said unto him, "How went the matter? I pray thee, tell me." And he answered, "The people are fled from the battle, and many of the people also are fallen and dead, and Saul and Jonathan his son are dead also." And David said unto the young man that told him, "How knowest thou that Saul and Jonathan his son be dead?"

And the young man that told him said, "As I happened by chance upon mount Gilboa, behold, Saul leaned upon his spear: and lo, the chariots and horsemen followed hard after him. And when he looked behind him, he saw me, and called unto me: and I answered, 'Here am I.' And he said unto me, 'Who art thou?' And I answered him, 'I am an Amalekite.' He said unto me again, 'Stand, I pray thee, upon me, and slay me: for anguish is come upon me, because my life is yet whole in me.' So I stood upon him, and slew him, because I was sure that he could not live after that he was fallen: and I took the crown that was upon his head, and the bracelet that was on his arm, and have brought them hither unto my lord."

Then David took hold on his clothes, and rent them, and likewise all the men that were with him. And they mourned and wept, and fasted until even, for Saul and for Jonathan his son, and for the people of the Lord, and for the house of Israel, because they were fallen by the sword.

And David said unto the young man that told him, "Whence art thou?" And he answered, "I am the son of a stranger, an Amalekite." And David said unto him, "How wast thou not afraid to stretch forth thine hand to destroy the Lord's anointed?" And David called one of the young men, and said, "Go near, and fall upon him." And he smote him, that he died. And David said unto him, "Thy blood be upon thy head: for thy mouth hath testified against thee, saying, 'I have slain the Lord's anointed.' "

And David lamented with this lamentation[1] over Saul, and over Jonathan his son (also he bade them teach the children of Judah the use of the bow: behold, it is written in the Book of Jasher):

> "The beauty of Israel is slain upon thy high
>   places: how are the mighty fallen!
> Tell it not in Gath, publish it not in the streets of
>   Askalon: lest the daughters of the Philistines
>   rejoice, lest the daughters of the uncircumcised
>   triumph.
> Ye mountains of Gilboa, let there be no dew,
>   neither let there be rain upon you, nor fields of
>   offerings: for there the shield of the mighty is
>   vilely cast away, the shield of Saul, as though he
>   had not been anointed with oil.
> From the blood of the slain, from the fat of the
>   mighty, the bow of Jonathan turned not back,
>   and the sword of Saul returned not empty.

---

[1] *this lamentation:* Most scholars agree that David himself wrote this elegy for Saul and Jonathan.

>Saul and Jonathan were lovely and pleasant in
>their lives, and in their death they were not
>divided: they were swifter than eagles, they
>were stronger than lions.
>Ye daughters of Israel, weep over Saul, who
>clothed you in scarlet, with other delights, who
>put on ornaments of gold upon your apparel.
>How are the mighty fallen in the midst of battle!
>O Jonathan, thou wast slain in thine high
>places.
>I am distressed for thee, my brother Jonathan,
>very pleasant hast thou been unto me: thy love
>to me was wonderful, passing the love of women.
>How are the mighty fallen, and the weapons of
>war perished!"

David Rules in Israel

Five Then came all the tribes of Israel to David unto Hebron, and spake, saying, "Beloved, we are thy bone and thy flesh. Also in time past when Saul was king over us, thou wast he that leddest out and broughtest in Israel: and the Lord said to thee, 'Thou shalt feed my people Israel, and thou shalt be a captain over Israel.' " So all the elders of Israel came to the king to Hebron; and King David made a league with them in Hebron before the Lord: and they anointed David king over Israel.

David was thirty years old when he began to reign, and he reigned forty years. . . .

David and Bathsheba

Eleven And it came to pass, that after the year was expired, at the time when kings go forth to battle, that David sent Joab, and his servants with him, and all Israel; and they destroyed the children of Ammon, and besieged Rabbah: but David tarried still at Jerusalem.

And it came to pass in an eveningtide, that David arose from off his bed, and walked upon the roof of the king's house: and from the roof he saw a woman washing herself; and the woman was very beautiful to look upon. And David sent and inquired after the woman. And one said, "Is not this Bathsheba the daughter of Eliam, the wife of Uriah the Hittite?"

And David sent messengers, and took her; and she came in unto him, and he lay with her (for she was purified from her uncleanness): and she returned unto her house. And the woman conceived, and sent and told David, and said, "I am with child."

And David sent to Joab, saying, "Send me Uriah the Hittite." And Joab sent Uriah to David. And when Uriah was come unto him, David demanded of him how Joab did, and how the people did, and how the war prospered. And David said to Uriah, "Go down to thy house, and wash thy feet." And Uriah departed out of the king's house, and there followed him a mess of meat from the king. But Uriah slept at the door of the king's house, with all the servants of his lord and went not down to his house.

And when they had told David, saying, "Uriah went not down unto his house," David said unto Uriah, "Camest thou not from thy journey? why then didst thou not go down unto thine house?" And Uriah said unto David, "The ark, and Israel, and Judah abide in tents; and my lord Joab, and the servants of my lord, are encamped in the open fields; shall I then go into mine house, to eat and to drink, and to lie with my wife? As thou livest, and as thy soul liveth, I will not do this thing."

And David said to Uriah, "Tarry here today also, and tomorrow I will let thee depart." So Uriah abode in Jerusalem that day, and the morrow. And when David had called him, he did eat and drink before him, and he made him drunk: and at even he went out to lie on his bed with the servants of his lord, but went not down to his house.

And it came to pass in the morning, that David wrote a letter to Joab, and sent it by the hand of Uriah. And he wrote in the letter, saying, "Set ye Uriah in the forefront of the hottest battle, and retire ye from him, that he may be smitten, and die." And it came to pass when Joab observed the city, that he assigned Uriah unto a place where he knew that valiant men were. And the men of the city went out, and fought with Joab: and there fell some of the people of the servants of David, and Uriah the Hittite died also.

Then Joab sent, and told David all the things concerning the war: and charged the messenger, saying, "When thou hast made an end of telling the matters of the war unto the king, and if so be that the king's wrath arise, and he say unto thee, 'Wherefore approached ye so nigh unto the city when ye did fight? knew ye not that they would shoot from the wall? Who smote Abimelech the son of Jerubbesheth? did not a woman cast a piece of millstone upon him from the wall, that he died in Thebez? why went ye nigh the wall?' then say thou, 'Thy servant Uriah the Hittite is dead also.' "

So the messenger went, and came and showed David all that Joab had sent him for. And the messenger said unto David, "Surely the men prevailed against us, and came out unto us into the field, and we were upon them even unto the entering of the gate. And the shooters shot from off the wall upon thy servants, and some of the king's servants be dead, and thy servant Uriah the Hittite is dead also." Then David said unto the messenger, "Thus shalt thou say unto Joab, 'Let not this thing displease thee: for the sword devoureth one as well as another: make thy battle more strong against the city, and overthrow it'; and encourage thou him."

And when the wife of Uriah heard that Uriah her husband was dead, she mourned for her husband. And when the mourning was past, David sent, and fetched her to his house, and she became his wife, and bare him a son. But the thing that David had done displeased the Lord.

Twelve And the Lord sent Nathan unto David: and he came unto him, and said unto him, "There were two men in one city; the one rich, and the other poor. The rich man had exceeding many flocks and herds. But the poor man had nothing save one little ewe lamb, which he had bought and nourished up: and it grew up together with him, and with his children; it did eat of his own meat, and drank of his own cup, and lay in his bosom, and was unto him as a daughter. And there came a traveller unto the rich man, and he spared to take of his own flock, and of his own herd, to dress for the wayfaring man that was come unto him, but took the poor man's lamb, and dressed it for the man that was come to him."

And David's anger was greatly kindled against the man, and he said to Nathan, "As the Lord liveth, the man that hath done this thing shall surely die. And he shall restore the lamb fourfold, because he did this thing, and because he had no pity."

And Nathan said to David, "Thou art the man. Thus saith the Lord God of Israel, 'I anointed thee king over Israel, and I delivered thee out of the hand of Saul, and I gave thee thy master's house, and thy master's wives into thy bosom, and gave thee the house of Israel and of Judah, and if that had been too little, I would moreover have given unto thee such and such things. Wherefore hast thou despised the commandment of the Lord, to do evil in his sight? thou hast killed Uriah the Hittite with the sword, and hast taken his wife to be thy wife, and hast slain him with the sword of the children of Ammon. Now therefore the sword shall never depart from thine house, because thou hast despised me, and hast taken the wife of Uriah the Hittite to be thy wife.'

"Thus saith the Lord, 'Behold, I will raise up evil against thee out of thine own house, and I will take thy wives before thine eyes, and give them unto thy neighbour, and he shall lie with thy wives in the sight of this sun. For thou didst it secretly: but I will do this thing before all Israel, and before the sun.' "

And David said unto Nathan, "I have sinned against the Lord." And Nathan said unto David, "The Lord also hath put away thy sin; thou shalt not die. Howbeit, because by this deed thou hast given great occasion to the enemies of the Lord to blaspheme, the child also that is born unto thee shall surely die."

MY SON, DESPISE NOT THE CHASTENING OF THE LORD; NEITHER BE WEARY OF HIS CORRECTION. FOR WHOM THE LORD LOVETH HE CORRECTETH; EVEN AS A FATHER THE SON IN WHOM HE DELIGHTETH.

PROVERBS 3:11–12

And Nathan departed unto his house. And the Lord struck the child that Uriah's wife bare unto David, and it was very sick. David therefore besought God for the child; and David fasted, and went in, and lay all night upon the earth. And the elders of his house arose, and went to him, to raise him up from the earth: but he would not, neither did he eat bread with them.

And it came to pass on the seventh day, that the child died. And the servants of David feared to tell him that the child was dead: for they said, "Behold, while the child was yet alive, we spake unto him, and he would not hearken unto our voice: how will he then vex himself, if we tell him that the child is dead?"

But when David saw that his servants whispered, David perceived that the child was dead: therefore David said unto his servants, "Is the child dead?" And they said, "He is dead." Then David arose from the earth and washed and anointed himself, and changed his apparel, and came into the house of the Lord, and worshipped: then he came to his own house, and when he required, they set bread before him, and he did eat.

Then said his servants unto him, "What thing is this that thou hast done? thou didst fast and weep for the child, while it was alive, but when the child was dead, thou didst rise and eat bread." And he said, "While the child was yet alive, I fasted and wept: for I said, 'Who can tell whether God will be gracious to me, that the child may live?' But now he is dead, wherefore should I fast? Can I bring him back again? I shall go to him, but he shall not return to me."

And David comforted Bathsheba his wife, and went in unto her, and lay with her: and she bare a son, and he called his name Solomon, and the Lord loved him. And he sent by the hand of Nathan the prophet, and he called his name Jedidiah, because of the Lord.

And Joab fought against Rabbah of the children of Ammon, and took the royal city. And Joab sent messengers to David, and said, "I have fought against Rabbah, and have taken the city of waters. Now therefore, gather the rest of the people together, and encamp against the city, and take it: lest I take the city, and it be called after my name."

And David gathered all the people together, and went to Rabbah, and fought against it, and took it. And he took their king's crown from off his head, the weight whereof was a talent of gold, with the precious stones: and it was set on David's head.

And he brought forth the spoil of the city in great abundance. And he brought forth the people that were therein, and put them under saws, and under harrows of iron, and under axes of iron, and made them pass through the brick-kiln.[2] And thus did he unto all the cities of the children of Ammon. So David and all the people returned unto Jerusalem.

Absalom Avenges Tamar

Thirteen   And it came to pass after this, that Absalom the son of David had a fair sister, whose name was Tamar; and Amnon the son of David loved her. And Amnon was so vexed, that he fell sick for his sister Tamar; for she was a virgin, and Amnon thought it hard for him to do any thing to her. But Amnon had a friend, whose name was Jonadab, the son of Shimeah, David's brother: and Jonadab was a very subtle man. And he said unto him, "Why art thou, being a king's son, lean from day to day? Wilt thou not tell me?" And Amnon said unto him, "I love Tamar my brother Absalom's sister." And Jonadab said unto him, "Lay thee down on thy bed, and make thyself sick: and when thy father cometh to see thee, say unto him, 'I pray thee, let my sister Tamar come, and give me meat, and dress the meat in my sight, that I may see it, and eat it at her hand.' "

So Amnon lay down, and made himself sick: and when the king was come to see him, Amnon said unto the king, "I pray thee, let Tamar my sister come, and make me a couple of cakes in my sight, that I may eat at her hand." Then David sent home to Tamar, saying, "Go now to thy brother Amnon's house, and dress him meat." So Tamar went to her brother Amnon's house (and he was laid down), and she took flour, and kneaded it, and made cakes in his sight, and did bake the cakes. And she took a pan, and poured them out before him, but he refused to eat. And Amnon said, "Have out all men from me." And they went out every man from him.

2 *put them . . . brick kiln: i.e.,* David put the captives to work with saws, harrows, and axes and made them operate brick furnaces.

And Amnon said unto Tamar, "Bring the meat into the chamber, that I may eat of thine hand." And Tamar took the cakes which she had made, and brought them into the chamber to Amnon her brother. And when she had brought them unto him to eat, he took hold of her, and said unto her, "Come lie with me, my sister." And she answered him, "Nay, my brother, do not force me; for no such thing ought to be done in Israel: do not thou this folly. And I, whither shall I cause my shame to go? and as for thee, thou shalt be as one of the fools in Israel. Now therefore, I pray thee, speak unto the king, for he will not withhold me from thee." Howbeit he would not hearken unto her voice, but being stronger than she, forced her, and lay with her.

Then Amnon hated her exceedingly; so that the hatred wherewith he hated her was greater than the love wherewith he had loved her. And Amnon said unto her, "Arise, be gone." And she said unto him, "There is no cause: this evil in sending me away is greater than the other that thou didst unto me." But he would not hearken unto her. Then he called his servant that ministered unto him, and said, "Put now this woman out from me, and bolt the door after her." And she had a garment of diverse colours upon her, for with such robes were the king's daughters that were virgins apparelled. Then his servant brought her out, and bolted the door after her.

And Tamar put ashes on her head, and rent her garment of diverse colours that was on her, and laid her hand on her head, and went on, crying. And Absalom her brother said unto her, "Hath Amnon thy brother been with thee? But hold now thy peace, my sister: he is thy brother; regard not this thing." So Tamar remained desolate in her brother Absalom's house.

But when King David heard of all these things, he was very wroth. And Absalom spake unto his brother Amnon neither good nor bad: for Absalom hated Amnon, because he had forced his sister Tamar.

And it came to pass after two full years, that Absalom had sheep-shearers in Baal-hazor, which is beside Ephraim: and Absalom invited all the king's sons. And Absalom came to the king, and said, "Behold now, thy servant hath sheep-shearers; let the king, I beseech thee, and his servants, go with thy servant."

And the king said to Absalom, "Nay, my son, let us not all now go, lest we be chargeable unto thee." And he pressed him: howbeit he would not go, but blessed him. Then said Absalom, "If not, I pray thee, let my brother Amnon go with us." And the king said unto him, "Why should he go with thee?" But Absalom pressed him, that he let Amnon and all the king's sons go with him.

Now Absalom had commanded his servants, saying, "Mark ye now when Amnon's heart is merry with wine, and when I say unto you, 'Smite Amnon,' then kill him, fear not: have not I commanded you? Be courageous, and be valiant." And the servants of Absalom did unto Amnon as Absalom had commanded. Then all the king's sons arose, and every man got him up upon his mule, and fled.

And it came to pass, while they were in the way, that tidings came to David, saying, "Absalom hath slain all the king's sons, and there is not one of them left." Then the king arose, and tore his garments, and lay on the earth; and all his servants stood by with their clothes rent. And Jonadab, the son of Shimeah, David's brother, answered and said, "Let not my lord suppose that they have slain all the young men the king's sons; for Amnon only is dead: for by the appointment of Absalom this hath been determined, from the day that he forced his sister Tamar. Now therefore let not my lord the king take the thing to his heart, to think that all the king's sons are dead: for Amnon only is dead."

But Absalom fled. And the young man that kept the watch lifted up his eyes, and looked, and behold, there came much people by the way of the hillside behind him. And Jonadab said unto the king, "Behold, the king's sons come: as thy servant said, so it is." And it came to pass as soon as he had made an end of speaking, that behold, the king's sons came, and lifted up their voice, and wept: and the king also and all his servants wept very sore.

But Absalom fled, and went to Talmai the son of Ammihud, king of Geshur: and David mourned for his son every day. So Absalom fled, and went to Geshur, and was there three years. And the soul of King David longed to go forth unto Absalom: for he was comforted concerning Amnon, seeing he was dead.

The Rift between David and Absalom

Fourteen Now Joab the son of Zeruiah perceived that the king's heart was toward Absalom. And Joab sent to Tekoah, and fetched thence a wise woman, and said unto her, "I pray thee, feign thyself to be a mourner, and put on now mourning apparel, and anoint not thyself with oil, but be as a woman that had a long time mourned for the dead: and come to the king, and speak on this manner unto him." So Joab put the words in her mouth.

And when the woman of Tekoah spake to the king, she fell on her face to the ground, and did obeisance, and said, "Help, O king." And the king said unto her, "What aileth thee?" And she answered, "I am indeed a widow woman, and mine husband is dead. And thy handmaid had two sons, and they two strove together in the field, and there was none to part them, but the one smote the other, and slew him. And behold, the whole family is risen against thine handmaid, and they said, 'Deliver him that smote his brother, that we may kill him, for the life of his brother whom he slew; and we will destroy the heir also': and so they shall quench my coal which is left, and shall not leave to my husband neither name nor remainder upon the earth."

And the king said unto the woman, "Go to thine house, and I will give charge concerning thee." And the woman of Tekoah said unto the king, "My lord, O king, the iniquity be on me, and on my father's house: and the king and his throne be guiltless." And the king said, "Whosoever saith aught unto thee, bring him to me, and he shall not touch thee any more."

Then said she, "I pray thee, let the king remember the Lord thy God, that thou wouldst not suffer the revengers of blood to destroy any more, lest they destroy my son." And he said, "As the Lord liveth, there shall not one hair of thy son fall to the earth." Then the woman said, "Let thine handmaid, I pray thee, speak one word unto my lord the king." And he said, "Say on."

And the woman said, "Wherefore then hast thou thought such a thing against the people of God? For the king doth speak this thing as one which is faulty, in that the king doth not fetch home again his banished. For we must needs die, and are as water spilt on the ground, which cannot be gathered up again: neither doth God respect any person: yet doth he devise means, that his banished be not expelled from him.

"Now therefore that I am come to speak of this thing unto my lord the king, it is because the people have made me afraid: and thy handmaid said, 'I will now speak unto the king, it may be that the king will perform the request of his handmaid. For the king will hear, to deliver his handmaid out of the hand of the man that would destroy me and my son together out of the inheritance of God.' Then thine handmaid said, 'The word of my lord the king shall now be comfortable': for as an angel of God, so is my lord the king to discern good and bad: therefore the Lord thy God will be with thee."

Then the king answered and said unto the woman, "Hide not from me, I pray thee, the thing that I shall ask thee." And the woman said, "Let my lord the king now speak." And the king said, "Is not the hand of Joab with thee in all this?" And the woman answered and said, "As thy soul liveth, my lord the king, none can turn to the right hand or to the left from aught that my lord the king hath spoken: for thy servant Joab, he bade me, and he put all these words in the mouth of thine handmaid. To fetch about this form of speech hath thy servant Joab done this thing: and my lord is wise, according to the wisdom of an angel of God, to know all things that are in the earth."

And the king said unto Joab, "Behold now, I have done this thing: go therefore, bring the young man Absalom again." And Joab fell to the ground on his face, and bowed himself, and thanked the king: and Joab said, "Today thy servant knoweth that I have found grace in thy sight, my lord, O king, in that the king hath fulfilled the request of his servant."

So Joab arose, and went to Geshur, and brought Absalom to Jerusalem. And the king said, "Let him turn to his own house, and let him not see my face." So Absalom returned to his own house, and saw not the king's face.

But in all Israel there was none to be so much praised as Absalom for his beauty: from the sole of his foot even to the crown of his head, there was no blemish in him. And when he polled his head, (for it was at every year's end that he polled it:

because the hair was heavy on him, therefore he polled it), he weighed the hair of his head at two hundred shekels after the king's weight. And unto Absalom there were born three sons, and one daughter, whose name was Tamar: she was a woman of a fair countenance.

So Absalom dwelt two full years in Jerusalem, and saw not the king's face. Therefore Absalom sent for Joab, to have sent him to the king, but he would not come to him: and when he sent again the second time, he would not come. Therefore he said unto his servants, "See, Joab's field is near mine, and he hath barley there; go, and set it on fire." And Absalom's servants set the field on fire. Then Joab arose, and came to Absalom unto his house, and said unto him, "Wherefore have thy servants set my field on fire?" And Absalom answered Joab, "Behold, I sent unto thee, saying, 'Come hither, that I may send thee to the king, to say, "Wherefore am I come from Geshur? It had been good for me to have been there still": now therefore let me see the king's face; and if there be any iniquity in me, let him kill me.' "

So Joab came to the king, and told him: and when he had called for Absalom, he came to the king, and bowed himself on his face to the ground before the king: and the king kissed Absalom.

Absalom's Conspiracy against David

Fifteen And it came to pass after this, that Absalom prepared him chariots and horses, and fifty men to run before him. And Absalom rose up early, and stood beside the way of the gate: and it was so, that when any man that had a controversy came to the king for judgment, then Absalom called unto him, and said, "Of what city art thou?" And he said, "Thy servant is of one of the tribes of Israel." And Absalom said unto him, "See, thy matters are good and right, but there is no man deputed of the king to hear thee." Absalom said moreover, "Oh that I were made judge in the land, that every man which hath any suit or cause might come unto me, and I would do him justice!" And it was so, that when any man came nigh to him, to do him obeisance, he put forth his hand, and took him, and kissed him. And on this manner did

Absalom to all Israel that came to the king for judgment: so Absalom stole the hearts of the men of Israel.

And it came to pass after forty[3] years, that Absalom said unto the king, "I pray thee, let me go and pay my vow which I have vowed unto the Lord in Hebron. For thy servant vowed a vow while I abode at Geshur in Syria, saying, 'If the Lord shall bring me again indeed to Jerusalem, then I will serve the Lord.' " And the king said unto him, "Go in peace." So he arose, and went to Hebron.

But Absalom sent spies throughout all the tribes of Israel, saying, "As soon as ye hear the sound of the trumpet, then ye shall say, 'Absalom reigneth in Hebron.' " And with Absalom went two hundred men out of Jerusalem, that were called; and they went in their simplicity, and they knew not any thing. And Absalom sent for Ahithophel the Gilonite, David's counsellor, from his city, even from Giloh, while he offered sacrifices. And the conspiracy was strong; for the people increased continually with Absalom.

And there came a messenger to David, saying, "The hearts of the men of Israel are after Absalom." And David said unto all his servants that were with him at Jerusalem, "Arise, and let us flee; for we shall not else escape from Absalom: make speed to depart, lest he overtake us suddenly, and bring evil upon us, and smite the city with the edge of the sword." And the king's servants said unto the king, "Behold, thy servants are ready to do whatsoever my lord the king shall appoint."

And the king went forth, and all his household after him. And the king left ten women, which were concubines, to keep the house. And the king went forth, and all the people after him, and tarried in a place that was far off. And all his servants passed on beside him: and all the Cherethites, and all the Pelethites, and all the Gittites, six hundred men which came after him from Gath, passed on before the king.

Then said the king to Ittai the Gittite, "Wherefore goest thou also with us? Return to thy place, and abide with the king: for thou art a stranger, and also an exile. Whereas thou camest but

3 *forty:* "Four" is probably the true reading here.

yesterday, should I this day make thee go up and down with us? Seeing I go whither I may, return thou, and take back thy brethren: mercy and truth be with thee."

And Ittai answered the king, and said, "As the Lord liveth, and as my lord the king liveth, surely in what place my lord the king shall be, whether in death or life, even there also will thy servant be." And David said to Ittai, "Go and pass over." And Ittai the Gittite passed over, and all his men, and all the little ones that were with him. And all the country wept with a loud voice, and all the people passed over: the king also himself passed over the brook Kidron, and all the people passed over, toward the way of the wilderness.

And lo, Zadok also, and all the Levites were with him, bearing the ark of the covenant of God: and they set down the ark of God; and Abiathar went up, until all the people had done passing out of the city. And the king said unto Zadok, "Carry back the ark of God into the city: if I shall find favour in the eyes of the Lord, he will bring me again, and show me both it and his habitation. But if he thus say, 'I have no delight in thee': behold, here am I, let him do to me as seemeth good unto him." The king said also unto Zadok the priest, "Art not thou a seer? Return into the city in peace, and your two sons with you, Ahimaaz thy son, and Jonathan the son of Abiathar. See, I will tarry in the plain of the wilderness, until there come word from you to certify me." Zadok therefore and Abiathar carried the ark of God again to Jerusalem: and they tarried there.

And David went up by the ascent of mount Olivet, and wept as he went up, and had his head covered, and he went barefoot: and all the people that was with him covered every man his head, and they went up, weeping as they went up.

And one told David, saying, "Ahithophel is among the conspirators with Absalom." And David said, "O Lord, I pray thee turn the counsel of Ahithophel into foolishness." And it came to pass, that when David was come to the top of the mount, where he worshipped God, behold, Hushai the Archite came to meet him, with his coat rent, and earth upon his head: unto whom David said, "If thou passest on with me, then thou shalt be a burden unto me. But if thou return to the city, and say unto

Absalom, 'I will be thy servant, O king; as I have been thy father's servant hitherto, so will I now also be thy servant': then mayest thou for me defeat the counsel of Ahithophel. And hast thou not there with thee Zadok and Abiathar the priests? therefore it shall be, that what thing soever thou shalt hear out of the king's house, thou shalt tell it to Zadok and Abiathar the priests. Behold, they have there with them their two sons, Ahimaaz, Zadok's son, and Jonathan, Abiathar's son: and by them ye shall send unto me every thing that ye can hear." So Hushai David's friend came into the city, and Absalom came into Jerusalem.

Sixteen And when David was a little past the top of the hill, behold, Ziba the servant of Mephibosheth[4] met him with a couple of asses saddled, and upon them two hundred loaves of bread, and an hundred bunches of raisins, and an hundred of summer fruits, and a bottle of wine. And the king said unto Ziba, "What meanest thou by these?" And Ziba said, "The asses be for the king's household to ride on; and the bread and summer fruit for the young men to eat, and the wine, that such as be faint in the wilderness may drink."

And the king said, "And where is thy master's son?" And Ziba said unto the king, "Behold, he abideth at Jerusalem: for he said, 'Today shall the house of Israel restore me the kingdom of my father.'" Then said the king to Ziba, "Behold, thine are all that pertained unto Mephibosheth." And Ziba said, "I humbly beseech thee that I may find grace in thy sight, my lord, O king."

And when King David came to Bahurim, behold, thence came out a man of the family of the house of Saul, whose name was Shimei, the son of Gera: he came forth, and cursed still as he came. And he cast stones at David, and at all the servants of King David: and all the people, and all the mighty men were on his right hand and on his left. And thus said Shimei when he cursed, "Come out, come out, thou bloody man, and thou man of Belial. The Lord hath returned upon thee all the blood of the house of Saul, in whose stead thou hast reigned; and the

---

4 *Mephibosheth:* the lame son of Jonathan, to whom David had shown much kindness.

Lord hath delivered the kingdom into the hand of Absalom thy son: and behold, thou art taken in thy mischief, because thou art a bloody man."

Then said Abishai the son of Zeruiah unto the king, "Why should this dead dog curse my lord the king? let me go over, I pray thee, and take off his head." And the king said, "What have I to do with you, ye sons of Zeruiah? So let him curse, because the Lord hath said unto him, 'Curse David.' Who shall then say, 'Wherefore hast thou done so?'"

And David said to Abishai, and to all his servants, "Behold, my son, which came forth of my bowels, seeketh my life: how much more now may this Benjamite do it? let him alone, and let him curse; for the Lord hath bidden him. It may be that the Lord will look on mine affliction, and that the Lord will requite me good for his cursing this day."

And as David and his men went by the way, Shimei went along on the hill's side over against him, and cursed as he went, and threw stones at him, and cast dust. And the king, and all the people that were with him, came weary, and refreshed themselves there.

And Absalom, and all the people the men of Israel, came to Jerusalem, and Ahithophel with him. And it came to pass when Hushai the Archite, David's friend, was come unto Absalom, that Hushai said unto Absalom, "God save the king, God save the king." And Absalom said to Hushai, "Is this thy kindness to thy friend? Why wentest thou not with thy friend?" And Hushai said unto Absalom, "Nay, but whom the Lord, and this people, and all the men of Israel choose, his will I be, and with him will I abide. And again, whom should I serve? should I not serve in the presence of his son? As I have served in thy father's presence, so will I be in thy presence."

Then said Absalom to Ahithophel, "Give counsel among you what we shall do." And Ahithophel said unto Absalom, "Go in unto thy father's concubines, which he hath left to keep the house; and all Israel shall hear that thou art abhorred of thy father: then shall the hands of all that are with thee be strong." So they spread Absalom a tent upon the top of the house; and Absalom went in unto his father's concubines, in the sight of all

Israel. And the counsel of Ahithophel, which he counselled in those days, was as if a man had inquired at the oracle of God: so was all the counsel of Ahithophel both with David and with Absalom.

Seventeen Moreover Ahithophel said unto Absalom, "Let me now choose out twelve thousand men, and I will arise and pursue after David this night. And I will come upon him while he is weary and weak-handed, and will make him afraid: and all the people that are with him shall flee; and I will smite the king only. And I will bring back all the people unto thee: the man whom thou seekest is as if all returned: so all the people shall be in peace." And the saying pleased Absalom well, and all the elders of Israel.

Then said Absalom, "Call now Hushai the Archite also, and let us hear likewise what he saith." And when Hushai was come to Absalom, Absalom spake unto him, saying, "Ahithophel hath spoken after this manner: shall we do after his saying? if not, speak thou."

And Hushai said unto Absalom, "The counsel that Ahithophel hath given is not good at this time. For," said Hushai, "thou knowest thy father and his men, that they be mighty men, and they chafed in their minds, as a bear robbed of her whelps in the field: and thy father is a man of war, and will not lodge with the people. Behold, he is hid now in some pit, or in some other place: and it will come to pass, when some of them be overthrown at the first, that whosoever heareth it will say, 'There is a slaughter among the people that follow Absalom.' And he also that is valiant, whose heart is as the heart of a lion, shall utterly melt: for all Israel knoweth that thy father is a mighty man, and they which be with him are valiant men.

"Therefore I counsel that all Israel be generally gathered unto thee, from Dan even to Beer-sheba, as the sand that is by the sea for multitude, and that thou go to battle in thine own person. So shall we come upon him in some place where he shall be found, and we will light upon him as the dew falleth on the ground: and of him and of all the men that are with him, there shall not be left so much as one. Moreover, if he be gotten into a city, then shall all Israel bring ropes to that city, and we will draw it into the river, until there be not one small stone found there."

And Absalom and all the men of Israel said, "The counsel of Hushai the Archite is better than the counsel of Ahithophel." For the Lord had appointed to defeat the good counsel of Ahithophel, to the intent that the Lord might bring evil upon Absalom.

Then said Hushai unto Zadok and to Abiathar the priests, "Thus and thus did Ahithophel counsel Absalom and the elders of Israel; and thus have I counselled. Now therefore send quickly, and tell David, saying, 'Lodge not this night in the plains of the wilderness, but speedily pass over; lest the king be swallowed up, and all the people that are with him.' "

Now Jonathan and Ahimaaz stayed by En-rogel, for they might not be seen to come into the city: and a wench went and told them; and they went, and told King David. Nevertheless, a lad saw them, and told Absalom: but they went both of them away quickly, and came to a man's house in Bahurim, which had a well in his court, whither they went down. And the woman took and spread a covering over the well's mouth, and spread ground corn thereon; and the thing was not known. And when Absalom's servants came to the woman to the house, they said, "Where is Ahimaaz and Jonathan?" And the woman said unto them, "They be gone over the brook of water." And when they had sought, and could not find them, they returned to Jerusalem.

And it came to pass, after they had departed, that they came up out of the well, and went and told King David, and said unto David, "Arise, and pass quickly over the water: for thus hath Ahithophel counselled against you." Then David arose, and all the people that were with him, and they passed over Jordan: by the morning light there lacked not one of them that was not gone over Jordan.

And when Ahithophel saw that his counsel was not followed, he saddled his ass, and arose, and got him home to his house, to his city, and put his household in order, and hanged himself, and died, and was buried in the sepulchre of his father.

Then David came to Mahanaim. And Absalom passed over Jordan, he and all the men of Israel with him. And Absalom made Amasa captain of the host instead of Joab: which Amasa was a man's son whose name was Ithra, an Israelite, that went in to Abigail the daughter of Nahash, sister to Zeruiah, Joab's mother. So Israel and Absalom pitched in the land of Gilead.

And it came to pass, when David was come to Mahanaim, that Shobi the son of Nahash of Rabbah of the children of Ammon, and Machir the son of Ammiel of Lodebar, and Barzillai the Gileadite of Rogelim, brought beds, and basins, and earthen vessels, and wheat, and barley, and flour, and parched corn, and beans, and lentils, and parched pulse, and honey, and butter, and sheep, and cheese of kine for David, and for the people that were with him, to eat: for they said, "The people is hungry, and weary, and thirsty in the wilderness."

Eighteen And David numbered the people that were with him, and set captains of thousands and captains of hundreds over them. And David sent forth a third part of the people under the hand of Joab, and a third part under the hand of Abishai the son of Zeruiah, Joab's brother, and a third part under the hand of Ittai the Gittite. And the king said unto the people, "I will surely go forth with you myself also." But the people answered, "Thou shalt not go forth: for if we flee away, they will not care for us, neither if half of us die will they care for us: but now thou art worth ten thousand of us: therefore now it is better that thou succor us out of the city." And the king said unto them, "What seemeth you best I will do."

And the king stood by the gate side, and all the people came out by hundreds and by thousands. And the king commanded Joab, and Abishai, and Ittai, saying, "Deal gently for my sake with the young man, even with Absalom." And all the people heard when the king gave all the captains charge concerning Absalom.

So the people went out into the field against Israel: and the battle was in the woods of Ephraim, where the people of Israel were slain before the servants of David, and there was there a great slaughter that day of twenty thousand men. For the battle was there scattered over the face of all the country: and the wood devoured more people that day than the sword devoured.

Death of Absalom

And Absalom met the servants of David. And Absalom rode upon a mule, and the mule went under the thick boughs of a great oak, and his head caught hold of the oak, and he was taken up between the heaven and the earth; and the mule that was under him went away. And a certain man saw it, and told Joab, and said, "Behold, I saw Absalom hanged in an oak."

And Joab said unto the man that told him, "And behold, thou sawest him, and why didst thou not smite him there to the ground? and I would have given thee ten shekels of silver, and a girdle." And the man said unto Joab, "Though I should receive a thousand shekels of silver in mine hand, yet would I not put forth mine hand against the king's son: for in our hearing the king charged thee, and Abishai, and Ittai, saying, 'Beware that none touch the young man Absalom.' Otherwise, I should have wrought falsehood against mine own life: for there is no matter hid from the king, and thou thyself wouldest have set thyself against me."

Then said Joab, "I may not tarry thus with thee." And he took three darts in his hand, and thrust them through the heart of Absalom, while he was yet alive in the midst of the oak. And ten young men that bare Joab's armour compassed about and smote Absalom, and slew him. And Joab blew the trumpet, and the people returned from pursuing after Israel: for Joab held back the people. And they took Absalom, and cast him into a great pit in the wood, and laid a very great heap of stones upon him: and all Israel fled every one to his tent.

Now Absalom in his lifetime had taken and reared up for himself a pillar, which is in the king's dale: for he said, "I have no son to keep my name in remembrance." And he called the pillar after his own name: and it is called unto this day Absalom's place.

Then said Ahimaaz the son of Zadok, "Let me now run, and bear the king tidings, how that the Lord hath avenged him of his enemies." And Joab said unto him, "Thou shalt not bear tidings this day, but thou shalt bear tidings another day: but this day thou shalt bear no tidings, because the king's son is dead." Then said Joab to Cushi, "Go tell the king what thou hast seen." And

Cushi bowed himself unto Joab, and ran. Then said Ahimaaz the son of Zadok yet again to Joab, "But howsoever, let me, I pray thee, also run after Cushi." And Joab said, "Wherefore wilt thou run, my son, seeing that thou hast no tidings ready?" "But howsoever," said he, "let me run." And he said unto him, "Run." Then Ahimaaz ran by the way of the plain, and overran Cushi.

And David sat between the two gates: and the watchman went up to the roof over the gate unto the wall, and lifted up his eyes, and looked, and behold, a man running alone. And the watchman cried, and told the king. And the king said, "If he be alone, there is tidings in his mouth." And he came apace, and drew near. And the watchman saw another man running: and the watchman called unto the porter, and said, "Behold, another man running alone." And the king said, "He also bringeth tidings." And the watchman said, "Me thinketh the running of the foremost is like the running of Ahimaaz the son of Zadok." And the king said, "He is a good man, and cometh with good tidings."

And Ahimaaz called, and said unto the king, "All is well." And he fell down to the earth, upon his face before the king, and said, "Blessed be the Lord thy God which hath delivered up the men that lifted up their hand against my lord the king." And the king said, "Is the young man Absalom safe?" And Ahimaaz answered, "When Joab sent the king's servant, and me thy servant, I saw a great tumult, but I knew not what it was." And the king said unto him, "Turn aside and stand here." And he turned aside, and stood still.

And behold, Cushi came; and Cushi said, "Tidings my lord the king: for the Lord hath avenged thee this day of all them that rose up against thee." And the king said unto Cushi, "Is the young man Absalom safe?" And Cushi answered, "The enemies of my lord the king, and all that rise against thee to do thee hurt, be as that young man is."

And the king was much moved, and went up to the chamber over the gate, and wept: and as he went, thus he said, "O my son Absalom! my son, my son Absalom! would God I had died for thee, O Absalom, my son, my son!"

I Kings

The Death of David

One Now King David was old, and stricken in years, and they covered him with clothes, but he got no heat. Wherefore his servants said unto him, "Let there be sought for my lord the king a young virgin, and let her stand before the king, and let her cherish him, and let her lie in thy bosom, that my lord the king may get heat." So they sought for a fair damsel throughout all the coasts of Israel, and found Abishag a Shunammite, and brought her to the king. And the damsel was very fair, and cherished the king, and ministered to him: but the king knew her not.

Then Adonijah the son of Haggith exalted himself, saying, "I will be king": and he prepared him chariots and horsemen, and fifty men to run before him. And his father had not displeased him at any time in saying, "Why hast thou done so?" And he also was a very goodly man, and his mother bare him after Absalom. And he conferred with Joab the son of Zeruiah, and with Abiathar the priest: and they following Adonijah, helped him. But Zadok the priest, and Benaiah the son of Jehoiada, and Nathan the prophet, and Shimei, and Rei, and the mighty men which belonged to David, were not with Adonijah. And Adonijah slew sheep, and oxen, and fat cattle, by the stone of Zoheleth, which is by En-rogel, and called all his brethren the king's sons, and all the men of Judah the king's servants. But Nathan the prophet, and Benaiah, and the mighty men, and Solomon his brother, he called not.

Wherefore Nathan spake unto Bathsheba the mother of Solomon, saying, "Hast thou not heard that Adonijah the son of Haggith doth reign, and David our lord knoweth it not? Now therefore come, let me, I pray thee, give thee counsel, that thou mayest save thine own life, and the life of thy son Solomon. Go, and get thee in unto King David, and say unto him, 'Didst not thou, my lord, O king, swear unto thine handmaid, saying, "Assuredly Solomon thy son shall reign after me, and he shall sit upon my throne"? why then doth Adonijah reign?' Behold, while thou yet talkest there with the king, I also will come in after thee, and confirm thy words."

And Bathsheba went in unto the king into the chamber: and the king was very old, and Abishag the Shunammite ministered unto the king. And Bathsheba bowed, and did obeisance unto the king: and the king said, "What wouldest thou?" And she said unto him, "My lord, thou swarest by the Lord thy God unto thine handmaid, saying, 'Assuredly Solomon thy son shall reign after me, and he shall sit upon my throne.' And now behold, Adonijah reigneth; and now, my lord the king, thou knowest it not. And he hath slain oxen, and fat cattle, and sheep in abundance, and hath called all the sons of the king, and Abiathar the priest, and Joab the captain of the host: but Solomon thy servant hath he not called. And thou, my lord, O king, the eyes of all Israel are upon thee, that thou shouldest tell them who shall sit on the throne of my lord the king after him. Otherwise it shall come to pass, when my lord the king shall sleep with his fathers, that I and my son Solomon shall be counted offenders."

And lo, while she yet talked with the king, Nathan the prophet also came in. And they told the king, saying, "Behold Nathan the prophet." And when he was come in before the king, he bowed himself before the king with his face to the ground. And Nathan said, "My lord O king, hast thou said, 'Adonijah shall reign after me, and he shall sit upon my throne'? For he is gone down this day, and hath slain oxen, and fat cattle, and sheep in abundance, and hath called all the king's sons, and the captains of the host, and Abiathar the priest: and behold, they eat and drink before him, and say, 'God save King Adonijah.' But me, even me thy servant, and Zadok the priest, and Benaiah the son of

Jehoiada, and thy servant Solomon, hath he not called. Is this thing done by my lord the king, and thou hast not showed it unto thy servant, who should sit on the throne of my lord the king after him?"

Then King David answered, and said, "Call me Bathsheba." And she came into the king's presence, and stood before the king. And the king sware, and said, "As the Lord liveth, that hath redeemed my soul out of all distress, even as I sware unto thee by the Lord God of Israel, saying, 'Assuredly Solomon thy son shall reign after me, and he shall sit upon my throne in my stead'; even so will I certainly do this day." Then Bathsheba bowed with her face to the earth, and did reverence to the king, and said, "Let my lord King David live for ever."

And King David said, "Call me Zadok the priest, and Nathan the prophet, and Benaiah the son of Jehoiada." And they came before the king. The king also said unto them, "Take with you the servants of your lord, and cause Solomon my son to ride upon mine own mule, and bring him down to Gihon. And let Zadok the priest, and Nathan the prophet anoint him there king over Israel: and blow ye with the trumpet, and say, 'God save King Solomon.' Then ye shall come up after him, that he may come and sit upon my throne; for he shall be king in my stead: and I have appointed him to be ruler over Israel, and over Judah." And Benaiah the son of Jehoiada answered the king, and said, "Amen: the Lord God of my lord the king say so too. As the Lord hath been with my lord the king, even so be he with Solomon, and make his throne greater than the throne of my lord King David."

So Zadok the priest, and Nathan the prophet, and Benaiah the son of Jehoiada, and the Cherethites, and the Pelethites, went down, and caused Solomon to ride upon King David's mule, and brought him to Gihon. And Zadok the priest took an horn of oil out of the tabernacle, and anointed Solomon: and they blew the trumpet, and all the people said, "God save King Solomon." And all the people came up after him, and the people piped with pipes, and rejoiced with great joy, so that the earth rent with the sound of them.

And Adonijah and all the guests that were with him heard it as they had made an end of eating. And when Joab heard the sound of the trumpet, he said, "Wherefore is this noise of the city, being in an uproar?" And while he yet spake, behold, Jonathan the son of Abiathar the priest came, and Adonijah said unto him, "Come in, for thou art a valiant man, and bringest good tidings." And Jonathan answered, and said to Adonijah, "Verily our lord King David hath made Solomon king. And the king hath sent with him Zadok the priest, and Nathan the prophet, and Benaiah the son of Jehoiada, and the Cherethites, and the Pelethites, and they have caused him to ride upon the king's mule. And Zadok the priest and Nathan the prophet have anointed him king in Gihon: and they are come up from thence rejoicing, so that the city rang again: this is the noise that ye have heard. And also Solomon sitteth on the throne of the kingdom. And moreover, the king's servants came to bless our lord King David, saying, 'God make the name of Solomon better than thy name, and make his throne greater than thy throne.' And the king bowed himself upon the bed. And also thus said the king 'Blessed be the Lord God of Israel, which hath given one to sit on my throne this day, mine eyes even seeing it.'" And all the guests that were with Adonijah were afraid, and rose up, and went every man his way.

And Adonijah feared because of Solomon, and arose, and went, and caught hold on the horns of the altar. And it was told Solomon, saying, "Behold, Adonijah feareth King Solomon: for lo, he hath caught hold on the horns of the altar, saying, 'Let King Solomon swear unto me today that he will not slay his servant with the sword.'" And Solomon said, "If he will show himself a worthy man, there shall not an hair of him fall to the earth: but if wickedness shall be found in him, he shall die." So King Solomon sent, and they brought him down from the altar, and he came and bowed himself to King Solomon: and Solomon said unto him, "Go to thine house."

Two Now the days of David drew nigh, that he should die, and he charged Solomon his son, saying, "I go the way of all the earth: be thou strong therefore, and show thyself a man. And keep the

charge of the Lord thy god, to walk in his ways, to keep his statutes, and his commandments, and his judgments, and his testi-
monies as it is written in the law of Moses, that thou mayest prosper in all that thou doest, and whithersoever thou turnest thyself:
that the Lord may continue his word which he spake concerning
me, saying, 'If thy children take heed to their way, to walk
before me in truth, with all their heart, and with all their soul,
there shall not fail thee (said he) a man on the throne of Israel.'
Moreover thou knowest also what Joab the son of Zeruiah did to
me, and what he did to the two captains of the hosts of Israel,
unto Abner the son of Ner, and unto Amasa the son of Jether,
whom he slew, and shed the blood of war in peace, and put the
blood of war upon his girdle that was about his loins, and in his
shoes that were on his feet. Do therefore according to thy wisdom,
and let not his hoar head go down to the grave in peace. But
show kindness unto the sons of Barzillai the Gileadite, and let
them be of those that eat at thy table: for so they came to me
when I fled because of Absalom thy brother. And behold, thou
hast with thee Shimei the son of Gera, a Benjamite of Bahurim,
which cursed me with a grievous curse in the day when I went to
Mahanaim: but he came down to meet me at Jordan, and I sware
to him by the Lord, saying, 'I will not put thee to death with the
sword.' Now therefore hold him not guiltless: for thou art a wise
man, and knowest what thou oughtest to do unto him, but his
hoar head bring thou down to the grave with blood." So David
slept with his fathers, and was buried in the city of David. And the
days that David reigned over Israel were forty years: seven years
reigned he in Hebron, and thirty and three years reigned he in
Jerusalem.

Then sat Solomon upon the throne of David his father, and his
kingdom was established greatly. . . .

And the Lord took me as I followed the flock,
And the Lord said unto me,
"Go prophesy unto my people Israel."

Seated Old Man
National Gallery of Art, Washington, D.C.
Rosenwald Collection

The Prophets

As can be seen from the earlier stories, the children of Israel
had a tradition rich in prophecy of various sorts. There were
the "prophet-counselors" such as Moses, Samuel, and Nathan
who spoke to the consciences of princes and common people
alike. There were also the traveling bands of prophets who
foretold the future and were known by their ecstatic religious
behavior — dancing, singing, and falling into trances. Samuel
is referring to such men when he says to Saul, "Thou shalt meet
a company of prophets coming down from the high place, with
. . . a pipe, and a harp before them, and they shall prophesy.
And the spirit of the Lord will come upon thee, and thou shalt
prophesy with them, and shalt be turned into another man."

But the great age of prophecy begins with Amos in the 8th
century B.C. and lasts for three or four centuries. These men
are known as the "ethical" prophets because of the nature of
their teaching and as the "literary" prophets because unlike
their predecessors', their words were written down in separate
books. For the most part their prophecies are pessimistic and
often angry, concerned with personal ethics and uttered as a goad
to conscience. They express a new concern for the poor and
downtrodden and for social justice. Also from their writings
emerges a new concept of God — a God who is righteous, loving,
and just, who is not merely the God of Israel but of all nations,
who is the only God.

Amos

Amos was "an herdman, and a gatherer of sycamore fruit" who made his prophecies in about 750 B.C. Although he lived in Judah, the southern kingdom, he apparently preached only in Israel, the northern kingdom. (After the death of Solomon in 930 B.C. the kingdom of Israel was divided into two parts.) When Amos predicted that prosperous Israel would soon be destroyed — the punishment of a corrupt people by a righteous God — no one believed him. But shortly after Amos's prophecies, Israel's powerful neighbor Assyria began a march of conquest, and in 721 B.C. Israel was conquered and many of her people were deported to other parts of the Assyrian empire. It was almost exactly as Amos had predicted.

3   Hear this word that the Lord hath spoken against you, O children of Israel, against the whole family which I brought up from the land of Egypt, saying,

You only have I known of all the families of the earth: therefore I will punish you for all your iniquities.

Can two walk together, except they be agreed?

Will a lion roar in the forest, when he hath no prey? Will a young lion cry out of his den, if he have taken nothing?

Can a bird fall in a snare upon the earth, where no gin is for him? shall one take up a snare from the earth, and have taken nothing at all?

Shall a trumpet be blown in the city, and the people not be afraid? shall there be evil in a city, and the Lord hath not done it?

Surely the Lord God will do nothing, but he revealeth his secret unto his servants the prophets.

The lion hath roared, who will not fear? the Lord God hath spoken, who can but prophesy?

Publish in the palaces at Ashdod, and in the palaces in the land of Egypt, and say, "Assemble yourselves upon the mountains of Samaria," and behold the great tumults in the midst thereof, and the oppressed in the midst thereof.

For they know not to do right, saith the Lord, who store up violence and robbery in their palaces.

Therefore thus saith the Lord God; An adversary there shall be even round about the land; and he shall bring down thy strength from thee, and thy palaces shall be spoiled.

Thus saith the Lord; As the shepherd taketh out of the mouth of the lion two legs, or a piece of an ear; so shall the children of Israel be taken out that dwell in Samaria in the corner of a bed, and in Damascus in a couch.

Hear ye, and testify in the house of Jacob, saith the Lord God, the God of hosts,

That in the day that I shall visit the transgressions of Israel upon him I will also visit the altars of Bethel: and the horns of the altar shall be cut off, and fall to the ground.

And I will smite the winter house with the summer house; and the houses of ivory shall perish, and the great houses shall have an end, saith the Lord.

4 Hear this word, ye kine of Bashan, that are in the mountain of Samaria, which oppress the poor, which crush the needy, which say to their masters, "Bring, and let us drink."

The Lord God hath sworn by his holiness, that, lo, the days shall come upon you, that he will take you away with hooks, and your posterity with fishhooks. . . .

I have smitten you with blasting and mildew: when your gardens and your vineyards and your fig trees and your olive trees increased, the palmerworm devoured them: yet have ye not returned unto me, saith the Lord.

I have sent among you the pestilence after the manner of Egypt: your young men have I slain with the sword, and have taken away your horses; and I have made the stink of your camps to come up unto your nostrils: yet have ye not returned unto me, saith the Lord.

I have overthrown some of you, as God overthrew Sodom and Gomorrah, and ye were as a firebrand plucked out of the burning: yet have ye not returned unto me, saith the Lord.

Therefore thus will I do unto thee, O Israel: and because I will do this unto thee, prepare to meet thy God, O Israel.

For, lo, he that formeth the mountains, and createth the wind, and declareth unto man what is his thought, that maketh the morning darkness, and treadeth upon the high places of the earth, The Lord, The God of hosts, is his name.

5   . . . Seek the Lord, and ye shall live; lest he break out like fire in the house of Joseph, and devour it, and there be none to quench it in Bethel.

Ye who turn judgment to wormwood, and leave off righteousness in the earth,

Seek him that maketh the seven stars and Orion, and turneth the shadow of death into the morning, and maketh the day dark with night: that calleth for the waters of the sea, and poureth them out upon the face of the earth: The Lord is his name. . . .

Seek good, and not evil, that ye may live: and so the Lord, the God of hosts, shall be with you, as ye have spoken.

Hate the evil, and love the good, and establish judgment in the gate: it may be that the Lord God of hosts will be gracious unto the remnant of Joseph. . . .

I hate, I despise your feast days, and I will not smell in your solemn assemblies.

Though ye offer me burnt offerings and your meat offerings, I will not accept them: neither will I regard the peace offerings of your fat beasts.

Take thou away from me the noise of thy songs; for I will not hear the melody of thy viols.

But let judgment run down as waters, and righteousness as a mighty stream.

Have ye offered unto me sacrifices and offerings in the wilderness forty years, O house of Israel?

But ye have borne the tabernacle of your Moloch and Chiun your images, the star of your god, which ye made to yourselves.

Therefore will I cause you to go into captivity beyond Damascus, saith the Lord, whose name is The God of hosts.

7 . . . Then Amaziah the priest of Bethel sent to Jeroboam king of Israel, saying, "Amos hath conspired against thee in the midst of the house of Israel: the land is not able to bear all his words.

For thus Amos saith, 'Jeroboam shall die by the sword, and Israel shall surely be led away captive out of their own land.' "

Also Amaziah said unto Amos, "O thou seer, go, flee thee away into the land of Judah, and there eat bread, and prophesy there:

But prophesy not again any more at Bethel: for it is the king's chapel, and it is the king's court."

Then answered Amos, and said to Amaziah, "I was no prophet, neither was I a prophet's son; but I was an herdman, and a gatherer of sycamore fruit:

And the Lord took me as I followed the flock, and the Lord said unto me, 'Go, prophesy unto my people Israel.'

Now therefore hear thou the word of the Lord: Thou sayest, 'Prophesy not against Israel, and drop not thy word against the house of Isaac.'

Therefore thus saith the Lord; 'Thy wife shall be an harlot in the city, and thy sons and thy daughters shall fall by the sword, and thy land shall be divided by line; and thou shalt die in a polluted land: and Israel shall surely go into captivity forth of his land.' "

8 Thus hath the Lord God shewed unto me: and behold a basket of summer fruit.

And he said, "Amos, what seest thou?" And I said, "A basket of summer fruit." Then said the Lord unto me, "The end is come upon my people of Israel; I will not again pass by them any more."

And the songs of the temple shall be howlings in that day, saith the Lord God: there shall be many dead bodies in every place; they shall cast them forth with silence.

Hear this, O ye that swallow up the needy, even to make the poor of the land to fail,

Saying, "When will the new moon be gone, that we may sell corn? and the sabbath, that we may set forth wheat, making the ephah small, and the shekel great, and falsifying the balances by deceit?

That we may buy the poor for silver, and the needy for a pair of shoes; yea, and sell the refuse of the wheat?"

The Lord hath sworn by the excellency of Jacob, Surely I will never forget any of their works.

Shall not the land tremble for this, and every one mourn that dwelleth therein? and it shall rise up wholly as a flood; and it shall be cast out and drowned, as by the flood of Egypt.

And it shall come to pass in that day, saith the Lord God, that I will cause the sun to go down at noon, and I will darken the earth in the clear day:

And I will turn your feasts into mourning, and all your songs into lamentation; and I will bring up sackcloth upon all loins, and baldness upon every head; and I will make it as the mourning of an only son, and the end thereof as a bitter day.

Behold, the days come, saith the Lord God, that I will send a famine in the land, not a famine of bread, nor a thirst for water, but of hearing the words of the Lord:

And they shall wander from sea to sea, and from the north even to the east, they shall run to and fro to seek the word of the Lord, and shall not find it.

In that day shall the fair virgins and young men faint for thirst.

They that swear by the sin of Samaria, and say, "Thy god, O Dan, liveth"; and, "The manner of Beer-sheba liveth"; even they shall fall, and never rise up again.

Hosea

Writing a few years after Amos, the prophet Hosea saw Amos's prophecies begin to come true. Once prosperous Israel was falling apart — her kings were assassinated, her armies were defeated, and her very existence was threatened. Hosea may even have lived to see the destruction of Israel by the Assyrians in 721 B.C. Yet in the midst of the political, social, and moral collapse of his country, Hosea concentrates on the personal relationship between God and Israel and emphasizes love, mercy, and forgiveness.

4 Hear the word of the Lord, ye children of Israel: for the Lord hath a controversy with the inhabitants of the land, because there is no truth, nor mercy, nor knowledge of God in the land.

By swearing, and lying, and killing, and stealing, and committing adultery, they break out, and blood toucheth blood.

Therefore shall the land mourn, and every one that dwelleth therein shall languish, with the beasts of the field, and with the fowls of heaven; yea, the fishes of the sea also shall be taken away.

Yet let no man strive, nor reprove another: for thy people are as they that strive with the priest.

Therefore shalt thou fall in the day, and the prophet also shall fall with thee in the night, and I will destroy thy mother.

My people are destroyed for lack of knowledge: because thou hast rejected knowledge, I will also reject thee, that thou shalt be no priest to me: seeing thou hast forgotten the law of thy God, I will also forget thy children.

As they were increased, so they sinned against me: therefore will I change their glory into shame.

They eat up the sin of my people, and they set their heart on their iniquity.

And there shall be, like people, like priest: and I will punish them for their ways, and reward them their doings.

For they shall eat, and not have enough: they shall commit whoredom, and shall not increase: because they have left off to take heed to the Lord.

Whoredom and wine and new wine take away the heart.

My people ask counsel at their stocks, and their staff declareth unto them: for the spirit of whoredoms hath caused them to err, and they have gone a whoring from under their God.

They sacrifice upon the tops of the mountains, and burn incense upon the hills, under oaks and poplars and elms, because the shadow thereof is good: therefore your daughters shall commit whoredom, and your spouses shall commit adultery.

I will not punish your daughters when they commit whoredom, nor your spouses when they commit adultery: for themselves are separated with whores, and they sacrifice with harlots: therefore the people that doth not understand shall fall.

Though thou, Israel, play the harlot, yet let not Judah offend; and come not ye unto Gilgal, neither go ye up to Beth-aven, nor swear, "The Lord liveth."

For Israel slideth back as a backsliding heifer: now the Lord will feed them as a lamb in a large place. . . .

6 Come, and let us return unto the Lord: for he hath torn, and he will heal us; he hath smitten, and he will bind us up.

After two days will he revive us: in the third day he will raise us up, and we shall live in his sight.

Then shall we know, if we follow on to know the Lord: his going forth is prepared as the morning; and he shall come unto us as the rain, as the latter and former rain unto the earth.

O Ephraim, what shall I do unto thee? O Judah, what shall I do unto thee? for your goodness is as a morning cloud, and as the early dew it goeth away.

Therefore have I hewed them by the prophets; I have slain them by the words of my mouth: and thy judgments are as the light that goeth forth.

For I desired mercy, and not sacrifice; and the knowledge of God more than burnt offerings. . . .

8 Set the trumpet to thy mouth. He shall come as an eagle against the house of the Lord, because they have transgressed my covenant, and trespassed against my law.

Israel shall cry unto me, "My God, we know thee."

Israel hath cast off the thing that is good: the enemy shall pursue him.

They have set up kings, but not by me: they have made princes, and I knew it not: of their silver and their gold have they made them idols, that they may be cut off.

Thy calf, O Samaria, hath cast thee off; mine anger is kindled against them: how long will it be ere they attain to innocency?

For from Israel was it also: the workman made it; therefore it is not God: but the calf of Samaria shall be broken in pieces.

For they have sown the wind, and they shall reap the whirlwind: it hath no stalk: the bud shall yield no meal: if so be it yield, the strangers shall swallow it up.

Israel is swallowed up: now shall they be among the Gentiles as a vessel wherein is no pleasure.

For they are gone up to Assyria, a wild ass alone by himself: Ephraim hath hired lovers.

Yea, though they have hired among the nations, now will I gather them, and they shall sorrow a little for the burden of the king of princes.

Because Ephraim hath made many altars to sin, altars shall be unto him to sin.

I have written to him the great things of my law, but they were counted as a strange thing.

They sacrifice flesh for the sacrifices of mine offerings, and eat it; but the Lord accepteth them not; now will he remember their iniquity, and visit their sins: they shall return to Egypt.

For Israel hath forgotten his Maker, and buildeth temples; and Judah hath multiplied fenced cities: but I will send a fire upon his cities, and it shall devour the palaces thereof.

11 When Israel was a child, then I loved him, and called my son out of Egypt.

As they called them, so they went from them: they sacrificed unto Baalim, and burned incense to graven images.

I taught Ephraim also to go, taking them by their arms; but they knew not that I healed them.

I drew them with cords of a man, with bands of love: and I was to them as they that take off the yoke on their jaws, and I laid meat unto them.

He shall not return into the land of Egypt, but the Assyrian shall be his king, because they refused to return.

And the sword shall abide on his cities, and shall consume his branches, and devour them, because of their own counsels.

And my people are bent to backsliding from me: though they called them to the Most High, none at all would exalt him.

How shall I give thee up, Ephraim? how shall I deliver thee, Israel? how shall I make thee as Admah? how shall I set thee as Zeboim? mine heart is turned within me, my repentings are kindled together.

I will not execute the fierceness of mine anger, I will not return to destroy Ephraim: for I am God, and not man: the Holy One in the midst of thee: and I will not enter into the city. . . .

14 . . . I will heal their backsliding, I will love them freely; for mine anger is turned away from him.

I will be as the dew unto Israel: he shall grow as the lily, and cast forth his roots as Lebanon.

His branches shall spread, and his beauty shall be as the olive tree, and his smell as Lebanon.

They that dwell under his shadow shall return; they shall revive as the corn, and grow as the vine: the scent thereof shall be as the wine of Lebanon.

Ephraim shall say, "What have I to do any more with idols?" I have heard him, and observed him: I am like a green fir tree. From me is thy fruit found.

Who is wise, and he shall understand these things? prudent, and he shall know them? for the ways of the Lord are right, and the just shall walk in them: but the transgressors shall fall therein.

I Isaiah

*Contemporary with Hosea was the prophet known as First
Isaiah, an aristocrat and statesman who lived in Jerusalem, capital
of the southern kingdom. From 740 to 700 B.C. he served as
counselor to kings and spiritual leader to the people during the
troubled period under the shadow of the Assyrian colossus. Although Judah was left nominally independent after the fall of
Israel, the Assyrians made devastating raids upon the country and
forced the king to pay tribute and to worship Assyrian gods.*

*Drawing on the teachings of Amos and Hosea, Isaiah stressed
the holiness of God and the need for social justice and ethical
dealings among men. Although much of his message is pessimistic,
he predicted a glorious and warless future under "the prince of
peace."*

1 . . . Hear the word of the Lord, ye rulers of Sodom; give ear
unto the law of our God, ye people of Gomorrah.

To what purpose is the multitude of your sacrifices unto me?
saith the Lord: I am full of the burnt offerings of rams, and
the fat of fed beasts; and I delight not in the blood of bullocks,
or of lambs, or of he goats.

When ye come to appear before me, who hath required this at
your hand, to tread my courts?

Bring no more vain oblations; incense is an abomination unto
me; the new moons and sabbaths, the calling of assemblies, I
cannot away with; it is iniquity, even the solemn meeting.

Your new moons and your appointed feasts my soul hateth: they are a trouble unto me; I am weary to bear them.

And when ye spread forth your hands, I will hide mine eyes from you: yea, when ye make many prayers, I will not hear: your hands are full of blood.

Wash you, make you clean; put away the evil of your doings from before mine eyes; cease to do evil;

Learn to do well; seek judgment, relieve the oppressed, judge the fatherless, plead for the widow.

Come now, and let us reason together, saith the Lord: though your sins be as scarlet, they shall be as white as snow; though they be red like crimson, they shall be as wool.

If ye be willing and obedient, ye shall eat the good of the land:

But if ye refuse and rebel, ye shall be devoured with the sword: for the mouth of the Lord hath spoken it. . . .

2 . . . And it shall come to pass in the last days, that the mountain of the Lord's house shall be established in the top of the mountains, and shall be exalted above the hills; and all nations shall flow unto it.

And many people shall go and say, "Come ye, and let us go up to the mountain of the Lord, to the house of the God of Jacob; and he will teach us of his ways, and we will walk in his paths: for out of Zion shall go forth the law, and the word of the Lord from Jerusalem."

And he shall judge among the nations, and shall rebuke many people: and they shall beat their swords into plowshares, and their spears into pruninghooks: nation shall not lift up sword against nation, neither shall they learn war any more.

O house of Jacob, come ye, and let us walk in the light of the Lord. . . .

3 . . . The Lord standeth up to plead, and standeth to judge the people.

The Lord will enter into judgment with the ancients of his people, and the princes thereof: for ye have eaten up the vineyard; the spoil of the poor is in your houses.

What mean ye that ye beat my people to pieces, and grind the faces of the poor? saith the Lord God of hosts.

Moreover the Lord saith, Because the daughters of Zion are haughty, and walk with stretched forth necks and wanton eyes, walking and mincing as they go, and making a tinkling with their feet:

Therefore the Lord will smite with a scab the crown of the head of the daughters of Zion, and the Lord will discover their secret parts.

In that day the Lord will take away the bravery of their tinkling ornaments about their feet, and their cauls,[1] and their round tires[2] like the moon.

The chains, and the bracelets, and the mufflers,

The bonnets, and the ornaments of the legs, and the headbands, and the tablets,[3] and the earrings,

The rings, and nose jewels,

The changeable suits of apparel, and the mantles, and the wimples,[4], and the crisping pins,[5]

The glasses,[6] and the fine linen, and the hoods, and the veils.

And it shall come to pass, that instead of sweet smell there shall be stink; and instead of a girdle[7] a rent; and instead of well-set hair baldness; and instead of a stomacher[8] a girding of sackcloth;[9] and burning instead of beauty.

Thy men shall fall by the sword, and thy mighty in the war.

And her gates shall lament and mourn; and she being desolate shall sit upon the ground.

5   Now will I sing to my well-beloved a song of my beloved touching his vineyard. My well-beloved hath a vineyard in a very fruitful hill:

---

1 *cauls:* gold or silver headbands.

2 *tires:* probably necklaces made of crescents of gold.

3 *tablets:* perfumes.

4 *wimples:* perhaps cloaks.

5 *crisping pins:* handbags.

6 *glasses:* mirrors.

7 *girdle:* a belt or waistband.

8 *stomacher:* the part of a woman's dress that covered the breasts and the stomach, usually richly ornamented.

9 *sackcloth:* a coarse, dark cloth; its wearing is associated with rending one's clothes and putting ashes on one's head as a sign of penitence.

And he fenced it, and gathered out the stones thereof, and planted it with the choicest vine, and built a tower in the midst of it, and also made a winepress therein: and he looked that it should bring forth grapes, and it brought forth wild grapes.

And now, O inhabitants of Jerusalem, and men of Judah, judge, I pray you, betwixt me and my vineyard.

What could have been done more to my vineyard, that I have not done in it? wherefore, when I looked that it should bring forth grapes, brought it forth wild grapes?

And now go to; I will tell you what I will do to my vineyard: I will take away the hedge thereof, and it shall be eaten up; and break down the wall thereof, and it shall be trodden down:

And I will lay it waste: it shall not be pruned, nor digged; but there shall come up briers and thorns: I will also command the clouds that they rain no rain upon it.

For the vineyard of the Lord of hosts is the house of Israel, and the men of Judah his pleasant plant: and he looked for judgment, but behold oppression; for righteousness, but behold a cry.

Woe unto them that join house to house, that lay field to field, till there be no place, that they may be placed alone in the midst of the earth!

In mine ears said the Lord of hosts, "Of a truth many houses shall be desolate, even great and fair, without inhabitant.

Yea, ten acres of vineyard shall yield one bath, and the seed of an homer shall yield an ephah.[10]

Woe unto them that rise up early in the morning, that they may follow strong drink; that continue until night, till wine inflame them!

And the harp, and the viol, the tabret, and pipe, and wine, are in their feasts: but they regard not the work of the Lord, neither consider the operation of his hands.

Therefore my people are gone into captivity, because they have

---

[10] *bath . . . homer . . . ephah:* A bath is about nine gallons; a homer is about eleven bushels; an ephah is one-tenth of a homer. The gist of the passage is that the vineyards and fields will yield very little.

no knowledge: and their honourable men are famished, and their multitude dried up with thirst." ...

6   In the year that King Uzziah died I saw also the Lord sitting upon a throne, high and lifted up, and his train filled the temple.

Above it stood the seraphims: each one had six wings; with twain he covered his face, and with twain he covered his feet, and with twain he did fly.

And one cried unto another, and said, "Holy, holy, holy, is the Lord of hosts: the whole earth is full of his glory."

And the posts of the door moved at the voice of him that cried, and the house was filled with smoke.

Then said I, "Woe is me! for I am undone; because I am a man of unclean lips, and I dwell in the midst of a people of unclean lips: for mine eyes have seen the King, the Lord of hosts."

Then flew one of the seraphims unto me, having a live coal in his hand, which he had taken with the tongs from off the altar:

And he laid it upon my mouth, and said, "Lo, this hath touched thy lips; and thine iniquity is taken away, and thy sin purged."

Also I heard the voice of the Lord, saying, "Whom shall I send, and who will go for us?" Then said I, "Here am I; send me."

And he said, "Go, and tell this people: 'Hear ye indeed, but understand not; and see ye indeed, but perceive not.'

Make the heart of this people fat, and make their ears heavy, and shut their eyes; lest they see with their eyes, and hear with their ears, and understand with their heart, and convert, and be healed."

Then said I, "Lord, how long?" And he answered, "Until the cities be wasted without inhabitant, and the houses without man, and the land be utterly desolate,

And the Lord have removed men far away, and there be a great forsaking in the midst of the land." ...

9   . . . The people that walked in darkness have seen a great light: they that dwell in the land of the shadow of death, upon them hath the light shined.

Thou hast multiplied the nation, and not increased the joy: they joy before thee according to the joy in harvest, and as men rejoice when they divide the spoil.

For thou hast broken the yoke of his burden, and the staff of his shoulder, the rod of his oppressor, as in the day of Midian.

For every battle of the warrior is with confused noise, and garments rolled in blood; but this shall be with burning and fuel of fire.

For unto us a child is born, unto us a son is given: and the government shall be upon his shoulder: and his name shall be called Wonderful, Counseller, The mighty God, The everlasting Father, The Prince of Peace.

Of the increase of his government and peace there shall be no end, upon the throne of David, and upon his kingdom, to order it, and to establish it with judgment and with justice from henceforth even for ever. The zeal of the Lord of hosts will perform this. . . .

11 And there shall come forth a rod out of the stem of Jesse, and a Branch shall grow out of his roots:

And the spirit of the Lord shall rest upon him, the spirit of wisdom and understanding, the spirit of counsel and might, the spirit of knowledge and of the fear of the Lord;

And shall make him of quick understanding in the fear of the Lord: and he shall not judge after the sight of his eyes, neither reprove after the hearing of his ears:

But with righteousness shall he judge the poor, and reprove with equity for the meek of the earth: and he shall smite the earth with the rod of his mouth, and with the breath of his lips shall he slay the wicked.

And righteousness shall be the girdle of his loins, and faithfulness the girdle of his reins.

The wolf also shall dwell with the lamb, and the leopard shall lie down with the kid; and the calf and the young lion and the fatling together; and a little child shall lead them.

And the cow and the bear shall feed; their young ones shall lie down together: and the lion shall eat straw like the ox.

And the sucking child shall play on the hole of the asp,[11] and the weaned child shall put his hand on the cockatrice'[12] den.

They shall not hurt nor destroy in all my holy mountain: for the earth shall be full of the knowledge of the Lord, as the waters cover the sea.

And in that day there shall be a root of Jesse, which shall stand for an ensign of the people; to it shall the Gentiles seek: and his rest shall be glorious.

And it shall come to pass in that day, that the Lord shall set his hand again the second time to recover the remnant of his people, which shall be left, from Assyria, and from Egypt, and from Pathros, and from Cush, and from Elam, and from Shinar, and from Hamath, and from the islands of the sea.

And he shall set up an ensign for the nations, and shall assemble the outcasts of Israel, and gather together the dispersed of Judah from the four corners of the earth.

The envy also of Ephraim shall depart, and the adversaries of Judah shall be cut off: Ephraim shall not envy Judah, and Judah shall not vex Ephraim.

But they shall fly upon the shoulders of the Philistines toward the west; they shall spoil them of the east together: they shall lay their hand upon Edom and Moab; and the children of Ammon shall obey them.

And the Lord shall utterly destroy the tongue of the Egyptian sea; and with his mighty wind shall he shake his hand over the seven streams, and make men go over dryshod.

And there shall be an highway for the remnant of his people, which shall be left, from Assyria; like as it was to Israel in the day that he came up out of the land of Egypt.

11 *asp:* a serpent.
12 *cockatrice:* a serpent.

II Isaiah

During the two troubled centuries after First Isaiah mighty Assyria declined, and a new power, the Babylonian empire, dominated the Near Eastern world. In 586 B.C. Nebuchadnezzar, the Babylonian king, destroyed Jerusalem and deported most of her people to Babylon. It was during this period of "Babylonian Captivity" that Second Isaiah wrote his exultant prophecies. His expectation that Cyrus of Persia would bring freedom to the Jews was fulfilled; in 538 B.C. Cyrus captured Babylon and immediately offered the Jews and other captured peoples their freedom. The exile had ended. Some scholars think that Second Isaiah wrote chapters 49–55 in the year after Cyrus' edict freeing the exiles, when many Jews were preparing to return to Palestine.

The "Unknown Prophet" referred to as Second Isaiah has been appraised as "perhaps the greatest poet the Hebrew genius ever produced." He writes of one, universal, loving God, and his message is one of hope and gladness: "ye shall go out with joy, and be led forth with peace: the mountains and the hills shall break forth before you into singing, and all the trees of the field shall clap their hands."

40 Comfort ye, comfort ye my people, saith your God.
Speak ye comfortably to Jerusalem, and cry unto her, that her warfare is accomplished, that her iniquity is pardoned: for she hath received of the Lord's hand double for all her sins.

The voice of him that crieth in the wilderness, Prepare ye the way of the Lord, make straight in the desert a highway for our God.

Every valley shall be exalted, and every mountain and hill shall be made low: and the crooked shall be made straight, and the rough places plain:

And the glory of the Lord shall be revealed, and all flesh shall see it together: for the mouth of the Lord hath spoken it.

The voice said, "Cry." And he said, "What shall I cry?" All flesh is grass, and all the goodliness thereof is as the flower of the field:

The grass withereth, the flower fadeth: because the spirit of the Lord bloweth upon it: surely the people is grass.

The grass withereth, the flower fadeth: but the word of our God shall stand for ever.

O Zion, that bringest good tidings, get thee up into the high mountain; O Jerusalem, that bringest good tidings, lift up thy voice with strength; lift it up, be not afraid; say unto the cities of Judah, "Behold your God!"

Behold, the Lord God will come with strong hand, and his arm shall rule for him: behold, his reward is with him, and his work before him.

He shall feed his flock like a shepherd: he shall gather the lambs with his arm, and carry them in his bosom, and shall gently lead those that are with young.

Who hath measured the waters in the hollow of his hand, and meted out heaven with the span, and comprehended the dust of the art in a measure, and weighed the mountains in scales, and the hills in a balance?

Who hath directed the Spirit of the Lord, or being his counseller hath taught him?

With whom took he counsel, and who instructed him, and taught him in the path of judgment, and taught him knowledge, and showed to him the way of understanding?

Behold, the nations are as a drop of a bucket, and are counted as the small dust of the balance: behold, he taketh up the isles as a very little thing.

And Lebanon is not sufficient to burn, nor the beasts thereof sufficient for a burnt offering.

All nations before him are as nothing; and they are counted to
him less than nothing, and vanity.

To whom then will ye liken God? or what likeness will ye compare unto him?

The workman melteth a graven image, and the goldsmith
spreadeth it over with gold, and casteth silver chains.

He that is so impoverished that he hath no oblation chooseth
a tree that will not rot; he seeketh unto him a cunning workman to prepare a graven image, that shall not be moved.

Have ye not known? have ye not heard? hath it not been told
you from the beginning? have ye not understood from the
foundations of the earth?

It is he that sitteth upon the circle of the earth, and the inhabitants thereof are as grasshoppers; that stretcheth out the heavens
as a curtain, and spreadeth them out as a tent to dwell in:

That bringeth the princes to nothing; he maketh the judges of
the earth as vanity.

Yea, they shall not be planted; yea, they shall not be sown: yea,
their stock shall not take root in the earth: and he shall also
blow upon them, and they shall wither, and the whirlwind
shall take them away as stubble.

To whom then will ye liken me, or shall I be equal? saith the
Holy One.

Lift up your eyes on high, and behold who hath created these
things, that bringeth out their host by number: he calleth them
all by names by the greatness of his might, for that he is strong
in power; not one faileth.

Why sayest thou, O Jacob, and speakest, O Israel, "My way is
hid from the Lord, and my judgment is passed over from my
God"?

Hast thou not known? hast thou not heard that the everlasting
God, the Lord, the Creator of the ends of the earth, fainteth
not, neither is weary? there is no searching of his understanding.

He giveth power to the faint; and to them that have no might
he increaseth strength.

Even the youths shall faint and be weary, and the young men
shall utterly fall:

But they that wait upon the Lord shall renew their strength;

they shall mount up with wings as eagles; they shall run, and not be weary; and they shall walk, and not faint.

49 . . . And now, saith the Lord that formed me from the womb to be his servant, to bring Jacob again to him, Though Israel be not gathered, yet shall I be glorious in the eyes of the Lord, and my God shall be my strength.

And he said, It is a light thing that thou shouldest be my servant to raise up the tribes of Jacob, and to restore the preserved of Israel: I will also give thee for a light to the Gentiles, that thou mayest be my salvation unto the end of the earth.

Thus saith the Lord, the Redeemer of Israel, and his Holy One, to him whom man despiseth, to him whom the nation abhorreth, to a servant of rulers, kings shall see and arise, princes also shall worship, because of the Lord that is faithful, and the Holy One of Israel, and he shall choose thee.

Thus saith the Lord, In an acceptable time have I heard thee, and in a day of salvation have I helped thee: and I will preserve thee, and give thee for a covenant of the people, to establish the earth, to cause to inherit the desolate heritages;

That thou mayest say to the prisoners, "Go forth"; to them that are in darkness, "Show yourselves." They shall feed in the ways, and their pastures shall be in all high places.

They shall not hunger nor thirst; neither shall the heat nor sun smite them: for he that hath mercy on them shall lead them, even by the springs of water shall he guide them.

And I will make all my mountains a way, and my highways shall be exalted.

Behold, these shall come from far: and, lo, these from the north and from the west; and these from the land of Sinim.

Sing, O heavens; and be joyful, O earth; and break forth into singing, O mountains: for the Lord hath comforted his people, and will have mercy upon his afflicted.

But Zion said, "The Lord hath forsaken me, and my Lord hath forgotten me."

Can a woman forget her sucking child, that she should not have compassion on the son of her womb? yea, they may forget, yet will I not forget thee.

Behold, I have graven thee upon the palms of my hands; thy walls are continually before me. . . .

52 Awake, awake; put on thy strength, O Zion; put on thy beautiful garments, O Jerusalem, the holy city: for henceforth there shall no more come into thee the uncircumcised and the unclean.

Shake thyself from the dust; arise, and sit down, O Jerusalem: loose thyself from the bands of thy neck, O captive daughter of Zion.

For thus saith the Lord, Ye have sold yourselves for nought; and ye shall be redeemed without money.

For thus saith the Lord God, My people went down aforetime into Egypt to sojourn there; and the Assyrian oppressed them without cause.

Now therefore, what have I here, saith the Lord, that my people is taken away for nought? they that rule over them make them to howl, saith the Lord; and my name continually every day is blasphemed.

Therefore my people shall know my name: therefore they shall know in that day that I am he that doth speak: behold, it is I.

How beautiful upon the mountains are the feet of him that bringeth good tidings, that publisheth peace; that bringeth good tidings of good, that publisheth salvation; that saith unto Zion, "Thy God reigneth!"

Thy watchmen shall lift up the voice; with the voice together shall they sing: for they shall see eye to eye, when the Lord shall bring again Zion.

Break forth into joy, sing together, ye waste places of Jerusalem: for the Lord hath comforted his people, he hath redeemed Jerusalem.

The Lord hath made bare his holy arm in the eyes of all the nations; and all the ends of the earth shall see the salvation of our God. . . .

53 Who hath believed our report? and to whom is the arm of the Lord revealed?

For he shall grow up before him as a tender plant, and as a root out of a dry ground: he hath no form nor comeliness; and

when we shall see him, there is no beauty that we should desire
him.

He is despised and rejected of men; a man of sorrows, and acquainted with grief: and we hid as it were our faces from him;
he was despised, and we esteemed him not.

Surely he hath borne our griefs, and carried our sorrows: yet we
did esteem him stricken, smitten of God, and afflicted.

But he was wounded for our transgressions, he was bruised for
our iniquities: the chastisement of our peace was upon him;
and with his stripes we are healed.

All we like sheep have gone astray; we have turned every one
to his own way; and the Lord hath laid on him the iniquity of
us all.

He was oppressed, and he was afflicted, yet he opened not his
mouth: he is brought as a lamb to the slaughter, and as a sheep
before her shearers is dumb, so he openeth not his mouth.

He was taken from prison and from judgment: and who shall
declare his generation? for he was cut off out of the land of the
living: for the transgression of my people was he stricken.

And he made his grave with the wicked, and with the rich in his
death; because he had done no violence, neither was any deceit
in his mouth.

Yet it pleased the Lord to bruise him; he hath put him to grief:
when thou shalt make his soul an offering for sin, he shall see
his seed, he shall prolong his days, and the pleasure of the Lord
shall prosper in his hand.

He shall see of the travail of his soul, and shall be satisfied: by
his knowledge shall my righteous servant justify many; for he
shall bear their iniquities.

Therefore will I divide him a portion with the great, and he shall
divide the spoil with the strong; because he hath poured out
his soul unto death: and he was numbered with the transgressors; and he bare the sin of many, and made intercession
for the transgressors.

55 Ho, every one that thirsteth, come ye to the waters, and he
that hath no money; come ye, buy, and eat; yea, come, buy wine
and milk without money and without price.

Wherefore do ye spend money for that which is not bread? and your labour for that which satisfieth not? hearken diligently unto me, and eat ye that which is good, and let your soul delight itself in fatness.

Incline your ear, and come unto me: hear, and your soul shall live; and I will make an everlasting covenant with you, even the sure mercies of David.

Behold, I have given him for a witness to the people, a leader and commander to the people.

Behold, thou shalt call a nation that thou knowest not, and nations that knew not thee shall run unto thee because of the Lord thy God, and for the Holy One of Israel; for he hath glorified thee.

Seek ye the Lord while he may be found, call ye upon him while he is near:

Let the wicked forsake his way, and the unrighteous man his thoughts: and let him return unto the Lord, and he will have mercy upon him; and to our God, for he will abundantly pardon.

For my thoughts are not your thoughts, neither are your ways my ways, saith the Lord.

For as the heavens are higher than the earth, so are my ways higher than your ways, and my thoughts than your thoughts.

For as the rain cometh down, and the snow from heaven, and returneth not thither, but watereth the earth, and maketh it bring forth and bud, that it may give seed to the sower, and bread to the eater:

So shall my word be that goeth forth out of my mouth: it shall not return unto me void, but it shall accomplish that which I please, and it shall prosper in the thing whereto I sent it.

For ye shall go out with joy, and be led forth with peace: the mountains and the hills shall break forth before you into singing, and all the trees of the field shall clap their hands.

Instead of the thorn shall come up the fir tree, and instead of the brier shall come up the myrtle tree: and it shall be to the Lord for a name, for an everlasting sign that shall not be cut off.

Boaz Laying Barley on Ruth's Mantle
Rijksmuseum, Amsterdam

Two Short Stories

We have already seen from their writings that the ancient Hebrew authors could see and hear keenly and could tell vividly. With them as with other ancient peoples, story-telling was a respected art. Most people in times past, when books had to be copied by hand, derived pleasure from the oral telling of stories. Unlike many other cultures, however, the Hebrews also developed a written short story literature. Furthermore, they showed their regard for this art by including short stories among their sacred writings — they saw in the stories expressions of sacred truths. They must also have taken pride in the craft of the story, as revealed in the following selections.

Ruth

One Now it came to pass in the days when the judges ruled, that there was a famine in the land: and a certain man of Bethlehem-Judah went to sojourn in the country of Moab, he, and his wife, and his two sons. And the name of the man was Elimelech, and the name of his wife Naomi, and the name of his two sons Mahlon and Chilion, Ephrathites of Bethlehem-Judah: and they came into the country of Moab, and continued there.

And Elimelech, Naomi's husband, died; and she was left, and her two sons. And they took them wives of the women of Moab; the name of the one was Orpah, and the name of the other Ruth: and they dwelled there about ten years. And Mahlon and Chilion died also both of them, and the woman was left[1] of her two sons and her husband.

Then she arose with her daughters-in-law, that she might return from the country of Moab: for she had heard in the country of Moab how that the Lord had visited his people in giving them bread. Wherefore she went forth out of the place where she was, and her two daughters-in-law with her; and they went on the way to return unto the land of Judah.

And Naomi said unto her two daughters-in-law, "Go, return each to her mother's house: the Lord deal kindly with you, as ye have dealt with the dead, and with me. The Lord grant you that you may find rest, each of you in the house of her husband." Then she kissed them, and they lifted up their voice and wept.

1 *left:* bereft.

And they said unto her, "Surely we will return with thee, unto thy people."

And Naomi said, "Turn again, my daughters: why will you go with me? Are there yet any more sons in my womb, that they may be your husbands? Turn again, my daughters, go your way, for I am too old to have an husband. If I should say, 'I have hope,' if I should have a husband also tonight, and should also bear sons: would ye tarry for them till they were grown? would ye stay for them from having husbands? nay, my daughters; for it grieveth me much for your sakes that the hand of the Lord is gone out against me."

And they lifted up their voice and wept again: and Orpah kissed her mother-in-law, but Ruth clave unto her. And she said, "Behold, thy sister-in-law is gone back unto her people, and unto her gods: return thou after thy sister-in-law."

And Ruth said, "Entreat me not to leave thee, or to return from following after thee: for whither thou goest, I will go; and where thou lodgest, I will lodge: thy people shall be my people, and thy God my God. Where thou diest, will I die, and there will I be buried: the Lord do so to me, and more also, if aught but death part thee and me." When she saw that she was steadfastly minded to go with her, then she left speaking unto her.

So they two went until they came to Bethlehem. And it came to pass, when they were come to Bethlehem, that all the city was moved about them, and they said, "Is this Naomi?" And she said unto them, "Call me not Naomi; call me Mara:[2] for the Almighty hath dealt very bitterly with me. I went out full, and the Lord hath brought me home again empty: why then call ye me Naomi, seeing the Lord hath testified against me, and the Almighty hath afflicted me?" So Naomi returned, and Ruth the Moabitess, her daughter-in-law, with her, which returned out of the country of Moab: and they came to Bethlehem in the beginning of barley harvest.

Two And Naomi had a kinsman of her husband's, a mighty man of wealth, of the family of Elimelech; and his name was Boaz.

---

[2] *Mara:* Mara means "bitter"; Naomi means "pleasant."

And Ruth the Moabitess said unto Naomi, "Let me now go to the field, and glean ears of corn after him in whose sight I shall find grace." And she said unto her, "Go, my daughter." And she went, and came, and gleaned in the field after the reapers: and her hap was to light on a part of the field belonging unto Boaz, who was of the kindred of Elimelech.

And behold, Boaz came from Bethlehem, and said unto the reapers, "The Lord be with you." And they answered him, "The Lord bless thee." Then said Boaz unto his servant that was set over the reapers, "Whose damsel is this?" And the servant that was set over the reapers answered and said, "It is the Moabitish damsel that came back with Naomi out of the country of Moab. And she said, 'I pray you, let me glean and gather after the reapers amongst the sheaves': so she came, and hath continued even from the morning until now, that she tarried a little in the house."

Then said Boaz unto Ruth, "Hearest thou not, my daughter? Go not to glean in another field, neither go from hence, but abide here fast by my maidens. Let thine eyes be on the field that they do reap, and go thou after them: have I not charged the young men that they shall not touch thee? and when thou art athirst, go into the vessels, and drink of that which the young men have drawn."

Then she fell on her face, and bowed herself to the ground, and said unto him, "Why have I found grace in thine eyes, that thou shouldest take knowledge of me, seeing I am a stranger?" And Boaz answered and said unto her, "It hath fully been showed me all that thou hast done unto thy mother-in-law since the death of thine husband: and how thou hast left thy father and thy mother, and the land of thy nativity, and art come unto a people which thou knewest not heretofore. The Lord recompense thy work, and a full reward be given thee of the Lord God of Israel, under whose wings thou art come to trust."

Then she said, "Let me find favour in thy sight, my lord, for that thou hast comforted me, and for that thou hast spoken friendly unto thine handmaid, though I be not like unto one of thine handmaidens." And Boaz said unto her, "At mealtime come thou hither, and eat of the bread, and dip thy morsel in the vinegar." And she sat beside the reapers: and he reached her parched corn, and she did eat, and was sufficed, and left.

And when she was risen up to glean, Boaz commanded his young men, saying, "Let her glean even among the sheaves, and reproach her not. And let fall also some of the handfuls of purpose for her, and leave them that she may glean them, and rebuke her not." So she gleaned in the field until even, and beat out that she had gleaned: and it was about an ephah of barley.

And she took it up, and went into the city: and her mother-in-law saw what she had gleaned; and she brought forth, and gave to her that she had reserved after she was sufficed. And her mother-in-law said unto her, "Where hast thou gleaned today? and where wroughtest thou? blessed be he that did take knowledge of thee." And she showed her mother-in-law with whom she had wrought, and said, "The man's name with whom I wrought today is Boaz." And Naomi said unto her daughter-in-law, "Blessed be he of the Lord, who hath not left off his kindness to the living and to the dead." And Naomi said unto her, "The man is near of kin unto us, one of our next kinsmen." And Ruth the Moabitess said, "He said unto me also, 'Thou shalt keep fast by my young men, until they have ended all my harvest.' " And Naomi said unto Ruth her daughter-in-law, "It is good, my daughter, that thou go out with his maidens, that they meet thee not in any other field." So she kept fast by the maidens of Boaz to glean unto the end of barley harvest and of wheat harvest, and dwelt with her mother-in-law.

Three Then Naomi her mother-in-law said unto her, "My daughter, shall I not seek rest for thee, that it may be well with thee? And now is not Boaz of our kindred, with whose maidens thou wast? Behold, he winnoweth barley tonight in the threshing floor. Wash thyself therefore, and anoint thee, and put thy raiment upon thee, and get thee down to the floor: but make not thyself known unto the man, until he shall have done eating and drinking. And it shall be when he lieth down, that thou shalt mark the place where he shall lie, and thou shalt go in, and uncover his feet, and lay thee down; and he will tell thee what thou shalt do." And she said unto her, "All that thou sayest unto me I will do."

And she went down unto the floor, and did according to all that her mother-in-law bade her. And when Boaz had eaten and drunk, and his heart was merry, he went to lie down at the end of the heap of corn: and she came softly, and uncovered his feet, and laid her down.

And it came to pass at midnight, that the man was afraid, and turned himself: and behold, a woman lay at his feet. And he said, "Who art thou?" And she answered, "I am Ruth thine handmaid: spread therefore thy skirt over thine handmaid, for thou art a near kinsman."

And he said, "Blessed be thou of the Lord, my daughter: for thou hast showed more kindness in the latter end than at the beginning, inasmuch as thou followedst not young men, whether poor or rich. And now, my daughter, fear not, I will do to thee all that thou requirest: for all the city of my people doth know that thou art a virtuous woman. And now it is true that I am thy near kinsman: howbeit there is a kinsman nearer than I. Tarry this night, and it shall be in the morning, that if he will perform unto thee the part of a kinsman,[3] well; let him do the kinsman's part: but if he will not do the part of a kinsman to thee then will I do the part of a kinsman to thee, as the Lord liveth: lie down until the morning."

And she lay at his feet until the morning: and she rose up before one could know another. And he said, "Let it not be known that a woman came into the floor." Also he said, "Bring the veil that thou hast upon thee, and hold it." And when she held it, he measured six measures of barley, and laid it on her: and she went into the city.

And when she came to her mother-in-law, she said, "Who art thou, my daughter?" And she told her all that the man had done to her. And she said, "These six measures of barley gave he me, for he said to me, 'Go not empty unto thy mother-in-law.' " Then

---

[3] *the part of a kinsman:* According to ancient custom a childless widow was to be married by the nearest kinsman of her dead husband.

said she, "Sit still, my daughter, until thou know how the matter will fall: for the man will not be in rest, until he have finished the thing this day."

Four Then went Boaz up to the gate, and sat him down there: and behold the kinsman of whom Boaz spake came by, unto whom he said, "Ho, such a one! turn aside, sit down here." And he turned aside, and sat down. And he took ten men of the elders of the city, and said, "Sit ye down here." And they sat down. And he said unto the kinsman, "Naomi, that is come again out of the country of Moab, selleth a parcel of land, which was our brother Elimelech's. And I thought to advertise[4] thee, saying, 'Buy it before the inhabitants, and before the elders of my people.' If thou wilt redeem it, redeem it: but if thou wilt not redeem it, then tell me, that I may know: for there is none to redeem it besides thee; and I am after thee." And he said, "I will redeem it." Then said Boaz, "What day thou buyest the field of the hand of Naomi, thou must buy it also of Ruth the Moabitess, the wife of the dead, to raise up the name of the dead upon his inheritance."

And the kinsman said, "I cannot redeem it for myself, lest I mar mine own inheritance: redeem thou my right to thyself, for I cannot redeem it." Now this was the manner in former time in Israel, concerning redeeming and concerning changing, for to confirm all things; a man plucked off his shoe, and gave it to his neighbour: and this was a testimony in Israel. Therefore the kinsman said unto Boaz, "Buy it for thee": so he drew off his shoe.

And Boaz said unto the elders, and unto all the people, "Ye are witnesses this day, that I have bought all that was Elimelech's, and all that was Chilion's, and Mahlon's, of the hand of Naomi. Moreover, Ruth the Moabitess, the wife of Mahlon, have I purchased to be my wife, to raise up the name of the dead upon his inheritance, that the name of the dead be not cut off from among his brethren, and from the gate of his place: ye are witnesses this day."

And all the people that were in the gate, and the elders said, "We are witnesses. The Lord make the woman that is come into

4 *advertise:* inform, tell.

thine house like Rachel and like Leah, which two did build the house of Israel: and do thou worthily in Ephratah, and be famous in Bethlehem. And let thy house be like the house of Pharez, whom Tamar bare unto Judah, of the seed which the Lord shall give thee of this young woman."

So Boaz took Ruth, and she was his wife: and when he went in unto her, the Lord gave her conception, and she bare a son. And the women said unto Naomi, "Blessed be the Lord, which hath not left thee this day without a kinsman, that his name may be famous in Israel. And he shall be unto thee a restorer of thy life, and a nourisher of thine old age: for thy daughter-in-law, which loveth thee, which is better to thee than seven sons, hath borne him." And Naomi took the child, and laid it in her bosom, and became nurse unto it. And the women her neighbours gave it a name, saying, "There is a son born to Naomi"; and they called his name Obed: he is the father of Jesse, the father of David. . . .

Jonah

One Now the word of the Lord came unto Jonah the son of Amittai, saying, "Arise, go to Nineveh, that great city, and cry against it; for their wickedness is come up before me." But Jonah rose up to flee unto Tarshish, from the presence of the Lord, and went down to Joppa; and he found a ship going to Tarshish: so he paid the fare thereof, and went down into it, to go with them unto Tarshish from the presence of the Lord.

But the Lord sent out a great wind into the sea, and there was a mighty tempest in the sea, so that the ship was like to be broken. Then the mariners were afraid, and cried every man unto his god, and cast forth the wares that were in the ship, into the sea, to lighten it of them. But Jonah was gone down into the sides of the ship; and he lay, and was fast asleep. So the shipmaster came to him, and said unto him, "What meanest thou, O sleeper? Arise, call upon thy God, if so be that God will think upon us, that we perish not." And they said every one to his fellow, "Come, and let us cast lots, that we may know for whose cause this evil is upon us."

So they cast lots, and the lot fell upon Jonah. Then said they unto him, "Tell us, we pray thee, for whose cause this evil is upon us: what is thine occupation? and whence comest thou? What is thy country? and of what people art thou?" And he said unto them, "I am an Hebrew; and I fear the Lord the God of heaven, which hath made the sea and the dry land." Then were the men exceedingly afraid, and said unto him, "Why hast thou done this?"

For the men knew that he fled from the presence of the Lord, because he had told them.

Then said they unto him, "What shall we do unto thee, that the sea may be calm unto us?" For the sea wrought and was tempestuous. And he said unto them, "Take me up, and cast me forth into the sea; so shall the sea be calm unto you: for I know that for my sake this great tempest is upon you."

Nevertheless the men rowed hard to bring it to the land; but they could not: for the sea wrought, and was tempestuous against them. Wherefore they cried unto the Lord, and said, "We beseech thee, O Lord, we beseech thee, let us not perish for this man's life, and lay not upon us innocent blood: for thou, O Lord, hast done as it pleased thee." So they took up Jonah, and cast him forth into the sea: and the sea ceased from her raging. Then the men feared the Lord exceedingly, and offered a sacrifice unto the Lord, and made vows.

Now the Lord had prepared a great fish to swallow up Jonah, and Jonah was in the belly of the fish three days, and three nights.

Two Then Jonah prayed unto the Lord his God, out of the fish's belly, and said, "I cried by reason of mine affliction unto the Lord, and he heard me; out of the belly of hell cried I, and thou heardest my voice. For thou hadst cast me into the deep, in the midst of the seas; and the floods compassed me about: all thy billows and thy waves passed over me. Then I said, 'I am cast out of thy sight; yet I will look again toward thy holy temple.' The waters compassed me about even to the soul: the depth closed me round about; the weeds were wrapped about my head. I went down to the bottoms of the mountains; the earth with her bars was about me for ever: yet hast thou brought up my life from corruption, O Lord my God.

"When my soul fainted within me, I remembered the Lord: and my prayer came in unto thee, into thine holy temple. They that observe lying vanities forsake their own mercy. But I will sacrifice unto thee with the voice of thanksgiving; I will pay that that I have vowed. Salvation is of the Lord."

And the Lord spake unto the fish, and it vomited out Jonah upon the dry land.

Three And the word of the Lord came unto Jonah the second time, saying, "Arise, go unto Nineveh, that great city, and preach unto it the preaching that I bid thee." So Jonah arose and went unto Nineveh, according to the word of the Lord. Now Nineveh was an exceeding great city of three days' journey.[1] And Jonah began to enter into the city a day's journey, and he cried, and said, "Yet forty days, and Nineveh shall be overthrown."

So the people of Nineveh believed God, and proclaimed a fast, and put on sackcloth from the greatest of them even to the least of them. For word came unto the king of Nineveh, and he arose from his throne, and he laid his robe from him, and covered him with sackcloth, and sat in ashes. And he caused it to be proclaimed and published through Nineveh by the decree of the king and his nobles, saying, "Let neither man nor beast, herd nor flock, taste any thing: let them not feed, nor drink water. But let man and beast be covered with sackcloth, and cry mightily unto God: yea, let them turn every one from his evil way, and from the violence that is in their hands. Who can tell if God will turn and repent, and turn away from his fierce anger, that we perish not?"

And God saw their works, that they turned from their evil way; and God repented of the evil that he had said that he would do unto them; and he did it not.

Four But it displeased Jonah exceedingly, and he was very angry. And he prayed unto the Lord, and said, "I pray thee, O Lord, was not this my saying, when I was yet in my country? Therefore I fled before unto Tarshish: for I knew that thou art a gracious God, and merciful, slow to anger, and of great kindness, and repentest thee of the evil. Therefore now, O Lord, take, I beseech thee, my life from me; for it is better for me to die than to live."

Then said the Lord, "Doest thou well to be angry?" So Jonah went out of the city, and sat on the east side of the city, and there made him a booth, and sat under it in the shadow, till he might see what would become of the city.

---

[1] *three day's journey:* a day's journey was a common Hebrew measure for distance. Nineveh was so large it took three days to walk across it.

And the Lord God prepared a gourd, and made it to come up over Jonah, that it might be a shadow over his head, to deliver him from his grief. So Jonah was exceeding glad of the gourd. But God prepared a worm when the morning rose the next day, and it smote the gourd that it withered.

And it came to pass when the sun did arise, that God prepared a vehement east wind; and the sun beat upon the head of Jonah, that he fainted, and wished in himself to die, and said, "It is better for me to die than to live." And God said to Jonah, "Doest thou well to be angry for the gourd?" And he said, "I do well to be angry, even unto death."

Then said the Lord, "Thou hast had pity on the gourd, for the which thou hast not laboured, neither madest it grow, which came up in a night, and perished in a night: and should not I spare Nineveh that great city, wherein are more than sixscore thousand persons that cannot discern between their right hand and their left hand,[2] and also much cattle?"

[2] *persons . . . hand: i.e.,* children so young they do not know their right from their left.

Job and His Friends
Private Collection, Switzerland

Wisdom
Literature

*Under the heading of wisdom literature are grouped two of
the major works of the Old Testament, Ecclesiastes and Job.
Ecclesiastes, the urbane philosopher-poet, is the most existential
of the thinkers in the Bible. Writing in the era just before
Christianity, he questions the prophetic thesis that good deeds
are rewarded or sins punished. Nonetheless he counsels a
temperate, generous, scholarly life as that most suitable to the
complete human being.*

*The Book of Job, considered the supreme literary masterpiece
of the Bible, asks the ultimate questions of human faith: Why
do the good so often suffer? What pattern is there to God's
justice among men? The book is based on an ancient folk tale
expanded by an unknown poet to a dialogue between the
tormented Job and his three dutiful comforters. Climaxed by a
confrontation between Job and God, it contains some of the
loftiest poetry and some of the most profound thought ever
uttered on the relationship of man to his God.*

Ecclesiastes

One The words of the Preacher, the son of David, king in Jerusalem. Vanity of vanities, saith the Preacher, vanity of vanities, all is vanity. What profit hath a man of all his labour which he taketh under the sun? One generation passeth away, and another generation cometh: but the earth abideth for ever. The sun also ariseth, and the sun goeth down, and hasteth to the place where he arose. The wind goeth toward the south, and turneth about unto the north; it whirleth about continually, and the wind returneth again according to his circuits. All the rivers run into the sea, yet the sea is not full; unto the place from whence the rivers come, thither they return again.

All things are full of labour, man cannot utter it: the eye is not satisfied with seeing, nor the ear filled with hearing. The thing that hath been, it is that which shall be; and that which is done is that which shall be done: and there is no new thing under the sun. Is there any thing whereof it may be said, "See, this is new"? it hath been already of old time, which was before us. There is no remembrance of former things; neither shall there be any remembrance of things that are to come with those that shall come after.

I the Preacher was king over Israel in Jerusalem. And I gave my heart to seek and search out by wisdom, concerning all things that are done under heaven: this sore travail hath God given to the sons of man to be exercised therewith. I have seen all the works that are done under the sun; and behold, all is vanity and vexation of spirit. That which is crooked cannot be made straight: and that which is wanting cannot be numbered.

I communed with mine own heart, saying, "Lo, I am come to great estate, and have gotten more wisdom than all they that have been before me in Jerusalem: yea, my heart had great experience of wisdom and knowledge." And I gave my heart to know wisdom, and to know madness and folly: I perceived that this also is vexation of spirit. For in much wisdom is much grief: and he that increaseth knowledge increaseth sorrow.

Two I said in mine heart, "Go to now, I will prove thee with mirth, therefore enjoy pleasure": and behold, this also is vanity. I said of laughter, "It is mad": and of mirth, "What doeth it?" I sought in mine heart to give myself unto wine, yet acquainting mine heart with wisdom, and to lay hold on folly, till I might see what was that good for the sons of men, which they should do under the heaven all the days of their life. I made me great works, I builded me houses, I planted me vineyards. I made me gardens and orchards, and I planted trees in them of all kind of fruits. I made me pools of water, to water therewith the wood that bringeth forth trees.

I got me servants and maidens, and had servants born in my house; also I had great possessions of great and small cattle, above all that were in Jerusalem before me. I gathered me also silver and gold, and the peculiar treasure of kings and of the provinces. I gat me men singers and women singers, and the delights of the sons of men, as musical instruments, and that of all sorts.

So I was great, and increased more than all that were before me in Jerusalem: also my wisdom remained with me. And whatsoever mine eyes desired, I kept not from them; I withheld not my heart from any joy; for my heart rejoiced in all my labour: and this was my portion of all my labour. Then I looked on all the works that my hands had wrought, and on the labour that I had laboured to do: and behold, all was vanity, and vexation of spirit, and there was no profit under the sun.

And I turned myself to behold wisdom, and madness, and folly: for what can the man do that cometh after the king? even that which hath been already done. Then I saw that wisdom excelleth folly, as far as light excelleth darkness. The wise man's eyes are in his head; but the fool walketh in darkness: and I myself perceived also that one event happeneth to them all. Then said I in my heart, "As it happeneth to the fool, so it happeneth even to me; and why was I then more wise?" Then I said in my heart, that this also is vanity. For there is no remembrance of the wise more than of the fool for ever; seeing that which now is, in the days to come shall all be forgotten. And how dieth the wise man? as the fool. Therefore I hated life, because the work that is wrought under the sun is grievous unto me: for all is vanity, and vexation of spirit.

Yea, I hated all my labour which I had taken under the sun: because I should leave it unto the man that shall be after me. And who knoweth whether he shall be a wise man or a fool? yet shall he have rule over all my labour, wherein I have laboured, and wherein I have showed myself under the sun. This is also vanity.

Therefore I went about to cause my heart to despair of all the labour which I took under the sun. For there is a man whose labour is in wisdom, and in knowledge, and in equity; yet to a man that hath not laboured therein shall he leave it for his portion. This also is vanity and a great evil. For what hath man of all his labour, and of the vexation of his heart, wherein he hath laboured under the sun? For all his days are sorrows, and his travail grief, yea, his heart taketh not rest in the night. This is also vanity.

There is nothing better for a man, than that he should eat and drink, and that he should make his soul enjoy good in his labour. This also I saw, that it was from the hand of God. For who can eat, or who else can hasten hereunto, more than I? For God giveth to a man that is good in his sight, wisdom, and knowledge, and joy: but to the sinner he giveth travail, to gather and to heap up, that he may give to him that is good before God. This also is vanity and vexation of spirit.

Three To every thing there is a season, and a time to every purpose under the heaven: A time to be born, and a time to die; a time to plant, and a time to pluck up that which is planted; a time to kill, and a time to heal; a time to break down, and a time to build up; a time to weep, and a time to laugh; a time to mourn, and a time to dance; a time to cast away stones, and a time to gather stones together; a time to embrace, and a time to refrain from embracing; a time to get, and a time to lose; a time to keep, and a time to cast away; a time to rend, and a time to sew; a time to keep silence, and a time to speak; a time to love, and a time to hate; a time of war, and a time of peace.

What profit hath he that worketh in that wherein he laboureth? I have seen the travail which God hath given to the sons of men, to be exercised in it. He hath made every thing beautiful in his time: also he hath set the world in their heart, so that no man can find out the work that God maketh from the beginning to the end. I know that there is no good in them, but for a man to rejoice, and to do good in his life. And also that every man should eat and drink, and enjoy the good of all his labour: it is the gift of God.

I know that, whatsoever God doeth, it shall be for ever: nothing can be put to it nor any thing taken from it: and God doeth it, that men should fear before him. That which hath been, is now: and that which is to be hath already been, and God requireth that which is past.

And moreover, I saw under the sun the place of judgment, that wickedness was there; and the place of righteousness, that iniquity was there. I said in mine heart, "God shall judge the righteous and the wicked: for there is a time there for every purpose and for every work."

I said in mine heart concerning the estate of the sons of men, that God might manifest them, and that they might see that they themselves are beasts. For that which befalleth the sons of men befalleth beasts; even one thing befalleth them: as the one dieth, so dieth the other; yea, they have all one breath; so that a man hath no preeminence above a beast: for all is vanity.

All go unto one place, all are of the dust, and all turn to dust again. Who knoweth the spirit of man that goeth upward, and the spirit of the beast that goeth downward to the earth? Wherefore I perceive that there is nothing better, than that a man should rejoice in his own works; for that is his portion; for who shall bring him to see what shall be after him?

Seven A good name is better than precious ointment: and the day of death than the day of one's birth.

It is better to go to the house of mourning, than to go to the house of feasting: for that is the end of all men; and the living will lay it to his heart. Sorrow is better than laughter: for by the sadness of the countenance the heart is made better. The heart of the wise is in the house of mourning: but the heart of fools is in the house of mirth. It is better to hear the rebuke of the wise, than for a man to hear the song of fools. For as the crackling of thorns under a pot, so is the laughter of the fool: this also is vanity.

Surely oppression maketh a wise man mad: and a gift destroyeth the heart. Better is the end of a thing than the beginning thereof: and the patient in spirit is better than the proud in spirit. Be not hasty in thy spirit to be angry: for anger resteth in the bosom of fools. Say not thou, "What is the cause that the former days were better than these?" for thou dost not inquire wisely concerning this.

Wisdom is good with an inheritance: and by it there is profit to them that see the sun. For wisdom is a defense, and money is a defense: but the excellency of knowledge is, that wisdom giveth life to them that have it. Consider the work of God: for who can make that straight, which he hath made crooked? In the day of prosperity be joyful, but in the day of adversity consider: God also hath set the one over against the other, to the end that man should find nothing after him.

All things have I seen in the days of my vanity: there is a just man that perisheth in his righteousness, and there is a wicked man that prolongeth his life in his wickedness. Be not righteous overmuch, neither make thyself overwise: why shouldest thou destroy thyself? Be not overmuch wicked, neither be thou foolish: why shouldest thou die before thy time? It is good that thou shouldest take hold of this; yea, also from this withdraw not thine hand: for he that feareth God shall come forth of them all.

Wisdom strengtheneth the wise more than ten mighty men which are in the city. For there is not a just man upon earth, that doeth good, and sinneth not. Also take no heed unto all words that are spoken; lest thou hear thy servant curse thee. For oftentimes also thine own heart knoweth that thou thyself likewise hast cursed others.

All this have I proved by wisdom: I said, "I will be wise," but it was far from me. That which is far off, and exceeding deep, who can find it out? I applied mine heart to know, and to search, and to seek out wisdom, and the reason of things, and to know the wickedness of folly, even of foolishness and madness.

And I find more bitter than death the woman whose heart is snares and nets, and her hands as bands: whoso pleaseth God shall escape from her, but the sinner shall be taken by her. Behold, this have I found, saith the preacher, counting one by one to find out the account: which yet my soul seeketh, but I find not: one man among a thousand have I found, but a woman among all those have I not found. Lo, this only have I found, that God hath made man upright: but they have sought out many inventions.

Nine . . . I returned, and saw under the sun, that the race is not to the swift, nor the battle to the strong, neither yet bread to the wise, nor yet riches to men of understanding, nor yet favour to men of skill; but time and chance happeneth to them all. For man also knoweth not his time: as the fishes that are taken in an evil net, and as the birds that are caught in the snare, so are the sons of men snared in an evil time, when it falleth suddenly upon them.

This wisdom have I seen also under the sun, and it seemed great unto me. There was a little city, and few men within it; and there came a great king against it, and besieged it, and built great bulwarks against it. Now there was found in it a poor wise man, and he by his wisdom delivered the city; yet no man remembered that same poor man. Then said I, "Wisdom is better than strength": nevertheless, the poor man's wisdom is despised, and his words are not heard. The words of wise men are heard in quiet, more than the cry of him that ruleth among fools. Wisdom is better than weapons of war: but one sinner destroyeth much good.

Eleven Cast thy bread upon the waters: for thou shalt find it after many days. Give a portion to seven, and also to eight; for thou knowest not what evil shall be upon the earth. If the clouds be full of rain, they empty themselves upon the earth: and if the tree fall toward the south, or toward the north, in the place where the tree falleth, there it shall be. He that observeth the wind shall not sow: and he that regardeth the clouds shall not reap. As thou knowest not what is the way of the spirit, nor how the bones do grow in the womb of her that is with child: even so thou knowest not the works of God who maketh all. In the morning sow thy seed, and in the evening withhold not thine hand: for thou knowest not whether shall prosper, either this or that, or whether they both shall be alike good.

Truly the light is sweet, and a pleasant thing it is for the eyes to behold the sun. But if a man live many years, and rejoice in them all; yet let him remember the days of darkness, for they shall be many. All that cometh is vanity.

Rejoice, O young man, in thy youth, and let thy heart cheer thee in the days of thy youth, and walk in the ways of thine heart, and in the sight of thine eyes: but know thou, that for all these things, God will bring thee into judgment. Therefore remove sorrow from thy heart, and put away evil from thy flesh: for childhood and youth are vanity.

Twelve Remember now thy Creator in the days of thy youth, while the evil days come not, nor the years draw nigh, when thou shalt say, "I have no pleasure in them"; while the sun, or the light, or the moon, or the stars, be not darkened, nor the clouds return after the rain. In the day when the keepers of the house shall tremble, and the strong men shall bow themselves, and the grinders cease because they are few, and those that look out of the windows be darkened, and the doors shall be shut in the streets, when the sound of the grinding is low, and he shall rise up at the voice of the bird, and all the daughters of music shall be brought low.

Also when they shall be afraid of that which is high, and fears shall be in the way, and the almond tree shall flourish, and the grasshopper shall be a burden, and desire shall fail: because man goeth to his long home, and the mourners go about the streets: or ever the silver cord be loosed, or the golden bowl be broken, or the pitcher be broken at the fountain, or the wheel broken at the cistern. Then shall the dust return to the earth as it was: and the spirit shall return unto God who gave it.

Vanity of vanities, saith the preacher, all is vanity. And moreover because the preacher was wise, he still taught the people knowledge; yea, he gave good heed, and sought out, and set in order many proverbs. The preacher sought to find out acceptable words: and that which was written was upright, even words of truth. The words of the wise are as goads, and as nails fastened by the masters of assemblies, which are given from one shepherd. And further, by these, my son, be admonished: of making many books there is no end; and much study is a weariness of the flesh.

Let us hear the conclusion of the whole matter: Fear God, and keep his commandments; for this is the whole duty of man. For God shall bring every work into judgment, with every secret thing, whether it be good, or whether it be evil.

Job

The Prologue

1 There was a man in the land of Uz, whose name was Job, and that man was perfect and upright, and one that feared God, and eschewed evil. And there were born unto him seven sons and three daughters. His substance also was seven thousand sheep, and three thousand camels, and five hundred yoke of oxen, and five hundred she-asses, and a very great household; so that this man was the greatest of all the men of the east.

And his sons went and feasted in their houses, every one his day, and sent and called for their three sisters to eat and to drink with them. And it was so, when the days of their feasting were gone about, that Job sent and sanctified them, and rose up early in the morning, and offered burnt offerings according to the number of them all: for Job said, "It may be that my sons have sinned, and cursed God in their hearts." Thus did Job continually.

Now there was a day when the sons of God came to present themselves before the Lord, and Satan came also among them. And the Lord said unto Satan, "Whence comest thou?" Then Satan answered the Lord, and said, "From going to and fro in the earth, and from walking up and down in it." And the Lord said unto Satan, "Hast thou considered my servant Job, that there is none like him in the earth, a perfect and an upright man, one that feareth God, and escheweth evil?"

Then Satan answered the Lord, and said, "Doth Job fear God for nought? Hast not thou made an hedge about him, and about his house, and about all that he hath on every side? thou hast blessed the work of his hands, and his substance is increased in the land. But put forth thine hand now, and touch all that he hath, and he will curse thee to thy face." And the Lord said unto Satan, "Behold, all that he hath is in thy power, only upon himself put not forth thine hand."

Job's Sufferings

And there was a day when his sons and his daughters were eating and drinking wine in their eldest brother's house. And there came a messenger unto Job, and said, "The oxen were plowing, and the asses feeding beside them, and the Sabeans fell upon them, and took them away; yea, they have slain the servants with the edge of the sword; and I only am escaped alone to tell thee."

While he was yet speaking, there came also another, and said, "The fire of God is fallen from heaven, and hath burnt up the sheep, and the servants, and consumed them; and I only am escaped alone to tell thee."

While he was yet speaking, there came also another, and said, "The Chaldeans made out three bands, and fell upon the camels, and have carried them away, yea, and slain the servants with the edge of the sword; and I only am escaped alone to tell thee."

While he was yet speaking, there came also another, and said, "Thy sons and thy daughters were eating and drinking wine in their eldest brother's house. And behold, there came a great wind from the wilderness, and smote the four corners of the house, and it fell upon the young men, and they are dead; and I only am escaped alone to tell thee."

Then Job arose, and rent his mantle, and shaved his head, and fell down upon the ground, and worshipped, and said, "Naked came I out of my mother's womb, and naked shall I return thither: the Lord gave, and the Lord hath taken away; blessed be the name of the Lord." In all this Job sinned not, nor charged God foolishly.

2 Again there was a day when the sons of God came to present themselves before the Lord, and Satan came also among them to present himself before the Lord. And the Lord said unto

Satan, "From whence comest thou?" And Satan answered the Lord, and said, "From going to and fro in the earth, and from walking up and down in it."

And the Lord said unto Satan, "Hast thou considered my servant Job, that there is none like him in the earth, a perfect and an upright man, one that feareth God, and escheweth evil? and still he holdeth fast his integrity, although thou movedst me against him, to destroy him without cause." And Satan answered the Lord, and said, "Skin for skin, yea, all that a man hath, will he give for his life. But put forth thine hand now, and touch his bone and his flesh, and he will curse thee to thy face." And the Lord said unto Satan, "Behold, he is in thine hand, but save his life."

So went Satan forth from the presence of the Lord, and smote Job with sore boils, from the sole of his foot unto his crown. And he took him a potsherd to scrape himself withal; and he sat down among the ashes.

Then said his wife unto him, "Dost thou still retain thine integrity? curse God, and die." But he said unto her, "Thou speakest as one of the foolish women speaketh. What? shall we receive good at the hand of God, and shall we not receive evil?" In all this did not Job sin with his lips.

Now when Job's three friends heard of all this evil that was come upon him, they came every one from his own place: Eliphaz the Temanite, and Bildad the Shuhite, and Zophar the Naamathite: for they had made an appointment together to come to mourn with him, and to comfort him. And when they lifted up their eyes afar off, and knew him not, they lifted up their voice, and wept; and they rent every one his mantle, and sprinkled dust upon their heads toward heaven. So they sat down with him upon the ground seven days and seven nights, and none spake a word unto him: for they saw that his grief was very great.

Job's Lament

3 After this, opened Job his mouth, and cursed his day. And Job spake, and said,

"Let the day perish wherein I was born, and the night in which it was said, 'There is a man-child conceived.'

Let that day be darkness, let not God regard it from above, neither let the light shine upon it.

Let darkness and the shadow of death stain it; let a cloud dwell upon it, let the blackness of the day terrify it.

As for that night, let darkness seize upon it; let it not be joined unto the days of the year, let it not come into the number of the months.

Lo, let that night be solitary, let no joyful voice come therein.

Let them curse it that curse the day, who are ready to raise up their mourning.

Let the stars of the twilight thereof be dark; let it look for light but have none; neither let it see the dawning of the day:

Because it shut not up the doors of my mother's womb, nor hid sorrow from mine eyes.

Why died I not from the womb? why did I not give up the ghost when I came out of the belly?

Why did the knees prevent me? or why the breasts, that I should suck?

For now should I have lain still and been quiet, I should have slept; then had I been at rest,

With kings and counsellors of the earth, which built desolate places for themselves,

Or with princes that had gold, who filled their houses with silver:

Or as an hidden untimely birth, I had not been; as infants which never saw light." . . .

First Cycle of Debate

ELIPHAZ

4 Then Eliphaz the Temanite answered, and said,

"If we assay to commune with thee, wilt thou be grieved? But who can withhold himself from speaking?

Behold, thou hast instructed many, and thou hast strengthened the weak hands.

Thy words have upholden him that was falling, and thou hast strengthened the feeble knees.

But now it is come upon thee, and thou faintest; it toucheth thee, and thou art troubled.

Is not this thy fear, thy confidence, thy hope, and the uprightness of thy ways?

Remember, I pray thee, who ever perished, being innocent? or where were the righteous cut off?

Even as I have seen, they that plow iniquity, and sow wickedness, reap the same.

By the blast of God they perish, and by the breath of his nostrils are they consumed." . . .

JOB

6 But Job answered, and said,

"Oh that my grief were thoroughly weighed, and my calamity laid in the balances together.

For now it would be heavier than the sand of the sea, therefore my words are swallowed up.

For the arrows of the Almighty are within me, the poison whereof drinketh up my spirit: the terrors of God do set themselves in array against me. . . .

O that I might have my request! and that God would grant me the thing that I long for!

Even that it would please God to destroy me, that he would let loose his hand, and cut me off. . . .

Teach me, and I will hold my tongue: and cause me to understand wherein I have erred.

How forcible are right words? but what doth your arguing reprove?

Do ye imagine to reprove words, and the speeches of one that is desperate, which are as wind?

Yea, ye overwhelm the fatherless, and you dig a pit for your friend.

Now therefore be content, look upon me, for it is evident unto you if I lie.

Return, I pray you, let it not be iniquity; yea return again: my righteousness is in it.

Is there iniquity in my tongue? cannot my taste discern perverse things?

7 ... My flesh is clothed with worms and clods of dust, my skin is broken, and become loathsome.

My days are swifter than a weaver's shuttle, and are spent without hope.

O remember that my life is wind: mine eye shall no more see good.

The eye of him that hath seen me shall see me no more: thine eyes are upon me, and I am not.

As the cloud is consumed and vanisheth away: so he that goeth down to the grave shall come up no more.

He shall return no more to his house: neither shall his place know him any more.

Therefore I will not refrain my mouth; I will speak in the anguish of my spirit, I will complain in the bitterness of my soul." ...

BILDAD

8 Then answered Bildad the Shuhite, and said,

"How long wilt thou speak these things? and how long shall the words of thy mouth be like a strong wind?

Doth God pervert judgment? or doth the Almighty pervert justice?

If thy children have sinned against him, and he have cast them away for their transgression:

If thou wouldst seek unto God betimes, and make thy supplication to the Almighty;

If thou wert pure and upright, surely now he would awake for thee, and make the habitation of thy righteousness prosperous.

Though thy beginning was small, yet thy latter end should greatly increase.

For inquire, I pray thee, of the former age, and prepare thyself to the search of their fathers. ...

Behold, God will not cast away a perfect man, neither will he help the evildoers." ...

JOB

9 Then Job answered, and said,

"I know it is so of a truth: but how should man be just with God?

If he will contend with him, he cannot answer him one of a thousand. . . .

If I had called, and he had answered me, yet would I not believe that he had hearkened unto my voice.

For he breaketh me with a tempest, and multiplieth my wounds without cause.

He will not suffer me to take my breath, but filleth me with bitterness.

If I speak of strength, lo, he is strong: and if of judgment, who shall set me a time to plead?

If I justify myself, mine own mouth shall condemn me: If I say, 'I am perfect,' it shall also prove me perverse.

Though I were perfect, yet would I not know my soul: I would despise my life.

This is one thing, therefore I said it: 'He destroyeth the perfect and the wicked.' . . .

10 My soul is weary of my life, I will leave my complaint upon myself; I will speak in the bitterness of my soul.

I will say unto God, 'Do not condemn me; show me wherefore thou contendest with me.

Is it good unto thee that thou shouldest oppress? that thou shouldest despise the work of thine hands? and shine upon the counsel of the wicked?

Hast thou eyes of flesh? or seest thou as man seeth?

Are thy days as the days of man? are thy years as man's days,

That thou inquirest after mine iniquity, and searchest after my sin?

Thou knowest that I am not wicked, and there is none that can deliver out of thine hand.

Thine hands have made me and fashioned me together round about; yet thou dost destroy me.

Remember, I beseech thee, that thou hast made me as the clay, and wilt thou bring me into dust again?

Hast thou not poured me out as milk, and curdled me like cheese?
Thou hast clothed me with skin and flesh, and hast fenced me
with bones and sinews.
Thou hast granted me life and favour, and thy visitation hath
preserved my spirit.
And these things hast thou hid in thine heart; I know that this is
with thee.
If I sin, then thou markest me, and thou wilt not acquit me from
mine iniquity.
If I be wicked, woe unto me; and if I be righteous, yet will I not
lift up my head: I am full of confusion, therefore see thou mine
affliction:
For it increaseth: thou huntest me as a fierce lion: and again thou
showest thyself marvelous upon me.
Thou renewest thy witnesses against me, and increasest thine in-
dignation upon me; changes and war are against me.
Wherefore then hast thou brought me forth out of the womb? Oh
that I had given up the ghost, and no eye had seen me!
I should have been as though I had not been, I should have been
carried from the womb to the grave.
Are not my days few? cease then, and let me alone that I may
take comfort a little,
Before I go whence I shall not return, even to the land of darkness
and the shadow of death,
A land of darkness, as darkness itself, and of the shadow of death,
without any order, and where the light is as darkness.' "

ZOPHAR

11 Then answered Zophar the Naamathite, and said,
"Should not the multitude of words be answered? and should a
man full of talk be justified?
Should thy lies make men hold their peace? and when thou mock-
est, shall no man make thee ashamed?
For thou hast said, 'My doctrine is pure, and I am clean in thine
eyes.'
But O that God would speak, and open his lips against thee;

And that he would show thee the secrets of wisdom, that they are
double to that which is! Know therefore that God exacteth of
thee less than thine iniquity deserveth." . . .

JOB

12 And Job answered, and said,
"No doubt but ye are the people, and wisdom shall die with
you.
But I have understanding as well as you, I am not inferior to you:
yea who knoweth not such things as these?
I am as one mocked of his neighbour, who calleth upon God, and
he answereth him: the just upright man is laughed to scorn. . . .

13 Lo, mine eye hath seen all this, mine ear hath heard and
understood it.
What ye know, the same do I know also: I am not inferior unto
you.
Surely I would speak to the Almighty, and I desire to reason with
God.
But ye are forgers of lies, ye are all physicians of no value.
O that you would altogether hold your peace! and it should be
your wisdom.
Hear now my reasoning, and hearken to the pleadings of my lips.
Will you speak wickedly for God? and talk deceitfully for him?
Will ye accept his person? will ye contend for God?
Is it good that he should search you out? or as one man mocketh
another, do ye so mock him?
He will surely reprove you, if ye do secretly accept persons.
Shall not his excellency make you afraid? and his dread fall upon
you?
Your remembrances are like unto ashes, your bodies to bodies of
clay.
Hold your peace, let me alone that I may speak, and let come on
me what will.
Wherefore do I take my flesh in my teeth, and put my life in
mine hand?

Though he slay me, yet will I trust in him: but I will maintain
mine own ways before him."

Second Cycle of Debate

ELIPHAZ

15 Then answered Eliphaz the Temanite, and said,
"Should a wise man utter vain knowledge, and fill his belly with
the east wind?
Should he reason with unprofitable talk? or with speeches where-
with he can do no good?
Yea thou castest off fear, and restrainest prayer before God.
For thy mouth uttereth thine iniquity, and thou choosest the
tongue of the crafty.
Thine own mouth condemneth thee, and not I: yea, thine own
lips testify against thee.
Art thou the first man that was born? or wast thou made before
the hills?
Hast thou heard the secret of God? and dost thou restrain wisdom
to thyself?
What knowest thou that we know not? what understandest thou
which is not in us?
With us are both the grayheaded and very aged men, much elder
than thy father.
Are the consolations of God small with thee? is there any secret
thing with thee?
Why doth thine heart carry thee away? and what do thine eyes
wink at,
That thou turnest thy spirit against God, and lettest such words
go out of thy mouth?" . . .

JOB

16 Then Job answered, and said,
"I have heard many such things: miserable comforters are ye all.

Shall vain words have an end? or what emboldeneth thee that thou answerest?

I also could speak as ye do: if your soul were in my soul's stead, I could heap up words against you, and shake mine head at you.

But I would strengthen you with my mouth, and the moving of my lips should assuage your grief.

Though I speak, my grief is not assuaged: and though I forbear, what am I eased?

But now he hath made me weary: thou hast made desolate all my company.

And thou hast filled me with wrinkles, which is a witness against me: and my leanness rising up in me beareth witness to my face.

He teareth me in his wrath, who hateth me: he gnasheth upon me with his teeth; mine enemy sharpeneth his eyes upon me.

They have gaped upon me with their mouth; they have smitten me upon the cheek reproachfully; they have gathered themselves together against me.

God hath delivered me to the ungodly, and turned me over into the hands of the wicked.

I was at ease, but he hath broken me asunder: he hath also taken me by my neck, and shaken me to pieces, and set me up for his mark.

His archers compass me round about, he cleaveth my reins asunder, and doth not spare; he poureth out my gall upon the ground.

He breaketh me with breach upon breach, he runneth upon me like a giant.

I have sewed sackcloth upon my skin, and defiled my horn in the dust.

My face is foul with weeping, and on mine eyelids is the shadow of death;

Not for any injustice in mine hands: also my prayer is pure.

O earth, cover not thou my blood, and let my cry have no place.

Also now, behold, my witness is in heaven, and my record is on high.

My friends scorn me: but mine eye poureth out tears unto God.

O that one might plead for a man with God, as a man pleadeth for his neighbor.

When a few years are come, then I shall go the way whence I shall not return.

17 . . . My days are past, my purposes are broken off, even the thoughts of my heart:
They change the night into day: the light is short because of darkness.
If I wait, the grave is mine house: I have made my bed in the darkness.
I have said to corruption, 'Thou art my father': to the worm, 'Thou art my mother, and my sister.'
And where is now my hope? as for my hope, who shall see it?
They shall go down to the bars of the pit, when our rest together is in the dust."

BILDAD

18 Then answered Bildad the Shuhite, and said,
"How long will it be ere you make an end of words? Mark, and afterwards we will speak.
Wherefore are we counted as beasts, and reputed vile in your sight?
He teareth himself in his anger: shall the earth be forsaken for thee? and shall the rock be removed out of his place?
Yea, the light of the wicked shall be put out, and the spark of his fire shall not shine.
The light shall be dark in his tabernacle, and his candle shall be put out with him.
The steps of his strength shall be straitened, and his own counsel shall cast him down.
For he is cast into a net by his own feet, and he walketh upon a snare. . . .
His remembrance shall perish from the earth, and he shall have no name in the street.
He shall be driven from light into darkness, and chased out of the world.
He shall neither have son nor nephew among his people, nor any remaining in his dwellings.

They that come after him shall be astonished at his day, as they that went before were affrighted.

Surely such are the dwellings of the wicked, and this is the place of him that knoweth not God."

JOB

19 Then Job answered, and said,

"How long will ye vex my soul, and break me in pieces with words?

These ten times have ye reproached me: you are not ashamed that you make yourselves strange to me.

And be it indeed that I have erred, mine error remaineth with myself.

If indeed ye will magnify yourselves against me, and plead against me my reproach:

Know now that God hath overthrown me, and hath compassed me with his net.

Behold, I cry out of wrong, but I am not heard: I cry aloud, but there is no judgment.

He hath fenced up my way that I cannot pass; and he hath set darkness in my paths.

He hath stripped me of my glory, and taken the crown from my head.

He hath destroyed me on every side, and I am gone: and mine hope hath he removed like a tree.

He hath also kindled his wrath against me, and he counteth me unto him as one of his enemies.

His troops come together, and raise up their way against me, and encamp round about my tabernacle.

He hath put my brethren far from me, and mine acquaintance are verily estranged from me.

My kinsfolk have failed, and my familiar friends have forgotten me. . . .

My breath is strange to my wife, though I entreated for the children's sake of mine own body.

Yea, young children despised me; I arose, and they spake against me.

All my inward friends abhorred me: and they whom I loved are turned against me.

My bone cleaveth to my skin, and to my flesh, and I am escaped with the skin of my teeth.

Have pity upon me, have pity upon me, O ye my friends; for the hand of God hath touched me.

Why do ye persecute me as God, and are not satisfied with my flesh?

Oh that my words were now written, oh that they were printed in a book!

That they were graven with an iron pen and lead in the rock for ever!

For I know that my redeemer liveth, and that he shall stand at the latter day upon the earth:

And though after my skin worms destroy this body, yet in my flesh shall I see God:

Whom I shall see for myself, and mine eyes shall behold, and not another, though my reins be consumed within me.

But ye should say, 'Why persecute we him?' seeing the root of the matter is found in me.

Be ye afraid of the sword: for wrath bringeth the punishments of the sword, that ye may know there is a judgment."

ZOPHAR

20 Then answered Zophar the Naamathite, and said,

"Therefore do my thoughts cause me to answer, and for this I make haste.

I have heard the check of my reproach, and the spirit of my understanding causeth me to answer.

Knowest thou not this of old, since man was placed upon earth,

That the triumphing of the wicked is short, and the joy of the hypocrite but for a moment?

Though his excellency mount up to the heavens, and his head reach unto the clouds:

Yet he shall perish for ever, like his own dung: they which have seen him, shall say, 'Where is he?' . . .

The heaven shall reveal his iniquity: and the earth shall rise up
against him.

The increase of his house shall depart, and his goods shall flow
away in the day of his wrath.

This is the portion of a wicked man from God, and the heritage
appointed unto him by God."

JOB

21 But Job answered, and said,

"Hear diligently my speech, and let this be your consolations.

Suffer me that I may speak, and after that I have spoken, mock
on.

As for me, is my complaint to man? and if it were so, why should
not my spirit be troubled?

Mark me, and be astonished, and lay your hand upon your mouth.

Even when I remember, I am afraid, and trembling taketh hold on
my flesh.

Wherefore do the wicked live, become old, yea, are mighty in
power?

Their seed is established in their sight with them, and their
offspring before their eyes.

Their houses are safe from fear, neither is the rod of God upon
them.

Their bull gendereth and faileth not, their cow calveth, and
casteth not her calf.

They send forth their little ones like a flock, and their children
dance.

They take the timbrel and harp, and rejoice at the sound of the
organ.

They spend their days in wealth, and in a moment go down to
the grave. . . .

Shall any teach God knowledge? seeing he judgeth those that are
high.

One dieth in his full strength, being wholly at ease and quiet.

His breasts are full of milk, and his bones are moistened with
marrow.

And another dieth in the bitterness of his soul, and never eateth
with pleasure.
They shall lie down alike in the dust, and the worms shall cover
them.
Behold, I know your thoughts, and the devices which ye wrong-
fully imagine against me. . . .
How then comfort ye me in vain, seeing in your answers there
remaineth falsehood?"

The Intervention of the Lord

THE LORD

38 Then the Lord answered Job out of the whirlwind, and said,
"Who is this that darkeneth counsel by words without knowledge?
Gird up now thy loins like a man; for I will demand of thee, and
answer thou me.
Where wast thou when I laid the foundations of the earth? declare,
if thou hast understanding.
Who hath laid the measures thereof, if thou knowest? or who
hath stretched the line upon it?
Whereupon are the foundations thereof fastened? or who laid the
cornerstone thereof;
When the morning stars sang together, and all the sons of God
shouted for joy?
Or who shut up the sea with doors, when it brake forth as if it
had issued out of the womb?
When I made the cloud the garment thereof, and thick darkness
a swaddling band for it,
And brake up for it my decreed place, and set bars and doors,
And said, 'Hitherto shalt thou come, but no further: and here
shall thy proud waves be stayed'?
Hast thou commanded the morning since thy days? and caused
the day-spring to know his place,
That it might take hold of the ends of the earth, that the wicked
might be shaken out of it?

It is turned as clay to the seal, and they stand as a garment.

And from the wicked their light is withholden, and the high arm shall be broken.

Hast thou entered into the springs of the sea? or hast thou walked in the search of the depth?

Have the gates of death been opened unto thee? or hast thou seen the doors of the shadow of death?

Hast thou perceived the breadth of the earth? Declare if thou knowest it all.

Where is the way where light dwelleth? and as for darkness, where is the place thereof,

That thou shouldest take it to the bound thereof, and that thou shouldest know the paths to the house thereof?

Knowest thou it, because thou wast then born? or because the number of thy days is great?

Hast thou entered into the treasures of the snow? or hast thou seen the treasures of the hail,

Which I have reserved against the time of trouble, against the day of battle and war?

By what way is the light parted, which scattereth the east wind upon the earth?

Who hath divided a watercourse for the overflowing of waters? or a way for the lightning of thunder,

To cause it to rain on the earth, where no man is: on the wilderness wherein there is no man;

To satisfy the desolate and waste ground, and to cause the bud of the tender herb to spring forth?

Hath the rain a father? or who hath begotten the drops of dew?

Out of whose womb came the ice? and the hoary frost of heaven, who hath gendered it?

The waters are hid as with a stone, and the face of the deep is frozen.

Canst thou bind the sweet influences of Pleiades? or loose the bands of Orion?

Canst thou bring forth Mazzaroth[1] in his season, or canst thou guide Arcturus with his sons?

---

1 *Mazzaroth:* probably the Zodiacal circle of stars.

Knowest thou the ordinances of heaven? canst thou set the dominion thereof in the earth?

Canst thou lift up thy voice to the clouds, that abundance of waters may cover thee?

Canst thou send lightnings, that they may go, and say unto thee, 'Here we are'?

Who hath put wisdom in the inward parts? or who hath given understanding to the heart?

Who can number the clouds in wisdom? or who can stay the bottles of heaven,

When the dust groweth into hardness, and the clods cleave fast together?

Wilt thou hunt the prey for the lion? or fill the appetite of the young lions,

When they couch in their dens, and abide in the covert to lie in wait?

Who provideth for the raven his food? when his young ones cry unto God, they wander for lack of meat.

39 Knowest thou the time when the wild goats of the rock bring forth?

Canst thou number the months that they fulfill? or knowest thou the time when they bring forth?

They bow themselves, they bring forth their young ones, they cast out their sorrows.

Their young ones are in good liking, they grow up with corn: they go forth, and return not unto them.

Who hath sent out the wild ass free? or who hath loosed the bands of the wild ass?

Whose house I have made the wilderness, and the barren land his dwellings.

He scorneth the multitude of the city, neither regardeth he the crying of the driver.

The range of the mountains is his pasture, and he searcheth after every green thing.

Will the unicorn[2] be willing to serve thee? or abide by thy crib?

---

[2] *unicorn:* probably a large and ferocious wild ox with double horns.

Canst thou bind the unicorn with his band in the furrow? or will he harrow the valleys after thee?

Wilt thou trust him because his strength is great? or wilt thou leave thy labour to him?

Wilt thou believe him that he will bring home thy seed? and gather it into thy barn?

Gavest thou the goodly wings unto the peacocks, or wings and feathers unto the ostrich?

Which leaveth her eggs in the earth, and warmeth them in the dust,

And forgetteth that the foot may crush them, or that the wild beast may break them.

She is hardened against her young ones, as though they were not hers: her labour is in vain without fear:

Because God hath deprived her of wisdom, neither hath he imparted to her understanding.

What time she lifteth up herself on high, she scorneth the horse and his rider.

Hast thou given the horse strength? hast thou clothed his neck with thunder?

Canst thou make him afraid as a grasshopper? the glory of his nostrils is terrible.

He paweth in the valley, and rejoiceth in his strength: he goeth on to meet the armed men.

He mocketh at fear, and is not affrighted: neither turneth he back from the sword.

The quiver rattleth against him, the glittering spear and the shield.

He swalloweth the ground with fierceness and rage: neither believeth he that it is the sound of the trumpet.

He saith among the trumpets, 'Ha, ha': and he smelleth the battle afar off, the thunder of the captains, and the shouting.

Doth the hawk fly by thy wisdom, and stretch her wings toward the south?

Doth the eagle mount up at thy command? and make her nest on high?

She dwelleth and abideth on the rock, upon the crag of the rock, and the strong place.

From thence she seeketh the prey, and her eyes behold afar off.
Her young ones also suck up blood: and where the slain are,
there is she."

40 Moreover the Lord answered Job, and said,
"Shall he that contendeth with the Almighty instruct him? he that
reproveth God, let him answer it."

JOB

Then Job answered the Lord, and said,
"Behold, I am vile, what shall I answer thee? I will lay my hand
upon my mouth.
Once have I spoken, but I will not answer: yea twice, but I will
proceed no further."

THE LORD

Then answered the Lord unto Job out of the whirlwind, and said,
"Gird up thy loins now like a man: I will demand of thee, and
declare thou unto me.
Wilt thou also disannul my judgment? wilt thou condemn me,
that thou mayest be righteous?
Hast thou an arm like God? or canst thou thunder with a voice
like him?
Deck thyself now with majesty and excellency, and array thyself
with glory and beauty.
Cast abroad the rage of thy wrath: and behold every one that is
proud, and abase him.
Look on every one that is proud, and bring him low: and tread
down the wicked in their place.
Hide them in the dust together, and bind their faces in secret.
Then will I also confess unto thee, that thine own right hand can
save thee.
Behold now behemoth[3] which I made with thee, he eateth grass
as an ox.

---

3 *behemoth:* commonly identified with the hippopotamus.

Lo now, his strength is in his loins, and his force is in the navel of his belly.

He moveth his tail like a cedar: the sinews of his stones are wrapped together.

His bones are as strong pieces of brass: his bones are like bars of iron.

He is the chief of the ways of God: he that made him can make his sword to approach unto him.

Surely the mountains bring him forth food, where all the beasts of the field play.

He lieth under the shady trees, in the covert of the reed, and fens.

The shady trees cover him with their shadow: the willows of the brook compass him about.

Behold, he drinketh up a river, and hasteth not: he trusteth that he can draw up Jordan into his mouth.

He taketh it with his eyes: his nose pierceth through snares.

41 Canst thou draw out leviathan[4] with an hook? or his tongue with a cord which thou lettest down?

Canst thou put an hook into his nose? or bore his jaw through with a thorn?

Will he make many supplications unto thee? will he speak soft words unto thee?

Will he make a covenant with thee? wilt thou take him for a servant for ever?

Wilt thou play with him as with a bird? or wilt thou bind him for thy maidens?

Shall the companions make a banquet of him? shall they part him among the merchants?

Canst thou fill his skin with barbed irons? or his head with fish spears?

Lay thine hand upon him, remember the battle: do no more.

Behold, the hope of him is in vain: shall not one be cast down even at the sight of him?

None is so fierce that dare stir him up: who then is able to stand before me?

---

4 *leviathan:* either a dolphin or a fanciful crocodile.

Who hath prevented me that I should repay him? whatsoever is under the whole heaven is mine.

I will not conceal his parts, nor his power, nor his comely proportion.

Who can discover the face of his garment? or who can come to him with his double bridle?

Who can open the doors of his face? his teeth are terrible round about.

His scales are his pride, shut up together as with a close seal.

One is so near to another that no air can come between them.

They are joined one to another, they stick together, that they cannot be sundered.

By his neesings[5] a light doth shine, and his eyes are like the eyelids of the morning.

Out of his mouth go burning lamps, and sparks of fire leap out.

Out of his nostrils goeth smoke, as out of a seething pot or caldron.

His breath kindleth coals, and a flame goeth out of his mouth.

In his neck remaineth strength, and sorrow is turned into joy before him.

The flakes of his flesh are joined together: they are firm in themselves, they cannot be moved.

His heart is as firm as a stone, yea as hard as a piece of the nether millstone.

When he raiseth up himself, the mighty are afraid: by reason of breakings they purify themselves.

The sword of him that layeth at him cannot hold: the spear, the dart, nor the habergeon.[6]

He esteemeth iron as straw, and brass as rotten wood.

The arrow cannot make him flee: slingstones are turned with him into stubble.

Darts are counted as stubble: he laugheth at the shaking of a spear.

Sharp stones are under him: he spreadeth sharp pointed things upon the mire.

---

5 *neesings:* snortings.
6 *habergeon:* coat of mail.

He maketh the deep to boil like a pot: he maketh the sea like a
pot of ointment.

He maketh a path to shine after him; one would think the deep
to be hoary.

Upon earth there is not his like, who is made without fear.

He beholdeth all high things: he is a king over all the children of
pride."

JOB

42 Then Job answered the Lord, and said,

"I know that thou canst do every thing, and that no thought can
be withholden from thee.

Who is he that hideth counsel without knowledge? therefore have
I uttered that I understood not, things too wonderful for me,
which I knew not.

Hear, I beseech thee, and I will speak: I will demand of thee,
and declare thou unto me.

I have heard of thee by the hearing of the ear: but now mine eye
seeth thee.

Wherefore I abhor myself, and repent in dust and ashes."

Epilogue

And it was so, that after the Lord had spoken these words unto
Job, the Lord said to Eliphaz the Temanite, "My wrath is kindled
against thee, and against thy two friends: for ye have not spoken of
me the thing that is right, as my servant Job hath. Therefore take
unto you now seven bullocks, and seven rams, and go to my servant
Job, and offer up for yourselves a burnt offering; and my servant
Job shall pray for you; for him will I accept: lest I deal with you
after your folly, in that ye have not spoken of me the thing which
is right, like my servant Job."

So Eliphaz the Temanite, and Bildad the Shuhite, and Zophar
the Naamathite went, and did according as the Lord commanded
them: the Lord also accepted Job. And the Lord turned the

captivity of Job, when he prayed for his friends: also the Lord gave Job twice as much as he had before.

Then came there unto him all his brethren, and all his sisters, and all they that had been of his acquaintance before, and did eat bread with him in his house: and they bemoaned him, and comforted him over all the evil that the Lord had brought upon him: every man also gave him a piece of money, and every one an earring of gold.

So the Lord blessed the latter end of Job more than his beginning: for he had fourteen thousand sheep, and six thousand camels, and a thousand yoke of oxen, and a thousand she-asses. He had also seven sons, and three daughters. And he called the name of the first Jemima, and the name of the second Kezia, and the name of the third Keren-happuch. And in all the land were no women found so fair as the daughters of Job: and their father gave them inheritance among their brethren. After this lived Job an hundred and forty years, and saw his sons, and his sons' sons, even four generations. So Job died, being old, and full of days.

Who can find a virtuous woman?
for her price is far above rubies.
Her children arise up, and call her blessed;
her husband also, and he praiseth her.

Two Women Teaching a Child to Walk
The British Museum, London

Lyric
Poetry

"Sing unto the Lord a new song!" sang the Psalmist. "Come before his presence with singing." For the Hebrews poetry was both an expression of faith and the noblest of art forms. So highly did they consider the craft of the poet that their two greatest collections of poetry, the Psalms and the Song of Songs, are associated with their two greatest kings, David and Solomon.

No other portion of the Bible contains more beautiful or more familiar passages than do Psalms. Its words, which express the entire range of human emotions, have been recited or sung in scores of tongues. As the Psalter it has served as the hymn book of many faiths. It has been called "perhaps the most perfect blending in all literature of poetry and of religion."

The Song of Solomon is unique in the Old Testament, both in its themes and in its form. Its inclusion in the sacred writings was sharply debated; it was finally accepted because many people thought the lyrics were written by Solomon himself, although we know now that they were written long after his reign. However we interpret the lyrics, whether as sacred allegory or as sensuous love poetry, they have lost none of their freshness and charm.

The poem from Proverbs about a virtuous woman is one of the best-known passages from the Old Testament. Its striking conception of the woman's role is expressed in a series of vivid, concrete images that beautifully sum up the Hebrew idea of a good woman.

Proverbs

A VIRTUOUS WOMAN

31 Who can find a virtuous woman? for her price is far above rubies.

The heart of her husband doth safely trust in her, so that he shall have no need of spoil.

She will do him good and not evil all the days of her life.

She seeketh wool, and flax, and worketh willingly with her hands.

She is like the merchants' ships; she bringeth her food from afar.

She riseth also while it is yet night, and giveth meat to household, and portion to her maidens.

She considered a field, and buyeth it: with the fruit of her hands she planteth a vineyard.

She girdeth her loins with strength, and strengtheneth her arms.

She perceiveth that her merchandise is good: her candle goeth not out by night.

She layeth her hands to the spindle, and her hands hold the distaff.

She stretcheth out her hand to the poor; yea, she reacheth forth her hands to the needy.

She is not afraid of the snow for her household: for all her household are clothed with scarlet.

She maketh herself coverings of tapestry; her clothing is silk and purple.

Her husband is known in the gates, when he sitteth among the elders of the land.

She maketh fine linen, and selleth it; and delivereth girdles[1] unto the merchant.

Strength and honour are her clothing; and she shall rejoice in time to come.

She openeth her mouth with wisdom; and in her tongue is the law of kindness.

She looketh well to the ways of her household, and eateth not the bread of idleness.

Her children arise up, and call her blessed; her husband also, and he praiseth her.

Many daughters have done virtuously, but thou excellest them all.

Favour is deceitful, and beauty is vain: but a woman that feareth the Lord, she shall be praised.

Give her of the fruit of her hands; and let her own works praise her in the gates.

(Verses 10–31)

[1] *girdles:* belts or waistbands.

Psalms

PSALM 1

Blessed is the man that walketh not in the counsel of the ungodly, nor standeth in the way of sinners, nor sitteth in the seat of the scornful.

But his delight is in the law of the Lord; and in his law doth he meditate day and night.

And he shall be like a tree planted by the rivers of water, that bringeth forth his fruit in his season; his leaf also shall not wither; and whatsoever he doeth shall prosper.

The ungodly are not so: but are like the chaff which the wind driveth away.

Therefore the ungodly shall not stand in the judgment, nor sinners in the congregation of the righteous.

For the Lord knoweth the way of the righteous: but the way of the ungodly shall perish.

PSALM 3

Lord, how are they increased that trouble me! many are they that rise against me.

Many there be which say of my soul, "There is no help for him in God." Selah.[1]

---

[1] *Selah:* a Hebrew musical term of uncertain meaning. It may have been a direction to the singers to lift their voices or to the orchestra to strike in during a pause in the singing.

But thou, O Lord, art a shield for me; my glory, and the lifter of mine head.

I cried unto the Lord with my voice, and he heard me out of his holy hill. Selah.

I laid me down and slept; I awaked, for the Lord sustained me.

I will not be afraid of ten thousands of people, that have set themselves against me round about.

Arise, O Lord; save me, O my God: for thou hast smitten all mine enemies upon the cheek bone; thou hast broken the teeth of the ungodly.

Salvation belongeth unto the Lord: thy blessing is upon my people. Selah.

PSALM 19

The heavens declare the glory of God; and the firmament showeth his handiwork.

Day unto day uttereth speech, and night unto night showeth knowledge.

There is no speech nor language, where their voice is not heard.

Their line is gone out through all the earth, and their words to the end of the world. In them hath he set a tabernacle for the sun,

Which is as a bridegroom coming out of his chamber, and rejoiceth as a strong man to turn a race.

His going forth is from the end of the heaven, and his circuit unto the ends of it: and there is nothing hid from the heat thereof.

The law of the Lord is perfect, converting the soul: the testimony of the Lord is sure, making wise the simple.

The statutes of the Lord are right, rejoicing the heart: the commandment of the Lord is pure, enlightening the eyes.

The fear of the Lord is clean, enduring for ever: the judgments of the Lord are true and righteous altogether.

More to be desired are they than gold, yea, than much fine gold: sweeter also than honey and the honeycomb.

Moreover by them is thy servant warned: and in keeping of them there is great reward.

Who can understand his errors? cleanse thou me from secret faults.
Keep back thy servant also from presumptuous sins; let them not
have dominion over me: then shall I be upright, and I shall
be innocent from the great transgression.
Let the words of my mouth, and the meditation of my heart,
be acceptable in thy sight, O Lord, my strength, and my redeemer.

PSALM 23

The Lord is my shepherd; I shall not want.
He maketh me to lie down in green pastures; he leadeth me beside
the still waters.
He restoreth my soul: he leadeth me in the paths of righteousness
for his name's sake.
Yea, though I walk through the valley of the shadow of death,
I will fear no evil: for thou art with me; thy rod and thy staff
they comfort me.
Thou preparest a table before me in the presence of mine enemies:
thou anointest my head with oil; my cup runneth over.
Surely goodness and mercy shall follow me all the days of my life:
and I will dwell in the house of the Lord for ever.

PSALM 24

The earth is the Lord's, and the fulness thereof; the world, and
they that dwell therein.
For he hath founded it upon the seas, and established it upon
the floods.
Who shall ascend into the hill of the Lord? or who shall stand in
his holy place?
He that hath clean hands, and a pure heart; who hath not lifted
up his soul unto vanity, nor sworn deceitfully.
He shall receive the blessing from the Lord, and righteousness
from the God of his salvation.
This is the generation of them that seek him, that seek thy face,
O Jacob. Selah.

Lift up your heads, O ye gates; and be ye lift up, ye everlasting doors; and the King of glory shall come in.

Who is this King of glory? The Lord strong and mighty, the Lord mighty in battle.

Lift up your heads, O ye gates; even lift them up, ye everlasting doors; and the King of glory shall come in.

Who is this King of glory? The Lord of hosts, he is the King of glory. Selah.

PSALM 51

Have mercy upon me, O God, according to thy loving kindness: according unto the multitude of thy tender mercies blot out my transgressions.

Wash me thoroughly from mine iniquity, and cleanse me from my sin.

For I acknowledge my transgressions: and my sin is ever before me.

Against thee, thee only, have I sinned, and done this evil in thy sight: that thou mightest be justified when thou speakest, and be clear when thou judgest.

Behold, I was shapen in iniquity; and in sin did my mother conceive me.

Behold, thou desirest truth in the inward parts: and in the hidden part thou shalt make me to know wisdom.

Purge me with hyssop,[1] and I shall be clean: wash me, and I shall be whiter than snow.

Make me to hear joy and gladness, that the bones which thou hast broken may rejoice.

Hide thy face from my sins, and blot out all mine iniquities.

Create in me a clean heart, O God; and renew a right spirit within me.

Cast me not away from thy presence; and take not thy holy spirit from me.

Restore unto me the joy of thy salvation; and uphold me with thy free spirit.

Then will I teach transgressors thy ways; and sinners shall be converted unto thee.

1 *hyssop:* a plant used in purification rites.

Deliver me from blood-guiltiness, O God, thou God of my salvation: and my tongue shall sing aloud of thy righteousness.

O Lord, open thou my lips; and my mouth shall show forth thy praise.

For thou desirest not sacrifice; else would I give it: thou delightest not in burnt offering.

The sacrifices of God are a broken spirit: a broken and a contrite heart, O God, thou wilt not despise.

Do good in thy good pleasure unto Zion: build thou the walls of Jerusalem.

Then shalt thou be pleased with the sacrifices of righteousness, with burnt offering and whole burnt offering: then shall they offer bullocks upon thine altar.

PSALM 90

Lord, thou hast been our dwelling place in all generations.

Before the mountains were brought forth, or ever thou hadst formed the earth and the world, even from everlasting to everlasting, thou art God.

Thou turnest man to destruction, and sayest, "Return, ye children of men."

For a thousand years in thy sight are but as yesterday when it is past, and as a watch in the night.

Thou carriest them away as with a flood; they are as a sleep: in the morning they are like grass which groweth up.

In the morning it flourisheth, and groweth up; in the evening it is cut down, and withereth.

For we are consumed by thine anger, and by thy wrath are we troubled.

Thou hast set our iniquities before thee, our secret sins in the light of thy countenance.

For all our days are passed away in thy wrath: we spend our years as a tale that is told.

The days of our years are threescore years and ten; and if by reason of strength they be fourscore years, yet is their strength labour and sorrow; for it is soon cut off, and we fly away.

Who knoweth the power of thine anger? even according to thy
fear, so is thy wrath.

So teach us to number our days, that we may apply our hearts
unto wisdom.

Return, O Lord, how long? and let it repent thee concerning thy
servants.

O satisfy us early with thy mercy; that we may rejoice and be glad
all our days.

Make us glad according to the days wherein thou hast afflicted us,
and the years wherein we have seen evil.

Let thy work appear unto thy servants, and thy glory unto their
children.

And let the beauty of the Lord our God be upon us: and establish
thou the work of our hands upon us; yea, the work of our hands
establish thou it.

PSALM 96

O sing unto the Lord a new song: sing unto the Lord, all the earth.

Sing unto the Lord, bless his name; show forth his salvation from
day to day.

Declare his glory among the heathen, his wonders among all
people.

For the Lord is great, and greatly to be praised: he is to be feared
above all gods.

For all the gods of the nations are idols: but the Lord made the
heavens.

Honour and majesty are before him: strength and beauty are in
his sanctuary.

Give unto the Lord, O ye kindreds of the people, give unto the
Lord glory and strength.

Give unto the Lord the glory due unto his name: bring an offering, and come into his courts.

O worship the Lord in the beauty of holiness: fear before him,
all the earth.

Say among the heathen that the Lord reigneth: the world also
shall be established that it shall not be moved: he shall judge
the people righteously.

Let the heavens rejoice, and let the earth be glad; let the sea roar, and the fulness thereof.

Let the field be joyful, and all that is therein: then shall all the trees of the wood rejoice

Before the Lord: for he cometh, for he cometh to judge the earth: he shall judge the world with righteousness, and the people with his truth.

PSALM 100

Make a joyful noise unto the Lord, all ye lands.

Serve the Lord with gladness: come before his presence with singing.

Know ye that the Lord he is God: it is he that hath made us, and not we ourselves; we are his people, and the sheep of his pasture.

Enter into his gates with thanksgiving, and into his courts with praise: be thankful unto him, and bless his name.

For the Lord is good; his mercy is everlasting; and his truth endureth to all generations.

PSALM 103

Bless the Lord, O my soul: and all that is within me, bless his holy name.

Bless the Lord, O my soul, and forget not all his benefits:

Who forgiveth all thine iniquities; who healeth all thy diseases;

Who redeemeth thy life from destruction; who crowneth thee with loving kindness and tender mercies;

Who satisfieth thy mouth with good things, so that thy youth is renewed like the eagle's.

The Lord executeth righteousness and judgment for all that are oppressed.

He made known his ways unto Moses, his acts unto the children of Israel.

The Lord is merciful and gracious, slow to anger, and plenteous in mercy.

He will not always chide: neither will he keep his anger forever.

He hath not dealt with us after our sins; nor rewarded us according to our iniquities.

For as the heaven is high above the earth, so great is his mercy toward them that fear him.

As far as the east is from the west, so far hath he removed our transgressions from us.

Like as a father pitieth his children, so the Lord pitieth them that fear him.

For he knoweth our frame; he remembereth that we are dust.

As for man, his days are as grass: as a flower of the field, so he flourisheth.

For the wind passeth over it, and it is gone; and the place thereof shall know it no more.

But the mercy of the Lord is from everlasting to everlasting upon them that fear him, and his righteousness unto children's children;

To such as keep his covenant, and to those that remember his commandments to do them.

The Lord hath prepared his throne in the heavens; and his kingdom ruleth over all.

Bless the Lord, ye his angels, that excel in strength, that do his commandments, hearkening unto the voice of his word.

Bless ye the Lord, all ye his hosts; ye minister of his, that do his pleasure.

Bless the Lord, all his works in all places of his dominion: bless the Lord, O my soul.

PSALM 114

When Israel went out of Egypt, the house of Jacob from a people of strange language;

Judah was his sanctuary, and Israel his dominion.

The sea saw it, and fled: Jordan was driven back.

The mountains skipped like rams, and the little hills like lambs.

What ailed thee, O thou sea, that thou fleddest? thou Jordan, that thou wast driven back?

Ye mountains, that ye skipped like rams; and ye little hills, like lambs?

Tremble, thou earth, at the presence of the Lord, at the presence of the God of Jacob;

Which turned the rock into a standing water, the flint into a fountain of waters.

PSALM 121

I will lift up mine eyes unto the hills, from whence cometh my help.

My help cometh from the Lord, which made heaven and earth.

He will not suffer thy foot to be moved: he that keepeth thee will not slumber.

Behold, he that keepeth Israel shall neither slumber nor sleep.

The Lord is thy keeper: the Lord is thy shade upon thy right hand.

The sun shall not smite thee by day, nor the moon by night.

The Lord shall preserve thee from all evil: he shall preserve thy soul.

The Lord shall preserve thy going out and thy coming in from this time forth, and even for evermore.

PSALM 137

By the rivers of Babylon, there we sat down, yea, we wept, when we remembered Zion.

We hanged our harps upon the willows in the midst thereof.

For there they that carried us away captive required of us a song; and they that wasted us required of us mirth, saying, "Sing us one of the songs of Zion."

How shall we sing the Lord's song in a strange land?

If I forget thee, O Jerusalem, let my right hand forget her cunning.

If I do not remember thee, let my tongue cleave to the roof of my mouth; if I prefer not Jerusalem above my chief joy. . . .

PSALM 139

O Lord, thou hast searched me, and known me.

Thou knowest my downsitting, and mine uprising: thou understandest my thought afar off.

Thou compassest my path, and my lying down, and art acquainted with all my ways.

For there is not a word in my tongue, but lo, O Lord, thou knowest it altogether.

Thou hast beset me behind, and before: and laid thine hand upon me.

Such knowledge is too wonderful for me: it is high, I cannot attain unto it.

Whither shall I go from thy spirit? or whither shall I fly from thy presence?

If I ascend up into heaven, thou art there: if I make my bed in hell, behold, thou art there.

If I take the wings of the morning, and dwell in the uttermost parts of the sea,

Even there shall thy hand lead me: and thy right hand shall hold me.

If I say, "Surely the darkness shall cover me": even the night shall be light about me.

Yea the darkness hideth not from thee, but the night shineth as the day: the darkness and the light are both alike to thee.

For thou hast possessed my reins: thou hast covered me in my mother's womb.

I will praise thee, for I am fearfully and wonderfully made, marvelous are thy works: and that my soul knoweth right well.

My substance was not hid from thee when I was made in secret, and curiously wrought in the lowest parts of the earth.

Thine eyes did see my substance yet being unperfect, and in thy book all my members were written, which in continuance were fashioned, when as yet there was none of them.

How precious also are thy thoughts unto me, O God: how great is the sum of them?

If I should count them, they are more in number than the sand: when I awake, I am still with thee.

Surely thou wilt slay the wicked, O God: depart from me therefore, ye bloody men.

For they speak against thee wickedly: and thine enemies take thy name in vain.

Do not I hate them, O Lord, that hate thee? and am not I grieved with those that rise up against thee?

I hate them with perfect hatred: I count them mine enemies.

Search me, O God, and know my heart: try me, and know my thoughts:

And see if there be any wicked way in me: and lead me in the way everlasting.

Song of Solomon

1 The song of songs, which is Solomon's.

Let him kiss me with the kisses of his mouth: for thy love is better than wine.

Because of the savour of thy good ointments, thy name is as ointment poured forth, therefore do the virgins love thee.

Draw me, we will run after thee: the king hath brought me into his chambers: we will be glad and rejoice in thee, we will remember thy love more than wine: the upright love thee.

I am black, but comely, O ye daughters of Jerusalem, as the tents of Kedar, as the curtains of Solomon.

Look not upon me, because I am black, because the sun hath looked upon me: my mother's children were angry with me; they made me the keeper of the vineyards, but mine own vineyard have I not kept.

Tell me, O thou whom my soul loveth, where thou feedest, where thou makest thy flock to rest at noon: for why should I be as one that turneth aside by the flocks of thy companions?

If thou know not, O thou fairest among women, go thy way forth by the footsteps of the flock, and feed thy kids beside the shepherds' tents.

I have compared thee, O my love, to a company of horses in Pharaoh's chariots.

Thy cheeks are comely with rows of jewels, thy neck with chains of gold.

We will make thee borders of gold with studs of silver.

While the king sitteth at his table, my spikenard[1] sendeth forth
the smell thereof.

A bundle of myrrh[2] is my well-beloved unto me; he shall lie all
night betwixt my breasts.

My beloved is unto me as cluster of camphire[3] in the vineyards
of Engedi.

Behold, thou art fair, my love; behold, thou art fair; thou hast
doves' eyes.

Behold, thou art fair, my beloved, yea pleasant: also our bed is
green.

The beams of our house are cedar, and our rafters of fir.

2 I am the rose of Sharon, and the lily of the valleys.

As the lily among thorns, so is my love among the daughters.

As the apple tree among the trees of the wood, so is my beloved
among the sons. I sat under his shadow with great delight, and
his fruit was sweet to my taste.

He brought me to the banqueting house, and his banner over me
was love.

Stay me with flagons,[4] comfort me with apples, for I am sick of[5]
love.

His left hand is under my head, and his right hand doth embrace
me.

I charge you, O ye daughters of Jerusalem, by the roes, and by the
hinds of the field, that ye stir not up, nor awake my love, till he
please.

The voice of my beloved! behold! he cometh leaping upon the
mountains, skipping upon the hills.

My beloved is like a roe or a young hart: behold, he standeth
behind our wall, he looketh forth at the window, showing himself through the lattice.

---

[1] *spikenard:* the fragrant oil of an Indian plant that grows with a "spike."
When pure, the perfume was very valuable.

[2] *myrrh:* a liquid with a pleasant smell, known also as the balsam of Mecca.

[3] *camphire:* a small shrub whose flowers were often worn in the hair to
scent it.

[4] *flagons:* pressed cakes with raisins.

[5] *of:* with.

My beloved spake, and said unto me, "Rise up, my love, my fair one, and come away.

"For lo, the winter is past, the rain is over, and gone.

"The flowers appear on the earth; the time of the singing of birds is come, and the voice of the turtle[6] is heard in our land.

"The fig tree putteth forth her green figs, and the vines with the tender grape give a good smell. Arise, my love, my fair one, and come away."

O my dove, that art in the clefts of the rock, in the secret places of the stairs, let me see thy countenance, let me hear thy voice, for sweet is thy voice, and thy countenance is comely.

Take us the foxes, the little foxes, that spoil the vines: for our vines have tender grapes.

My beloved is mine, and I am his: he feedeth among the lilies.

Until the day break, and the shadows flee away, turn, my beloved, and be thou like a roe, or a young hart, upon the mountains of Bether.

4   Behold, thou art fair; my love, behold thou art fair; thou hast doves' eyes within thy locks: thy hair is as a flock of goats, that appear from mount Gilead.

Thy teeth are like a flock of sheep that are even shorn, which came up from the washing; whereof every one bear twins, and none is barren among them.

Thy lips are like a thread of scarlet, and thy speech is comely: thy temples are like a piece of a pomegranate within thy locks.

Thy neck is like the tower of David builded for an armoury, whereon there hang a thousand bucklers,[7] all shields of mighty men.

Thy two breasts are like two young roes that are twins, which feed among the lilies.

Until the day break, and the shadows flee away, I will get me to the mountain of myrrh, and to the hill of frankincense.[8]

Thou art all fair, my love, there is no spot in thee.

6 *turtle:* turtledove.
7 *bucklers:* small shields.
8 *frankincense:* a sweet-smelling gum used in incense.

Come with me from Lebanon, my spouse, with me from Lebanon:
look from the top of Amana, from the top of Shenir and
Hermon, from the lions' dens, from the mountains of the
leopards.

Thou hast ravished my heart, my sister, my spouse; thou hast
ravished my heart with one of thine eyes, with one chain of thy
neck.

How fair is thy love, my sister, my spouse! how much better is thy
love than wine! and the smell of thine ointments than all spices!

Thy lips, O my spouse, drop as the honeycomb: honey and milk
are under thy tongue, and the smell of thy garments is like the
smell of Lebanon.

A garden inclosed is my sister, my spouse: a spring shut up, a
fountain sealed.

Thy plants are an orchard of pomegranates, with pleasant fruits,
camphire, with spikenard,

Spikenard and saffron, calamus[9] and cinnamon, with all trees of
frankincense, myrrh and aloes, with all the chief spices:

A fountain of gardens, a well of living waters, and streams from
Lebanon.

Awake, O north wind, and come thou south; blow upon my
garden, that the spices thereof may flow out. Let my beloved
come into his garden, and eat his pleasant fruits.

5 I am come into my garden, my sister, my spouse, I have
gathered my myrrh with my spice; I have eaten my honeycomb
with my honey, I have drunk my wine with my milk: eat, O
friends; drink, yea, drink abundantly, O beloved!

I sleep, but my heart waketh: it is the voice of my beloved that
knocketh, saying, "Open to me, my sister, my love, my dove, my
undefiled: for my head is filled with dew, and my locks with the
drops of the night."

I have put off my coat; how shall I put it on? I have washed my
feet, how shall I defile them?

My beloved put in his hand by the hole of the door, and my
bowels were moved for him.

9 *calamus:* aromatic bark.

I rose up to open to my beloved, and my hands dropped with myrrh, and my fingers with sweet-smelling myrrh, upon the handles of the lock.

I opened to my beloved, but my beloved had withdrawn himself, and was gone: my soul failed when he spake: I sought him, but I could not find him; I called him, but he gave me no answer.

The watchmen that went about the city found me, they smote me, they wounded me; the keepers of the walls took away my veil from me.

I charge you, O daughters of Jerusalem, if ye find my beloved, that ye tell him that I am sick of love.

What is thy beloved more than another beloved, O thou fairest among women? what is thy beloved more than another beloved, that thou dost so charge us?

My beloved is white and ruddy, the chiefest among ten thousand.

His head is as the most fine gold, his locks are bushy, and black as a raven.

His eyes are as the eyes of doves by the rivers of waters, washed with milk, and fitly set.

His cheeks are as a bed of spices, as sweet flowers: his lips like lilies, dropping sweet-smelling myrrh.

His hands are as gold rings set with the beryl: his belly is as bright ivory, overlaid with sapphires.

His legs are as pillars of marble, set upon sockets of fine gold: his countenance is as Lebanon, excellent as the cedars.

His mouth is most sweet, yea, he is altogether lovely. This is my beloved, and this is my friend, O daughters of Jerusalem.

6 Whither is thy beloved gone? O thou fairest among women, whither is thy beloved turned aside? that we may seek him with thee.

My beloved is gone down into his garden, to the beds of spices, to feed in the gardens, and to gather lilies.

I am my beloved's, and my beloved is mine: he feedeth among the lilies.

Thou art beautiful, O my love, as Tirzah, comely as Jerusalem, terrible as an army with banners.

Turn away thine eyes from me, for they have overcome me: thy hair is as a flock of goats that appear from Gilead.

Thy teeth are as a flock of sheep which go up from the washing, whereof every one beareth twins, and there is not one barren among them.

As a piece of a pomegranate are thy temples within thy locks.

There are threescore queens, and fourscore concubines, and virgins without number.

My dove, my undefiled is but one; she is the only one of her mother, she is the choice one of her that bare her. The daughters saw her, and blessed her; yea, the queens and the concubines, and they praised her.

Who is she that looketh forth as the morning, fair as the moon, clear as the sun, and terrible as an army with banners?

I went down into the garden of nuts to see the fruits of the valley, and to see whether the vine flourished, and the pomegranates budded.

Or ever I was aware, my soul made me like the chariots of Amminadib.

Return, return, O Shulamite; return, return, that we may look upon thee. What will ye see in the Shulamite? as it were the company of two armies.

7 How beautiful are thy feet with shoes, O prince's daughter! the joints of thy thighs are like jewels, the work of the hands of a cunning workman.

Thy navel is like a round goblet, which wanteth not liquor: thy belly is like an heap of wheat, set about with lilies.

Thy two breasts are like two young roes that are twins.

Thy neck is as a tower of ivory; thine eyes like the fish-pools in Heshbon, by the gate of Bathrabbim: thy nose is as the tower of Lebanon, which looketh toward Damascus.

Thine head upon thee is like Carmel, and the hair of thine head like purple; the king is held in the galleries.

How fair, and how pleasant art thou, O love, for delights!

This thy stature is like to a palm tree, and thy breasts to clusters of grapes.

I said, "I will go up to the palm tree, I will take hold of the boughs thereof": now also thy breasts shall be as clusters of the vine, and the smell of thy nose like apples;

And the roof of thy mouth like the best wine for my beloved, that goeth down sweetly, causing the lips of those that are asleep to speak.

I am my beloved's, and his desire is toward me.

Come, my beloved, let us go forth into the field; let us lodge in the villages.

Let us get up early to the vineyards; let us see if the vine flourish, whether the tender grape appear, and the pomegranates bud forth: there will I give thee my loves.

The mandrakes give a smell, and at our gates are all manner of pleasant fruits, new and old, which I have laid up for thee, O my beloved.

For Reading and Discussion

In the Beginning . . .

1. Describe the order of creation in the Genesis account. Some scientists believe that the universe evolved from gas to liquid to solid substance. Can you see any connection between the two versions of the origin of things?

2. The first thing Adam does to demonstrate his mastery over all other creatures is to name them. How does Adam's naming the animals suggest the power that ancient people believed resided in language? How is the power of language made clear at the very beginning of Creation? Watch for other examples.

3. What does the creation of woman from the rib of Adam suggest about their relative importance in the world order of the ancient Hebrews? In the incident of the eating of the forbidden fruit, who seems to take the leadership? To what weakness of Eve does the serpent appeal? What weakness of Adam leads him to accept the forbidden fruit?

4. If Eve only had eaten of the forbidden fruit, what would have been the result? Who, in your opinion, was most responsible for Adam's sin — Eve, the serpent, or Adam himself? Why? If God was the creator of them all and if he had wanted a perfect world, why do you think he did not interfere?

5. What reason does God give for expelling Adam and Eve from the Garden of Eden? What other punishments does God direct against Adam and Eve? How do these punishments reflect the actual condition of man in the world? What did God mean when he said that if Adam ate of the tree of knowledge, he would "surely die"? What punishment fulfills that warning? Note again the emphasis on the power of language inherent in God's words.

6. How does God appear to Adam in these chapters — as a human figure, as an abstraction? Cite passages that support your contention. Does God appear to Cain in the same form? If there is a difference, how do you account for it?

7. Why did Cain slay Abel, his brother? What was the punishment which God placed upon Cain? As in the story of Adam and Eve, the events leading up to Cain's exile are told dramatically, chiefly through

286

dialogue. What sentences help us to see Cain's changing expressions of sullenness and fear? What sentences contribute to the changing tone of the passage?

8. Why does God repent of his creation of life on earth at the opening of the story of Noah? Does God destroy only man? How do you account for this?

9. What promise did Noah receive from God after the Deluge? This promise is sometimes referred to as God's first covenant with man. What was the sign or symbol of this covenant?

10. Like the story of Creation, the Flood is also described twice. Of the two versions, which description more effectively portrays the terror aroused at the extinction of life on earth? Which details have been included to make it more vivid?

11. What human trait is illustrated in the story of the Tower of Babel? What condition of man is explained?

Abraham and Isaac

1. Describe how God appeared to Abram the first time, when his name was changed to Abraham, and the second time, on the Plains of Mamre. Are there any differences? How does this appearance to Abraham compare with the way God appeared to Adam, to Cain, to Noah? Is there a further change in how God appears to Abraham later in the story? As you read further in the Old Testament, keep alert to the ways in which God reveals himself to particular individuals.

2. In what ways does God express his confidence in Abraham throughout this story? What particular qualities of Abraham make him worthy of this confidence in God's eyes?

3. God debates with Abraham over the fate of Sodom and Gomorrah in one of many dialogues between God and man in the Old Testament. What is God's reason for initiating this particular discussion and telling Abraham of his plans for Sodom and Gomorrah? What is Abraham's attitude toward God during their debate? What is the attitude of God toward Abraham? What is the outcome of the debate?

4. The story of Lot and the destruction of Sodom and Gomorrah is an episode inserted into the main account of Abraham. What purpose is there in having the story of Lot follow the two previous episodes in Abraham's life? Because Lot is also a worthy man, he is rescued from the destruction of Sodom. Compare his discussion with the angels to Abraham's debate with God. (Note the differences here between the visitation of God's messengers to Abraham and to Lot.) What do you

learn about Near Eastern hospitality in this episode and in the previous visitation by the angels to Abraham?

5. The first covenant between God and man was symbolized by the rainbow. The second covenant was between God and Abraham and his descendants. What was the symbol of this covenant?

6. What was God's purpose in commanding Abraham to sacrifice his son Isaac? Why does God refer to Isaac as Abraham's "only son" when Ishmael is still living? Did Abraham really believe that God intended him to carry out the sacrifice? Could it be that Abraham, knowing of God's plan for Isaac, did not really believe that God intended Isaac to be sacrificed? What do you know of the character of Abraham to support your opinion? What is there in the description of events to support your opinion?

7. What details show the anguish of Abraham as he and Isaac journey to Mount Moriah, the place of sacrifice? How does the account create suspense as the moment of sacrifice draws near? In what dramatic way does the episode reach its climax? In what form does God appear to Abraham in this episode?

8. Why does Abraham send his servant on such a long journey to find a wife for Isaac? How does the servant recognize the proper wife to bring back? What details about her future bridegroom convince Rebekah to return with the servant? How does the servant back up his claims of wealth and greatness? Note the use of repetition in this episode as the servant prays to God, meets Rebekah, and recounts his mission to Rebekah's family. Tellers of Biblical stories use repetition frequently. Watch for other examples throughout the Old Testament.

Jacob and Esau

1. Prophecy is used in the Bible in much the same way as foreshadowing is used in later literature. What example of such foreshadowing can be found in the beginning of the story of Jacob and Esau? Cite other examples of prophecy as foreshadowing from earlier stories.

2. From the moment of their birth Jacob and Esau are in almost constant conflict. What are they struggling over? How is this struggle similar to the struggle between Cain and Abel? Can we find anything in the way of life of Abel, Abraham, Isaac, and Jacob that God seems to prefer over that of Cain, Ishmael, or Esau? Find the sentence which differentiates between the ways of life of Esau and of Jacob. Where are the sympathies of Isaac and Rebekah in this conflict?

3. What is the first step in Jacob's mastery over Esau? How does the Bible by implication justify the way in which Jacob wins his brother's

birthright? The account of the way in which Jacob overcomes Esau is a masterpiece of intrigue. What is the role of Rebekah in this intrigue? Why is Isaac unable to see through the plot?

4. One of the great dramatic moments of the Bible is Esau's anguish when he learns that his blessing as the firstborn has been given to Jacob. How does the narrator prepare us for this scene? Even though Jacob is God's chosen instrument, we feel sympathy for Esau. What in the scene arouses compassion for Esau? What compensation does Esau receive from Isaac? Why can't Isaac's blessing be revoked? How does Esau intend to retaliate against Jacob?

5. Show how Rebekah's suggestion that Jacob flee to Haran is part of God's plan. In addition to the safety of her son, what does Rebekah hope will be the result of this journey? Why does Esau go to Ishmael?

6. How does the appearance of God to Jacob differ from God's appearance to Abraham? What evidence is there of an abrupt change in the character of Jacob? How does Jacob's dream contribute to his sense of destiny? When Jacob refers to the place of his dream as a "dreadful" place, in what sense is he using the word? What statements by Jacob imply that the place of his dream is particularly holy?

7. Why do you think the narrator uses so much detail in Jacob's prolonged courtship of Rachel? What new elements are added to Jacob's characterization through this episode? What elements in Jacob are brought out through his conflict with Laban? What is the difference between Jacob's cleverness in this episode and in the earlier episodes with Esau?

8. A final change in the character of Jacob is marked by his mysterious wrestling match. With whom was this wrestling match? What inner question of conscience, growing out of his meeting with Esau, might Jacob also be wrestling with? How then might the wrestling match be viewed symbolically? What other changes in Jacob's life take place as a result of the wrestling match?

9. Like Abraham, his grandfather, Jacob is given a new name, but in two separate incidents. What is this new name and what meaning does it imply? Note also the names of Jacob's sons. These are the children of Israel who will become the twelve tribes and will be referred to repeatedly throughout the Old Testament.

Joseph

1. Joseph is first made aware of his future greatness through a dream. What is the reaction of his brothers when he tells them of the prophecy? What is the reaction of his father?

2. Judging from the reaction of his brothers to Joseph, there is more to the story than appears in the Old Testament text. What was Joseph like at this stage in his life? Do Joseph's brothers share the sins of Cain's jealousy or are there circumstances which justify their hatred?

3. Reuben intercedes to save Joseph. What is Reuben's plan? Does he succeed in carrying it out? What is Judah's plan? How do the brothers explain Joseph's absence to their father?

4. How does the Bible account for Joseph's initial success in the land of Egypt? What causes him to be thrown into prison? What new qualities in Joseph are brought out through this incident? What talent, demonstrated before his enslavement, wins him his release? What is Joseph's reward for advising Pharoah? In the biblical sense, has Joseph's achievement of power in Egypt fulfilled the dream he related to his brothers? Justify your answer.

5. The story of Joseph contains a very modern plot development, each event preparing for the next and leading to an eventual climax. How do events in Egypt and Canaan lead to a reunion between Joseph and his brothers? Which incidents add to the suspense in this scene? Which incidents increase the emotional impact? How is Joseph able to insist that his brothers bring Benjamin to him without betraying himself? To what do the brothers attribute their apparent difficulties in Egypt? What strange event on their journey home frightens them?

6. Describe the second meeting between Joseph and his brothers. What are Joseph's motivations in continually bewildering his brothers? Why does he plant a cup in the sack of Benjamin? Show how Judah's summary of events to Joseph leads to a resolution of the mystery. (Note the use of repetition in this passage.) What details are used to underscore the happy ending?

7. How does Jacob honor Joseph above all the other sons? Why was there no tribe of Joseph? In what way does the blessing of Ephraim follow a pattern already seen several times? Show how the details describing the death of Jacob bring out the following: Joseph's grief; Egypt's respect for Joseph; Joseph's forgiveness of his brothers.

Moses

1. Since the days of Joseph profound changes have taken place in the relationship between Egypt and the Hebrews. Describe the new status of the Hebrews. How does Pharaoh justify his treatment of them? What evidence is there that he may have other motivations?

2. What orders are given to the Hebrew midwives? What is their response to these orders? How does Moses escape Pharaoh's further orders?

3. How do we first know that Moses is aware of his identity as a Hebrew? Where does Moses flee? How is he accepted by Jethro?

4. How does God first appear to Moses in the land of Midian? Is this appearance similar to or different from his appearance to Abraham, to Jacob? What ceremonial rite is demanded of Moses as he stands on holy ground? Why does Moses fear to see God?

5. What is God's charge to Moses? In what ways does Moses deny his qualifications for the assignment? What different forms of help does God promise him? What signs does God give Moses to identify himself as God's messenger?

6. What is the initial reaction of the elders of Israel to the proposals of Moses and Aaron? What is the response of Pharaoh to the demands of Moses and Aaron? What indications does Moses have that the Hebrews will not always be reliable supporters? How did the earlier incident of the two slaves foreshadow this reaction?

7. What is God's purpose in sending the plagues to Egypt? Why does he "harden Pharaoh's heart" after each plague is lifted? What lessons does the plague serve for the Egyptians, for the Hebrews? What was the ultimate suffering imposed by God upon the Egyptians? In what ways is the Passover connected with that final plague?

8. In what form does God appear to the Israelites while leading them out of Egypt? Why does God harden Pharaoh's heart once more after the Exodus? How does Moses reveal the power of God to the consistently faithless Hebrews? What explanation does the Bible offer for the dividing of the waters?

9. After the safe passage across the Red Sea, the Hebrews celebrated their escape with a song. What characteristics of God are emphasized in this song? What new examples of faithlessness are shown by the Hebrews as they enter the desert?

10. Why do you think the Ten Commandments were given at the time of Moses rather than that of Noah or Abraham or Jacob? What are the provisions of the Ten Commandments?

Samson

1. Miraculous births are frequent in the Bible. The birth of Samson is but one example. Cite others in earlier Old Testament stories. What warnings are given in the announcement of Samson's birth? What de-

tails about the appearance of God to the parents of Samson are similar to that of God to Moses?

2. What is the earliest evidence of Samson's strength? What is the occasion of this adventure? What weaknesses in Samson are brought out by this incident? What later events are foreshadowed by it?

3. What happens to Samson's first wife? How does he avenge her? What other episodes reveal Samson's strength and ingenuity? What is the reaction of the men of Judah to Samson's exploits? Describe the episode in which Samson makes use of a jawbone as a weapon. What miracle shows that God is still with him?

4. What secret of Samson's does Delilah attempt to discover? Why does she wish to betray her husband? What tests does Delilah induce Samson to undergo? What previously revealed trait in Samson explains his telling his secret to Delilah? What are the consequences of Delilah's betrayal of Samson?

5. What details point up the agony of Samson at the hands of the Philistines? Show how the scene of Samson's degradation contrasts with earlier scenes in which he figures. How do you explain the failure of the Philistines to make certain that Samson remains shaven?

6. In the last verses of the story of Samson the pace of the telling suddenly slows down as the author focuses on the final moments in Samson's life. What sentences help the reader to sense the might in Samson's body? Show how the act of bowing by Samson is at once an act of justice and a sign of reverence and repentance.

Saul and David

1. Why does Saul seek out Samuel? In what way has Samuel been prepared by God for Saul's visit? Judging from Saul's mission and the fact that prophets were then called "seers," what seems to have been a common use of prophets in those days? What qualities of Saul are emphasized as he is introduced in the story?

2. What are the three signs by which Saul will recognize his destiny? How does Saul first react when he is summoned before the Israelites? According to the translation, how did the Israelites hail their king?

3. What indications are there that it will be difficult for any king to rule Israel? What is Saul's reaction to the first signs of disloyalty among his subjects? What seems to be Samuel's attitude toward Saul during the early period of his reign? In what sense is a power struggle between the two men implied?

4. What commandment of God does Samuel warn Saul to fulfill against Amalek? What is Saul's excuse for failing to follow the commands strictly? Is this failure a sign of strength or of weakness? Give reasons for your opinion.

5. What details increase the suspense in the meeting between Saul and Samuel after Saul's disobedience? According to Samuel, what is the most important aspect of worship? What is the only way in which Saul can be restored to God's favor? According to the Bible, why was Samuel justified in anointing David while Saul continues as king?

6. What seems to be meant by the "evil spirit from the Lord," which troubles Saul? What coincidence brings him and David together?

7. What precedents can David offer to support his chances against Goliath? What are David's reasons for refusing Saul's armor? Without a sword, how does he finally slay the Philistine giant? What change occurs in the Israelite fortunes as a result of David's success?

8. When the women of Israel sing of Saul and David, Saul is displeased. What sentence marks the turning point of Saul's feeling for David? How does Michal help to save David from her father's anger? What incidents mark the deep affection of Jonathan for David? What signs are there that Saul's inner conflict is affecting his mind?

9. David seeks help from many sources in Palestine, including non-Israelites. Cite some. Why do the priests support David against Saul? Why is Doeg the Edomite the only soldier willing to carry out Saul's orders against Ahimelech the priest?

10. In their meeting at the caves of En-gedi, why does David cut off part of Saul's robe? How does he demonstrate his loyalty to Saul? What is Saul's response? Is Saul able to keep his promise? Why?

11. Why is the witch of Endor afraid at first to serve as a medium for Saul? What does his going to her tell of his relationship with God? What is the prophecy of the ghost of Samuel? How does this episode show that Saul is still a noble and sympathetic figure? In the fighting of the next day, note the Roman style in which he dies. No other figure in the Bible dies in this manner.

12. In many ways the tragedy of Saul is reminiscent of the tragedy of Macbeth. Like Macbeth, Saul becomes king as the result of a prophecy, sinks deeper and deeper into crime to retain his throne, consults a witch on the eve of his death, and dies knowing that the throne will pass, not to his son, but to his adversary. What other parallels can you discover? How is Saul different from Macbeth?

David the King

1. What news does the young Amalekite bring to David? Is everything in his story the truth? What is David's reaction to the story? What justification can you offer for David's action toward the messenger?

2. David's beautiful lament for Saul and Jonathan is an example of Hebraic poetry. What does the lament tell us about Saul and Jonathan? What similes or metaphors point up their qualities as warriors and as men? Who will rejoice at their death? Who will grieve? What does the poem tell us about David, who composed it? Study the poem's form. Note how David uses parallelism, or the restatement of phrases, to reinforce his imagery. Find examples in the poem of synonymous or almost synonymous phrasing. Parallelism is characteristic of Hebrew poetry. We shall see other examples in the prophets and in the psalms.

3. Why was David still in Jerusalem during wartime on the evening he first saw Bathsheba? What does the phrase "but David tarried still at Jerusalem" suggest about his leadership at this time? What character trait of Uriah is shown in his brief dialogue with David? What message does David send to Joab by Uriah? What were the results of this action?

4. How does Nathan induce David to condemn himself? How is David punished by God for his crime? What is his reaction to his punishment? How does this punishment foreshadow later events in David's reign? The brief tale told by Nathan is called a parable, a story used to illustrate a moral or religious concept. Can you recall any parables from other parts of the Bible?

5. Why does Absalom slay his half brother Amnon? If David is "comforted concerning Amnon, seeing he was dead," what prevents his reconciliation with Absalom? Why does Absalom resent David? What traits of character of Absalom and of David are brought out in this episode? Describe the events leading to Absalom's rebellion. Why does Ahitophel's shift of allegiance seem so perilous to David's cause? How does David move to offset this threat? What incident during this period shows the low fortunes of David and his armies? Why was the work of David's secret agent so essential to David's victory?

6. What is Joab's plan to reconcile Absalom with David? Why is this plan unsuccessful? What do we learn about Absalom from his dealings with Joab? What details point up his pride?

7. Why does Joab disobey his king concerning Absalom? What qualities of Joab, David's chief of staff, are brought out in this episode? Why is Ahimaaz hesitant about telling David about Absalom's death? What incident can you recall about another bearer of bad news to David that

adds suspense to this scene? How does the lament for Absalom point up David's tragic recognition of his own failure as a father?
8. The chapters following the death of Absalom tell of the struggle over David's throne which ends with another of David's sons dead. Who are the two chief claimants to succeed David? Who are their supporters? Is there any objective evidence that David had actually "promised" the throne to anyone before Bathsheba "reminds" him of his oath? How does Nathan's news about Adonijah's banquet hasten the crisis at court? What is the result of David's choice of Solomon to succeed him? Compare the power struggles at the end of David's reign with similar struggles in such Shakespearean plays as Richard II, Richard III, and Henry IV.

The Prophets

Amos

1. What does Amos emphasize about the relation between God and the children of Israel? According to Amos, what is the purpose and responsibility of a prophet? Watch for a new note condemning social injustice which we hear for the first time in Amos.
2. The necessity of God's judgment on Israel is expressed in a series of expressive metaphors in chapter 3. What comparisons are made in these metaphors? Why are they appropriate? The literary prophets, such as Amos, make extensive use of this device. Note other examples as they occur.
3. The prophets also make many references to past and contemporary history of Israel. To what historical events does Amos make reference, particularly in chapter 7?
4. At the time Amos prophesied, the Hebrew nation had been divided into two kingdoms, Israel on the north and Judah on the south. How does Amaziah's accusation against Amos reveal the rivalry between the two kingdoms? Who is the accuser of Amos? Judging from the passage, how did the priests and the prophets differ in their attitude toward religion?
5. What do we learn about Amos himself from his reply to the charges against him? What did Amos do for a living before devoting his life to preaching and prophecy? Are most of the sources of his imagery from the city, from warfare, or from the fields? How does Amos' background explain the choice of language in which he expresses his prophetic visions? What examples of parallelism can you find in the selections from Amos?

HOSEA

1. Why has the Lord forgotten his children, according to Hosea? Which of the original Ten Commandments does Hosea accuse the Israelites of breaking ? What is the greatest sin of Israel? What reference is made to the division of the Hebrews in the opening prophecy of this section?

2. Like the other literary prophets, Hosea often speaks in the first person. Does the first person voice always indicate that it is Hosea himself speaking? Whose words does he sometimes seem to be uttering? Does God, as in the earlier books of the Old Testament, ever speak directly to men? How does the function of the prophet give him a privileged position in ancient Hebrew society?

3. To what extent is Hosea a prophet of doom? (Note that *Samaria*, which is a place name for northern Palestine; *Israel*, which is the name of the ten tribes united in the northern kingdom; and *Ephraim*, which is the name of the dominant northern tribe at that time, are used synonymously.) Which of the two kingdoms seems to be in greater danger of destruction? Which powerful neighbor is the greatest threat to Israel? What indications are there that some of the Hebrews have already been absorbed by larger neighbors, such as Syria?

4. In one portion of this selection, Hosea makes use of a father-child metaphor to show the relationship of God to his Chosen People. What other metaphors and similes does Hosea employ to describe this relationship? What details make these comparisons particularly poignant and effective?

5. Does Hosea end his prophecies on a positive or a negative note? Which passages support your contention? What images does Hosea use that are similar to those of Amos? In what way does Hosea see his purpose as more than that of rebuking the faithless?

FIRST ISAIAH

1. Isaiah directs his announcement of the word of God to the people of Judah, rather than Israel, by comparing them to what other ancient sinful people? In what ways does Isaiah echo Amos and Hosea in his criticism of the Judeans? Why does he reject (in the name of God) Judah's offerings? What is most important to God? What punishment will Judah face unless it returns to God? What vivid comparison does Isaiah make to illustrate the qualities of sin and righteousness?

2. Note the vivid detail with which Isaiah denounces the immorality of the women of Jerusalem. How does Isaiah use images of sight, of sound, even of smell, to contrast the sins of the women to their punishments? What does Isaiah think of emphasis on external appearances? What

does he suggest is the source of the wealth with which the daughters of the rich adorn themselves?

3. More than Amos and Hosea, Isaiah utters prophecies of the coming of a deliverer, a messiah, to reunite his people. This selection contains two such prophecies. What qualities do they attribute to the messiah? From what great king is he a direct descendant?

4. In another passage Isaiah records a personal vision of God's appearance to him. How does this appearance of God differ from those to Abraham, Jacob, and Moses? How do the details of Isaiah's acceptance of his mission recall a similar story of Moses? What differences are there in their reactions? What instructions does God give to Isaiah in this vision?

5. Unlike Amos, Isaiah uses imagery of the city, of the temple, and of war, as well as of the fields. One of his greatest extended metaphors, however, describes the vineyard of the Lord. Find the passage (ch. 5) and tell why Isaiah chooses this particular metaphor in which to present his message. Who is the well-beloved to whom the song is sung? Who is the owner of the vineyard? What is the message of this prophecy for Judah? A detailed and extended comparison of this kind is called an allegory. What other passage in this selection may also be considered an allegory?

SECOND ISAIAH

1. In the opening selections from the Unknown Prophet, referred to as Second Isaiah, what sudden change in the tone of the message is quickly apparent that distinguishes it from First Isaiah? What might such a change imply about the times in which the two prophets lived?

2. What attributes of God does Second Isaiah emphasize? What images does he employ to make vivid the power and the glory of God? Compare this description with the descriptions of God in First Isaiah. What aspects of God does each emphasize? What do the selections from each prophet suggest about them as human beings?

3. In the last part of chapter 40 Second Isaiah asks a series of rapid-fire questions: "Have ye not known? have ye not heard? hath it not been told to you?" How does the English translation suggest the excitement of this passage? What feeling on the part of the prophet is suggested by these questions? How does this passage and the one preceding suggest the magnitude of God? What does the passage contribute to your picture of Second Isaiah as a person?

4. Second Isaiah also contains passages foretelling the coming of a messiah. Find these passages. In what respects do they seem to differ

from the earlier messianic prophecies in First Isaiah? What new dimension is added to God in these passages? For example, is God in Second Isaiah primarily a God of justice or of vengeance or of war or of love? Which passages support your contention? At this point you may wish to review the development of the concept of God as he has appeared in the previous portions of the Old Testament included in this volume.

5. Throughout Second Isaiah, the tone is one of joyous excitement. What passages emphasize this joy? Why do you think Second Isaiah has been called "perhaps the greatest poet the Hebrew genius ever produced"?

THE PROPHETS: AN OVERVIEW

1. Although prophecy is usually thought of as spoken, some of the greatest prophets wrote their prophecies in the form of rich and beautiful poetry. We have already seen how simile, metaphor, and allegory illuminate the relationship between God and men. Other devices include Amos' use of antithesis, when he wrote, "I will turn your feasts into mourning and all your songs into lamentations." Hosea used personification in the haunting line, "the land shall mourn." First Isaiah combined antithesis and simile to create a striking image of divine forgiveness: "though your sins be as scarlet, they shall be as white as snow." Other uses of figures of speech abound in the prophetic selections you have read. You should be able to identify many more.

2. The prophets are also filled with allusions—references to previous material in the Old Testament. These allusions to familiar ideas or events of the past help clarify new concepts. Through careful re-reading find some of the allusions to events in the history of the Hebrew people.

3. The prophets wrote often about remarkably modern themes. One of their recurring concerns was for justice. "Learn to do well," says Isaiah, "seek judgment, relieve the oppressed, judge the fatherless, plead for the widow." What passages can you find in Amos or Hosea that voice a similar concern? Other themes besides justice and the future glory of Israel which can be found in the prophets are obedience to God and the importance of following God's laws. What other basic themes can you discover?

Two Short Stories

RUTH

1. The story of Ruth is a love story, a story of loyalty, and a lesson in religious tolerance. With what touching plea does Ruth cast her lot with

Naomi, her bereaved mother-in-law? Which one of the Ten Commandments is Ruth particularly credited with observing?

2. How is the young woman from Moab regarded by the Hebrew inhabitants of Bethlehem when she returns with Naomi? How does she win the respect of the Hebrews? What plan does Naomi have for Ruth?

3. What details show Boaz's kindness to Ruth, a stranger in his land? What aspects of Ruth's conduct in his presence increase his respect for her? How does Boaz let Ruth know of his respect and affection? What plan does Naomi suggest to Ruth to confirm Boaz's affection?

4. Boaz's reason for delaying his decision to marry Ruth is based on an old Hebraic law intended to protect widows. It is summarized in a passage in the Old Testament not included in this collection, Numbers 27:8–11. Look up this passage in a King James Bible. What it has to say about the laws of inheritance will help to clarify Boaz's sense of legal responsibility. Why does the man who is Naomi's nearest relative refuse to buy the inheritance that will entitle him to marry Ruth? Who witnesses the conversation between Boaz and his kinsman?

5. Ruth, the stranger who adopts the God of Israel as her own, testifies to the evolving interpretation of God from the deity of a single Semitic tribe to the God of many nations prophesied in Isaiah. What other reason for including this account in sacred Hebrew literature is suggested by the genealogy at the end of the story?

JONAH

1. As you read "Jonah" notice that it is a story with two distinct divisions. In what way is the pattern of chapters 1 and 2 repeated in chapters 3 and 4? What is the difference in the tone of these two sections? What portion of the second section repeats Jonah's prayer in chapter 2?

2. What mission does the Lord give to Jonah? Why does Jonah seek to evade this mission? How do the words of the ship's captain during the storm remind Jonah of his responsibility? What detail shows the compassion of the crew for Jonah? How does Jonah redeem himself?

3. What details of Jonah's prayer from the belly of the fish suggest the terror of his experience? What lesson does Jonah declare he has learned from his awesome adventure? Has he really learned it?

4. In what way do the citizens of Nineveh, in atoning for their sins, remind us of Jonah? What symbolic acts of penance do the people of Nineveh perform? How does the involvement of their king in these acts indicate the seriousness with which they view Jonah's message? How does Jonah react to their repentance?

5. An interesting interpretation of Jonah is found in *Moby Dick,* in the sermon given by Father Mapple in chapter 9. Read that account and

then decide how valid an interpretation it is, giving reasons for your opinion.

It is also possible to interpret Jonah as a parody of a prophet. Compare him with Samuel, Nathan, and Amos. What evidence can you find that the author intended his story to be funny?

Wisdom Literature

ECCLESIASTES

1. What were the various ways of life which the Preacher explored in his search for meaning in the world? Of what use was wisdom? pleasure? possessions? the arts? Which of these seems to be the most lasting? Why is none of them very permanent? What single sentence in chapter 2 summarizes what for Ecclesiastes is a good life? What do you think of this notion of the good life?

2. The writings under the title of Ecclesiastes are a collection of individual poems with related themes. One section, in chapter 3, begins with a poem that has become a popular song in our time. How does this poem suit the philosophy summarized in chapter 2? Find another statement in this section which also defines the good life, according to Ecclesiastes. In what sense is man no better than a beast? Does Ecclesiastes seem to believe in the concept of the immortality of the soul? Why do you think so?

3. What conclusions about life does Ecclesiastes seem to be drawing in the passage in which he says that he "saw under the sun, that the race is not to the swift, nor the battle to the strong"? How does this statement relate to Job's question, why do the good so often suffer while the wicked seem to prosper?

4. Note how Ecclesiastes writes many of his verses in balanced statements, one part of the sentence amplifying or contrasting with another. He is especially fond of placing opposites together: "The sun also ariseth, and the sun goeth down . . ."; "a time to be born, and a time to die." Find other examples of Ecclesiastes' poetry in which he uses synonymous or contrasting (antithetical) parallels.

JOB

1. The story of Job is written in two different styles. The first two chapters, sometimes called the Prologue, and the last chapter or Epilogue, are told in prose in the form of a folk tale, possibly from much earlier times. The intervening chapters consist of a series of poetic dialogues between Job and his friends and between Job and God. The

original story of Job may have been told for centuries before a brilliant but unknown literary artist adapted it into a work unique as to type, ranking with the supreme literary masterpieces of all time.

The frame story in the Prologue and Epilogue suggests that Job is a man of all seasons and all places by having him live in an undisclosed era in the imaginary land of Uz. What words and phrases define the important qualities of Job which the author wants us to recognize? What examples of Job's righteousness are given in the first chapter? How does Job try to protect his children from sin? Why is this detail added?

2. Why is Job tested by Satan? As implied in the Prologue, who is Satan and what are his duties? Who is really testing Job's faith? What final pain does Job suffer? What advice does Job's wife give him? What is Job's response?

3. In chapter 3 Job expresses his anguish through lamentation and prayer. How does Job hope to end his pain? Which lines best express this wish?

4. When Eliphaz first replies to Job in chapter 4, how does he show his respect for Job and his suffering? What does Eliphaz believe to be the reason for human misery? Job's reply to Eliphaz is that if he is to remain alive he wants to know the reason for his suffering. What lines in chapters 6 and 7 emphasize Job's desire to know God's purpose? What lines detail his suffering?

5. Bildad reproves Job in chapter 8 and reaffirms his belief that Job's suffering grows out of his sins. Show how Job's reply in chapters 9 and 10 implies both his devotion to God and his refusal to accept his pain without question. Note how at various points Job addresses God directly instead of his friends. What lines suggest Job's awareness of God's power to know all and to do all?

6. Summarize the debates between Job and the comforters. What differences, if any, can you discern between Eliphaz, Bildad, and Zophar? What lines in chapter 13 indicate Job's growing dissatisfaction with their advice? What lines in that chapter indicate Job's belief that the comforters slander God without intending to? Show how Eliphaz in chapter 15 relies on tradition to support his position.

7. In chapter 19 what lines demonstrate Job's unshakable faith in God? Compare Job's words in chapter 21 on the lives of the wicked with the writings of Ecclesiastes on the same subject. In what way do their views appear to differ?

8. Why does God, in speaking to Job from out of the whirlwind in chapters 38–41, contrast divine might with human frailty? What lines suggest the vastness of God? What lines suggest that God is all-knowing

(omniscient)? Why does God emphasize in his words to Job the strength and glory of the animal kingdom? Does God give a reason for his torment? Explain your answer. What is Job's response to God's words? Is Job satisfied with God's answer? What lines support your contention? 9. In the Epilogue, why does God rebuke the three comforters? In what ways have they misinterpreted God's dealings with men? In your opinion, why is God pleased with Job's questioning of God's purpose? Why is Job rewarded for demanding an answer? What rewards does he receive?

10. The poetry in Job is so rich and varied that it is impossible to deal with all of it as it deserves. The nature imagery, which is used to suggest many different emotions and insights, is especially beautiful. For example, in chapter 39, note how the imagery in God's words to Job shows the miraculous element that is present in everyday events. What forms does water take in these lines? How does the poetry invest each of these common events with wonder? Note in these chapters the range of geographic and scientific references. Would all of them be known through personal experience to a Hebrew poet? How might he have gained knowledge of these natural phenomena? Find other passages in Job that illustrate the poet's power to depict nature.

11. One of the most striking features of Hebrew poetry is the use of parallel structure which we have already seen in David's lament for Saul and Jonathan and in the poetry of the prophets. One phrase is followed by another that contains a parallel thought.

In Job the parallelism occurs most often in one of two forms. In *synonymous parallelism,* the second part is almost identical to the first, as in "Why died I not from the womb? why did I not give up the ghost when I came out of the belly?" (chapter 3). In *synthetic parallelism,* the second part supplements the first, as in "My flesh is clothed with worms and clods of dust, my skin is broken, and become loathsome" (chapter 7). Find other examples of both kinds of parallelism in Job.

Lyric Poetry

PROVERBS (*A Virtuous Woman*)
1. According to this poem, what are the characteristics of a good woman? Is this conception of a woman's role valid in today's world? Why or why not?
2. The poem is made up of twenty-two parallelistic couplets. What kind of parallelism is most often used? (For a discussion of parallelism, see question 11 under "Job" and question 4 under "Psalms.")

PSALMS

1. We will begin with Psalm 23 because it is the most familiar poem in the Bible and because it contains so many of the literary characteristics of the psalms. Note first of all its vivid imagery. With what metaphor or comparison does the poem begin? How does the poet amplify or *extend* this metaphor? Which words convey a sense of peace and security? For what purposes would a shepherd use a rod and a staff? What does this extended metaphor imply about the relationship between God and man? With what other images does the narrator convey God's love for him? What is suggested by the reference to anointing? to a cup running over? How do the final lines show God's eternal care for man?

2. Psalm 1 has a two-part construction in which a contrast is established. Who is being contrasted with whom? What are the chief qualities of the godly man? What image both suggests his steadfastness and implies his reward? What biblical figure does this imagery call to your mind? Why? What image describes the ungodly? In what ways does this image contrast with the simile used to describe the godly man? Show how the last lines summarize the meaning of the poem.

3. What does the narrator ask of God in Psalm 3? What role does this request imply about God that is different from the roles in Psalms 1 and 23? What specific details in the poem depict the might of God? What suggestion is there in the poem that the narrator speaks for an entire people and not just for himself?

4. Two kinds of parallelism, synonymous and synthetic, were discussed in question 11 under "Job." In the Psalms we find two other kinds of parallelism: antithetical and climactic. In *antithetical parallelism* the second part contrasts with or contradicts the first. In *climactic parallelism,* lines similar in form and rhythm build to a climax of thought and expression.

Explain why the first line of Psalm 19 is an example of synonymous parallelism. Explain why the second line contains both synonymous and antithetical parallelism. The second section of the poem begins with a long example of synthetic parallelism. How many parallels does it contain? Why is this parallelism also climactic? Find another example of synthetic parallelism in the very last line of this psalm.

5. Psalms 24, 100, 103, 114, and 121 show various aspects of God, again using a wide range of imagery and of narrative voice. Which qualities of God enumerated in Psalm 103 can also be found in one or more of the others? What new qualities of God do each of the others bring forth?

Find an example of climactic parallelism in Psalm 100. Find examples of synonymous parallelism in Psalms 24 and 100. Find examples of synthetic parallelism in Psalm 103. Find an example of antithetical parallelism in Psalm 121. How does this psalm resemble the 23rd Psalm in content and tone?

6. Psalms 90 and 137 are psalms of sorrow, possibly commemorating the exile of the children of Israel in Babylon. What is the central theme of Psalm 90? What images contrast the eternity of God with the brevity of human life? In modern English, what is the normal life span of man according to the Psalmist? Is the God of Psalm 90 a gentle God or an angry God? Which lines support your contention? In Psalm 137, how does the Psalmist convey the anguish and bitterness of the Israelites in captivity?

7. Psalm 139 is one of the most eloquent poems of personal awareness of God. Note how the poet builds the first half of the poem with antitheses, contrasting light and dark, for example. What other contrasts can you find? Although creation is a mystery to man, what does the psalm suggest about the creation of each individual? Psalm 139 has been singled out for its expression of childlike awe at the very thought of God. What lines or images bring out this quality?

THE SONG OF SOLOMON

1. Which passages in the Song of Solomon are about Solomon? What evidence do they offer, if any, that Solomon is indeed the author of the poems? Which stanzas in chapters 1 and 2 appear to be the words of a young woman in these interrelated poems? Which appear to be the words of a young man? What clues led you to your conclusions?

2. Some lines of the young man as he describes his beloved in chapter 4 suggest that he is a shepherd. What passages or phrases would be most appropriate if spoken by a shepherd? Look for references to agriculture or herding. Find contrasting lines in this chapter in which the imagery suggests that the speaker is a king. What similes are those which a king might use in describing his beloved? What similes are those which a shepherd might use?

3. In your own words describe the young man as he appears in chapter 5. What series of similes is used to describe him? In what ways does this series of similes seem more masculine that the similes used to describe the young woman in chapter 7?

4. It has been suggested that the Song of Solomon is a series of dialogues that tell a story involving King Solomon, a young woman in his harem, a shepherd whom she loves and prefers to the king, and a chorus made up of ladies of the court. With that suggestion in mind, see if you can construct a script from the text. (This is strictly a fanciful exercise and there is no one "right" construction.) Can you think of any other cast and story line that fit the text?